The things they say behind your back

The things
they say
behind your back

WILLIAM B. HELMREICH

DOUBLEDAY & COMPANY, INC.
GARDEN CITY, NEW YORK
1982

Library of Congress Cataloging in Publication Data

Helmreich, William B.
  The things they say behind your back.

  Includes index.
  1. Prejudices. 2. Stereotype (Psychology)
3. Ethnic attitudes. 4. Minorities. 5. Racism.
I. Title.
HM291.H513   305.8
AACR2
ISBN 0-385-15606-5
LIBRARY OF CONGRESS CATALOG CARD NUMBER 81-43854

Grateful acknowledgment is made to the following for permission to reprint
  their copyrighted material.
Excerpt from Whitetown U.S.A. by Peter Binzen. Copyright © 1971 by
  Random House, Inc. Reprinted by permission of the publisher.
Excerpt from WASP, Where Is Thy Sting? by Florence King. Copyright
  © 1977 by Florence King. Reprinted by permission of Stein & Day,
  Publishers.
Excerpt from China Men by Maxine Hong Kingston. Copyright © 1980
  by Alfred A. Knopf, Inc. Reprinted by permission of the publisher.
Excerpt from the play A Streetcar Named Desire by Tennessee Williams,
  from Theatre of Tennessee Williams Volume I. Copyright 1947 by
  Tennessee Williams. Reprinted by permission of New Directions
  Publishing Corp.
Excerpt from the poem "Coole Parke and Ballylee, 1931" by William
  Butler Yeats, reprinted from Collected Poems. Copyright 1933 by
  Macmillan Publishing Co., Inc., renewed © 1961 by Bertha Georgie
  Yeats. Reprinted by permission of Macmillan Publishing Co., Inc. and
  A. P. Watt Ltd.
Excerpt from the song "Juice of the Barley" by The Clancy Brothers &
  Tommy Makem. Copyright © 1963 by Tiparm Music Publishing, Inc.
  Reprinted by permission of the publisher.
Excerpt from the song "Love, Light and a Dream," reprinted by permission
  of Matsushita Electronic Industrial Company, Ltd.
Excerpt from BITCH (Black Intelligence Test of Cultural Homogeneity)
  Test. Reprinted by permission of Robert L. Williams Associates, Inc.,
  St. Louis, MO 63130.

To my wife, Helaine, to our sons, Jeffrey and Alan,
and in memory of Norma Helmreich

CONTENTS

Contents ix

ACKNOWLEDGMENTS

It is a pleasant task to thank the people who have helped me in writing this book. Professor Irving Louis Horowitz, mentor, friend, and colleague, read the entire manuscript, offering both valuable suggestions and encouragement, as did Professors William and Arline McCord. The same exemplary effort was made by Maxine Bernstein, Dr. David Pelcovitz, Lonnie Pelcovitz, and my agent, Arthur Schwartz.

The following people all either read specific chapters, contributing their expertise and wisdom, or made suggestions that were crucial to the development of the book. My debt to them is great and mere mention of their names is hardly sufficient to convey my appreciation to them. I hope they will understand: Dr. Henry Barbera, Professor Joseph Bensman, Professor Marshall Berman, Maris and Stu Blechner, Herman Cline, Mary Curtis, Lena and Richard Eng, Professor Feliks Gross, Professor Ray Hall, Professor Gerald Handel, Professor John Howard, Peter Johnston, Ruth and Nat Kalt, Professor David Kranzler, Professor Jerome Krase, Professor Salvatore De Lagumina, Nancy Miller, Professor Frank Miyamoto, Professor Richard Nagasawa, Professor Alelia Nelson, Professor Joseph O'Brien, Reverend Don Plasman, Dr. Carlos Rodriguez, Professor Bernard Rosenberg, Professor Edward Sagarin, Professor Jose Sanchez, Professor Betty Lee Sung, Professor Howard Taylor, Professor Betty Yorburg, and Ben Zaricor.

I want to especially express my gratitude to my editor, Eve Roshevsky, whose help in conceptualizing and guiding this book to its completion was incalculable. Special thanks also to Peter Schneider of Doubleday for his assistance in many small and large ways and to my copyeditor, Henry Krawitz, who did a magnificent job.

My indebtedness to my wife, Helaine, goes far beyond the ritualistic declarations sometimes made by authors. As friend, critic, and fellow sufferer, her good humor and encouragement were invaluable, and her observations were, as always, incisive and stimulating. Without her this project could literally not have been done.

ONE

All about stereotypes

"Everyone knows that most Italians either belong to the Mafia or have a relative who does. And of course they're great shoemakers and tailors, though they tend to gamble too much."

"Do you know that the first present the new Pope got was a pair of slippers with gold initials inside them that said T.G.I.F. Now you know what that stands for. Right?"

"Sure. It stands for Thank God It's Friday. We say it every week at the office."

"Wrong. It means Toes Go In First. You know how those Polacks are."

"The problem with this country is that the Jews control everything. They run the TV stations, movies, newspapers, and whatever else they can get their grubby hands on. Worst of all, they're cheap and sneaky."

"The Blacks think they got everything coming to them. They can't think ahead more than one day. They never come on time when you make an appointment with them. All they wanna do is drink, shoot up, and play the numbers."

"Now you take the Japanese. There's a people that are hardworking, smart, and ambitious. But remember—you can never turn your
backs on them, even for a minute. They're really sly and treacherous.
And don't ever talk politics with them. They're so chauvinistic it's ridiculous, even though, you know, they just imitate everything we
do."

The well-known journalist and writer Walter Lippmann called
"these pictures in our heads" stereotypes. Basically, a stereotype
is an exaggerated belief, oversimplification, or uncritical judgement about a category. The category may be a neighborhood, a
city, a newspaper, members of a profession, believers in a religion, or even a highway (e.g., "The Long Island Expressway is
always packed."). Although stereotypes are most often exaggerations or distortions of reality, they are often accepted by people
as fact. When they concern a highway, they do little damage,
but when they are used to indict an entire group of people, great
harm can be done.

Naturally, not all stereotypes about different nationalities are
negative. Some, in fact, are quite complimentary. "The Italians
are very family oriented," "the French are great lovers," and "the
Chinese are so courteous," are examples of stereotypes that
reflect well on various peoples. Nevertheless, they are equally
exaggerated generalizations and a person who accepts such
statements as factual can easily believe less positive views.

Groups are sometimes responsible for creating, or at least
abetting, their own stereotypes. This is especially true when the
stereotype is a positive one. Thus, an after-dinner speaker at an
Irish affair may begin his speech by saying something like, "As
we know, the Irish have always been regarded as good politicians." The Jewish American Princess (JAP) is another case in
point. While not a very positive statement about the Jewish people, it has been given a tremendous boost in popularity by the
Jews themselves, particularly Jewish comedians, who have found
it makes great copy.

When people employ stereotypes they are usually making
judgements about a given individual's potential to fit into a certain category based upon that person's racial or ethnic origins.
In other words, they say that a Pole is more likely to be stupid

because he is Polish, an Italian more apt to talk with his hands because he is Italian, and so forth. Some people even believe such traits to be true of *all* members of a given group. What needs to be determined is when a statement about a member of a certain group has little basis in fact and when it has a good deal of basis in fact. In short, to what extent is a stereotype based on reality?

Why do we often stereotype people, even when deep down we "know better than that"? A great deal has been written about this question, with almost as many answers given as there are types of people. Among the most common explanations is that it is simply a very efficient way of coping with our environment, an environment so complex that we have to break it down into categories before we can understand it. It would clearly be impossible for us to function if everything that happened were dealt with on an individual basis. Without stereotypes everything would be treated as if it were taking place for the first time. Thus, stereotypes are convenient though often inaccurate. Frequently they eliminate the need to learn about people for those who simply do not, either because of fear or sheer laziness, wish to make the effort.

Another cause of stereotypes may be the cultural background of the individual. Most cultures encourage prejudiced attitudes toward other groups. These attitudes are ingrained in people beginning with early childhood, and are therefore very difficult to overcome. In general, the longer one has such attitudes, the harder it is to change them. In one study done on this question, a group of whites were shown a photograph of a white person holding a razor blade while arguing with a Black person in a New York City subway. They were shown the photo for a split second and then asked to write down what they saw on a slip of paper. More than half of the respondents said that they saw a *Black* man holding a razor blade against the throat of a *white* man. Culture is such a strong factor that persons who do not themselves agree with particular stereotypes will remain silent simply because they "want to be like everybody else."

Quite often people are unable to accept the blame for their own shortcomings, and when this happens they search for convenient targets upon whom they can vent their frustrations.

Some of the more typical victims are friends, parents, and others who are "safe" because they won't reject you for such outbursts, providing that it doesn't happen too often. In many cases, however, people select minority group members as scapegoats because they are powerless, relatively speaking, and/or easily identifiable. Thus General Brown talked about "the Jewish lobby," as did Billy Carter, and former Governor George Wallace talked about "Nigras and pointyheads."

Professors Bruno Bettelheim and Morris Janowitz have argued that stereotypes are often caused by a complex process known as projection. When people accuse others of motives or characteristics they sense in themselves but can't admit to openly, it is called projection. Noted psychologist Gordon Allport, in his famous work *The Nature of Prejudice,* notes that in Europe, where there is no large Black population, the Jew is the one accused of unbridled sexual lust, violence, and filth. Americans, having peoples such as Blacks, Puerto Ricans, and Chicanos to personify these traits, find it unnecessary to use Jews for this purpose. As a result, Americans can attribute other, more specialized, traits to Jews, such as defensiveness, aggressiveness, and shrewdness.

Stereotypes also allow us to justify our behavior toward a group that we already dislike or are mistreating. In other words, they enable us to rationalize our actions. An example would be General Westmoreland's comment during the Vietnam War. When asked to justify the napalming of innocent villagers, he replied, "These Asians don't value life the way we do." Further evidence for the use of stereotypes to rationalize behavior comes from the fact that people often assign contradictory stereotypes to members of a group. The writer Harry Golden once said, "The Jew is probably the only person who can be called a communist and a capitalist—by the same person—and at the same time."

The media also play a role in stereotypes, though it is more a case of reinforcing rather than creating stereotypes. Certain TV shows portray the Irish, Jews, Blacks, and other groups in a stereotyped manner. The same is true of films, plays, and magazines. Still, the media mainly reflect our pre-existing attitudes as opposed to inventing them.

Do stereotypes actually cause prejudice? Not necessarily.

More often they justify prejudice, but in doing so they reinforce prejudice. It is difficult to separate one from the other. If one has a stereotyped view of a nationality, it can result in prejudice toward that group, and if one is prejudiced one can either create or find stereotypes justifying one's attitudes. Whatever the case, since stereotypes often guide our behavior, an understanding of them is extremely important.

Knowing the causes of stereotypes is indeed helpful—and there are many books on the subject—but it does not tell us *how particular stereotypes developed.* Growing up in a certain culture may result in a person having negative views toward, say, Italians, but it does not tell us how that culture *acquired* these views in the first place. Understanding that people pick on certain groups when they need a scapegoat does not tell us why *particular* groups are chosen as scapegoats and not others. Why the Jews and not the Danes? Why the Poles and not the Bulgarians? To answer this question, we need to know much more.

Many stereotypes change over time because they are often a function of political, economic, and social developments. For example, American views of the Chinese and Japanese have been linked by researchers to U.S. relations with China and Japan at different times in history. When such relations were good, the stereotypes in this country tended to be positive; when they deteriorated, the stereotypes focused on the negative characteristics.

How have particular groups come to be identified with particular characteristics? Puerto Ricans are not thought of as grasping in a business sense, but Jews are. Blacks are sometimes categorized as lazy and shiftless, but the Chinese are not. We have the fighting Irish, the stupid Poles, the clannish Italians, the cold and insensitive WASPs. Where did these ideas originate?

A major thesis of this book is that, contrary to what many people may think, a large number of stereotypes possess more than a kernel of truth. There is, as we shall demonstrate, some basis for saying that Jews are aggressive, Blacks musically gifted, the Irish heavy drinkers, and Orientals inscrutable. True, the *majority* of stereotypes do not fall into this category, but it is important to know which do, which do not, and why.

Another important thesis advanced here is that all racial and ethnic stereotypes stem, in some measure, either from the historical experiences and culture of the group or from the historical experiences and culture of the nations that had contact with the group. In cases where the stereotypes are negative but contain some truth, we will try to understand them and not deny their existence. Though certain unpleasant truths may emerge from such an analysis, the long-range effect will be to increase our understanding of why people do the things they do and how the group to which they belong helps shape their attitudes and values.

Stereotypes are often vicious and can be exceedingly dangerous. We have only to recall what happened to Jews in Europe because of the blood libels leveled against them by Christians, as well as the fate of Black men accused of lusting after white women. If this is so, then why bother to write about stereotypes, especially when many have some validity? Does such information simply become ammunition for the Archie Bunkers of America?

The answer to this last question is yes—if it is done in a flip, insensitive, and unscientific manner. Programs such as "All in the Family" can legitimate prejudice largely because they are only seen as family entertainment. Thus the message that is transmitted becomes, "It's okay to put down Poles, Hispanics, and Blacks, and anyone who objects is either oversensitive or a spoilsport." That is neither the intent nor approach of this book. While readers will hopefully find the material entertaining, the main goal is to inform and enlighten. By examining the various stereotypes logically, point by point, a clearer picture should emerge about the different groups that make up American society and why they are viewed in certain ways by others. A careful examination of this problem will, in this writer's view, reduce rather than increase prejudice.

There are some jokes in this book. They are there not to ridicule the members of the groups under discussion but to show how popular the stereotypes themselves are. It should in no way be assumed that telling such jokes will either increase or decrease prejudice. The evidence on this question is, as of now, inconclusive.

Some groups have far more negative stereotypes than others.

The reader glancing through the Contents will find, for example, that almost all of the stereotypes attributed to Blacks, namely, lazy and shiftless, violent, stupid, and so forth, are negative. This does not mean that any of them are true or that Blacks possess no positive traits. Black people have made enormous contributions throughout history and have innumerable positive characteristics. But it is not the purpose of this book to detail them. Rather, the focus is on how *others* perceive (read: stereotype) Blacks. That Afro-Americans are seen so negatively by white America is, more than anything else, a reflection of the depths of racism in this country, and it is this reality that a book like the present one attempts to evaluate.

The groups selected for discussion in this book were chosen either because of their size or because they are among the most maligned in American society. The stereotypes themselves are based both on general impressions and scientific studies that show how different groups are perceived by Americans. Some of the stereotypes exist in the country from which the people came, while others do not. The focus here is on how Americans see them.

It should be understood that what is being presented here is really an *overview* of some of the most commonly held stereotypes. Hundreds of pages could probably be devoted to each of the stereotypes, but that is not our goal here. The first group to be considered is one of the oldest and most often stereotyped peoples in the world—the Jews.

TWO

Jews

The Jewish mother

The story is told of a Jewish mother who went to the beach with her son and daughter-in-law. The son, a physician, swam a bit too far away from shore and began struggling in the water as he tried to make his way to safety. His mother, in an effort to attract attention to his plight, began running up and down the beach screaming at the top of her lungs, "Help! Somebody please help! My son, the Great Neck psychiatrist, he's drowning!"

Humor of this genre, depicting the Jewish mother obsessed with the status of her children, is almost passé by now. It received a great boost in popularity with the success of Philip Roth's novel *Portnoy's Complaint*, which sold several million copies. In it, Sophie Portnoy is described as overprotective, pushy, aggressive, and guilt-inducing. To some extent such adjectives could be ascribed to Italian mothers, Black mothers, and Puerto Rican mothers, all of whom share the anxieties and concerns emanating from minority status. It is, however, the Jewish mother that has been accorded the rather dubious distinction of stereotype par excellence. The answer may lie in an understanding of Jewish culture.

Judaism has always placed tremendous importance on home, family, and especially on children, who are seen as the center of family life. The task of child rearing was primarily the woman's responsibility. Although this was true of other cultures too, Judaism turned this role into a tremendous virtue. Both the Bible and the Talmud are full of references to this function. A good example is the poem "Woman of Valor" in Proverbs, attributed to King Solomon: "She looks well to the ways of her household, and never eats the bread of idleness. Her children rise up and bless her . . ." By ennobling the woman and making her feel secure as a wife and mother, Judaism ensured that she would take her responsibilities very seriously. Restricted to the home, the mother turned all of her energies to the family.

In difficult economic times her role became even more important. When, as was the case with the East European immigrants who came to this country around the turn of the century, the husband was forced to work long hours away from home, the mother occupied a central place in the lives of her children. It is here that the guilt factor became important. Having made a major contribution to the upbringing of her offspring, she was able to gain not only their affection but also their loyalty and dependence. Her children were often imbued with a strong sense of guilt when they failed to measure up to the expectations of their mother, who "worked so hard so that *you* should be happy." The values transmitted to the child were rooted in the strong sense of morality that permeated the culture. A mother said to her child, "Eat for the sake of your parents, who love you and want only the best for you. Study so that your parents will be proud of you." Thus the biblical notion of responsibility for others became part of the secular belief system.

If Jewish mothers (and fathers as well) pushed and fought for their children and taught them never to be satisfied ("So you got a 98. But who got the 100?"), it was in large part due to their perception of a world hostile to their kind. Since their names were not Stuart or Baker or Blake, it was necessary to give them strong egos. Only then would they have the confidence to offset the disadvantages of their religion. Unfortunately, this was sometimes carried too far, with the child brought up to think of himself or herself (the Jewish Prince and Jewish Princess syndromes) as number one.

The general view held by many non-Jews (as well as Jews who seem almost proud of it) is that Jewish parents spoil their children. In one community study, the sociologist Benjamin Ringer reported the following attitudes of Gentile parents in a Chicago suburb toward their Jewish neighbors:

Jewish parents . . . let them [children] run wild in the stores without reprimanding them. They don't care how much trouble they cause, they don't punish them enough . . . they're always Mama's angel . . . [They] raise their children to feel superior to Gentile children either materially or else purely defensively . . . For example, my gun is better than yours. My house is better . . . My daughter came home from a Jewish home and asked why we didn't have seven telephones. (*The Edge of Friendliness*, pp. 71–72)

Such indulgence can perhaps best be understood in light of the heavy demands Jewish parents make upon their children in other areas. Because they expect so much from their children in terms of getting good grades, being admitted to the right school, marrying well, and so forth, the parents compensate in other areas, buying them what they want, letting them talk back, and generally pampering them. This often leads to overprotectiveness. The Jewish mother has therefore been immortalized in countless jokes and novels as the woman who asphyxiates her child in warm clothing, drowns him in chicken soup, and is constantly yelling at him to put on his galoshes.

No one has yet interviewed a thousand Jewish and Gentile mothers to ascertain the validity of this stereotype, though its extensive use as a focal point by many Jews in their own writings does seem to give it a stamp of authenticity. Whatever the case, it ought to be noted that being brought up in this fashion must have some positive points if one is to judge by the considerable success enjoyed by Jews as a group. If nothing else, delaying independence in the child tends to increase the educational level of many children by increasing the amount of time they will spend in school. More fundamentally, the fact that the Jewish parent lets his children know how much he believes in them can often be a crucial factor in their ultimate success and confidence in themselves. Finally, the strong family structure gives the Jew a strong sense of family responsibility, thus giving rise to yet another Jewish stereotype—that Jews make good husbands. Whether or not this is true awaits further study in a more extended treatment of the subject.

The Jewish mother has also been given much of the credit for producing the whining, self-indulgent, and "I'm God's gift to the world" daughter, otherwise known as the JAP (Jewish American Princess). Since the son's fulfillment came from "the real world," where he became an attorney, a doctor, or a partner in the business with his father-in-law, all that was left for the daughter was fancy clothes, nose jobs (the excuse is usually a deviated septum, but everyone knows better), marrying well, and knowing how to "set a table" (with the help of a maid or two, of course). Unlike their own mothers, the JAPs who "married rich" no longer found it necessary to achieve fulfillment in the home, turning instead to shopping expeditions at Bloomingdale's or Bergdorf's (Rich's in Atlanta; Stix, Baer, and Fuller in St. Louis; etc.), brunches with fellow JAPs, tennis, Mah-Jongg, trips to art galleries and museums for the more intellectually inclined, and, of course, the weekly trip to the therapist and the daily call to mother.

It is, however, unlikely that the characteristics attributed to the Jewish mother, or the above caricature of the JAP, will survive beyond the present generation. In fact, they are dying out rather quickly. More and more Jewish mothers are career-oriented, and this competing interest threatens the structure of the child-centered family. Indeed, young Jewish women who become doctors and lawyers are apt to find that the self-confidence developed in a supportive environment serves them well in their chosen field. They are more likely to view the notion of "everything for the children" as archaic. Psychiatry and psychology have also contributed heavily to the demise of these stereotypes by frowning upon guilt and dependence and by encouraging their patients, Jewish or Gentile, to assert themselves and do what makes them "feel good." Finally, assimilation and intermarriage (currently estimated at over 40 percent) will result in a dilution of those attitudes toward the family that spring from Jewish culture.

Internationalists plotting to take over the world

This myth developed because nineteenth-century anti-Semites needed an image of the Jew frightening enough to make the Russian peasant see him as the enemy rather than the czar.

To give support to these accusations, Czar Nicholas II asked the monk Sergei Nilus to come up with "proof" of an international Jewish conspiracy. Nilus obligingly produced a set of forged documents in a book called *Protocols of the Elders of Zion*. The *Protocols* were partially based on an admittedly fictional work called *Biarritz*, written by Hermann Goedsche and published in 1868. It contains a rather imaginative chapter called "In the Jewish Cemetery in Prague." A secret meeting takes place in this cemetery between thirteen old, white-bearded Jews, each of whom is supposed to represent one of the twelve tribes of Israel, plus a thirteenth who speaks for "the unfortunates of the exiles." This is actually the latest in a series of meetings that have occurred once every century ever since the Jews were exiled from the land of Israel. The representatives report on how their activities, ranging from undermining the Church to fomenting revolution, have helped the Jews move toward their eventual goal of taking control of the world.

The *Protocols* was widely published, reprinted, and distributed. Millions throughout the world, including many Americans, accepted it as true. Its origins are fully discussed in Dr. Norman Cohn's *Warrant for Genocide*, which makes fascinating reading. Despite its exposure as a fraud, it is today still widely disseminated in Russia, the Arab lands, and in Latin America. Billy Carter's Libyan guests quoted from the *Protocols* during interviews given to newsmen here several years ago and were apparently unaware that the documents have been widely discredited.

It is easy to dismiss such attitudes as the views of a small minority. Yet, as Cohn points out in his book, lies of this sort can have terrible consequences:

There exists a subterranean world where pathological fantasies disguised as ideas are churned out by crooks and half-educated fanatics for the benefit of the ignorant and superstitious. There are times when this underworld emerges from the depths and suddenly fascinates, captures, and dominates multitudes of usually sane and responsible people, who thereupon take leave of sanity and responsibility . . . It is an incontestible fact that the forgotten eccentrics described in the first half of this book built up the myth which, years later, the masters of a great European nation were to use as a warrant for genocide. (p. 18)

Shrewd businessmen

A Jewish agent in a Catholic insurance firm did exceptionally well for a number of years and was recommended for a top executive post. His religion posed a serious problem, however, because the company felt it would harm their relations with top members of other firms. After a good deal of agonizing, they decided to call in a leading priest to convert the Jew. A meeting was held in the private office of the company's president, during which the clergyman attempted to persuade the Jew to accept the Christian faith.

Finally, after almost three hours, the two emerged.

"Well, Father," asked the president. "How did you make out? Do we have a new Catholic?"

"No, we don't," replied the priest, "but he did sell me a $50,000 policy."

Whether or not Jews are actually shrewder businessmen than others is impossible to prove. Certainly this is widely believed to be so, as can be seen from such popular expressions as "Jew you down." There are enough factors involved that would suggest that they might indeed have an edge in this area. For one thing, Jews have been in business for a long time. The feudal system of the Middle Ages, which lasted over a thousand years, excluded Jews. Forbidden to own land by the Church, denied entry into the various craft guilds that were so important in those times, Jews were forced to turn to moneylending in order to survive. The Church forbade its members to enter this occupation, since it regarded the charging of interest, no matter how small the amount, as sinful. The Talmud, on the other hand, permitted the charging of interest on business loans, so long as the rates were not excessive, taking the position that moneylending was necessary in order to stimulate trade and commerce. Since the Jews were damned and money was damned, the Church concluded that a marriage of the two was entirely fitting and appropriate.

As matters turned out, the Jews became indispensable to the feudal economy in this capacity. It was they who supplied the necessary funds when the farmer's crops failed or when his live-stock were killed off by disease. They also supplied the neces-sary capital when the nobles wanted to build castles, when they went off to war, when the Church purchased jewels, and so forth. Eventually the Christian majority came to the conclusion that moneylending wasn't such a bad idea, and when this hap-pened Jews found themselves forced out of the industry which they had pioneered in so many countries. Nevertheless, their ex-perience in money matters and continuing discrimination against them made it inevitable that they would remain involved in var-ious forms of business. For example, it was moneylending that was responsible for the entry of Jews into the diamond trade. This occurred because diamonds were often used as collateral for loans. Thus, in the sixteenth century Jews controlled the dia-mond trade in Portugal, which traded extensively with India, then the chief source of uncut diamonds. Later, when the Jews were forced to leave Portugal, Holland, which welcomed the Jews, became the new center of the diamond market.

The Jewish religion, with its emphasis on abstract thinking, may also account for the Jew's interest and skill in business. It was not merely the worship of an abstract God that could not be seen and the rejection of idol worship, for Christianity and Islam also shared such beliefs. Rather, it was the study of the Talmud and the focus on abstract ideas—which make up so much of that work—that sharpened the mind of the Jew to the point where he was able to transfer his intellectual acumen to the economic sphere. From childhood on, when he was first exposed to the Bible, the Jew's mind was geared toward explaining the seem-ingly incomprehensible. As an adolescent, he might spend hours discussing the conditions under which the ancient rabbinic sages would permit someone to purchase something that had not yet come into existence. Could one, for example, purchase a grove of palm trees even if there were no trees, simply because past expe-rience indicated that they were certain to spring up in a particu-lar location? And, if so, was it permissible to buy the wool from

a sheep before the time had come to shear it, or the as-yet-un-
born calves of a cow? Even those Jews who were not as
educated developed a profound respect and appreciation for
such thinking.

Thus, when capitalism became important in the modern
world, Jews were in a position to benefit from it. After all, interest, futures, options, stocks and, most importantly, money itself
were abstractions. They were representations of concrete items,
and the Jew, trained as he was to think in analogies that
spanned both time and space, was equipped to function in a
modern industrialized society that increasingly depended upon
commerce, banking, and financial investment. In this sense it
was not so much a question of superior skills as having the skills
that modern society most needed.

In *The Pawnbroker* there is a famous scene in which Rod
Steiger, who plays the Jewish immigrant pawnbroker, sternly
lectures a young Puerto Rican boy who works for him about the
importance of having and holding on to money. It is easy to see
in this film the caricature of the Jew as a greedy, money-hungry
man without taking into account the experiences sometimes responsible for such obsessions. Lacking a homeland for thousands
of years, always dependent on the whims of others, never certain
when persecution might strike, the Jew, perhaps more than any
other nationality, has come to see money as a means of survival.
In medieval times Jews often bartered their lives in exchange for
money, which they gave to local overlords for protection from a
hostile population. Unlike the Gentile, who could work the land
and benefit from its use, the Jew owed his shelter, safety, food,
and anything else of value he possessed to money. Small wonder
that it became so important to many Jews. During the Nazi era,
to take a case in point, many Jews survived because they were
able to purchase protection from individual Gentiles in various
occupied lands.

Jews today are far more likely to enter the professions than
business-related fields. This is a natural outgrowth of the desire
on the part of many Jews of a generation ago to have their children become doctors, lawyers, teachers, and so forth, because
they wanted to raise both their own status ("my son, the doctor") and that of their offspring. As a result, the image of the

Jew as a shrewd or good businessman may, like other stereotypes in this area, be headed for extinction. Still, such views often die a slow death, as this observer discovered during a visit to a non-Jewish resort in Pennsylvania's Pocono Mountains in 1980. An Italian comedian regaled his audience with story after story of Jews and their preoccupation with money. In one joke a Jewish watchdog was described as one who says to the burglar, "Take anything you want. It's all insured."

Have horns

This belief is not an exaggeration but rather a complete falsehood. It is clearly confined to those who have never seen a Jew. While few Americans fall into this category, the author was asked this question once while traveling through rural Iowa. Its roots can be traced to Aquila Ponticus, who translated the Old Testament from Hebrew into Greek during the second century. According to the Bible, Moses is described as descending from Mount Sinai carrying the tablets, with rays of light shining from his head. Unfortunately for the Jews, the word *koran* (shone) was incorrectly pronounced *keren*, the Hebrew word for horn. This was quite easy to do, since Hebrew relies on vowels beneath the letters for its pronunciation, and the vowels in the version consulted by Ponticus were probably missing.

This interpretation was given a powerful boost in popularity in the Renaissance. One of the greatest works during that time was Michelangelo's sculpture of Moses, and perched on his head are two small horns. The stereotype was also enhanced by the association, among Christians, of the Jew with the devil.

The chosen people

For you are a holy people unto the Lord your God: of all the peoples that are on the face of the earth the Lord your God has chosen you to be his treasured people. (Deut. 7:6)

The story is told of how God offered the Torah to several other nations before turning to the Jews, all of whom rejected it as too restrictive. The Jews, according to the legend, accepted it unquestioningly, agreeing to be bound by its commandments even before they knew what they were. Such acceptance implied a special responsibility but did not mean superiority. Thus one can understand the response to the English writer Hilaire Belloc's quip, "How odd of God to choose the Jews" that "It was not odd—the Jews chose God."

Regardless of who chose whom, there is certainly a kernel of truth to this theory, for many Jews, especially those who are observant, believe that God has a special relationship with "His people." Many view their meticulous observance of the hundreds of biblical commandments as meriting special consideration from God. In addition, Jews have used the idea of being chosen to explain the suffering and cruelties to which they were so often subjected by other peoples. It was often only by seeing himself as destined to play a special role in the world or in the hereafter that the Jew was able to justify his suffering.

Support for the concept of chosenness comes also from Christian fundamentalists, who cite such evidence as the survival of the Jews through the ages despite the efforts of others to destroy them, their success in so many areas, and the rebirth of the State of Israel. In his book *Israel's Final Holocaust* noted evangelist Dr. Jack Van Impe writes:

Frederick the Great said: "No nation ever persecuted the Jew and prospered." His correct observation is proof of God's faithfulness in keeping His promise to Abraham . . . This tiny scattered people has had such a definite date with destiny that no power on earth could destroy them. (pp. 56, 59)

If the Jews are "chosen," they are not unique in this sense. After all, Christianity and Islam, as well as most other religions, hold out the promise of divine grace and salvation only to believers. By contrast, Judaism believes that "all the righteous of the world have a place in the world to come." Nevertheless, it ought to be recognized that no faith or doctrine can demand the undivided loyalty of its adherents unless it believes its members occupy a special place in the scheme of life.

In modern times, as Jews have increased their contact with people outside their community, many leaders have become increasingly sensitive to this stereotype. Some have responded by asking, tongue in cheek, whether being chosen is such a great privilege when one considers that the Jews have been persecuted for so many centuries and have only recently been able to re-establish their homeland. Others have taken concrete steps to deal with the term by specifically denying its validity. The Reconstructionists, one of the denominations within the Jewish faith, have eliminated all such references from their prayer book, while Orthodox Jews have repeatedly emphasized that the concept means service and accountability, not an elite status.

Killed Jesus Christ

Nearly every Jew in America has been exposed, at one time or another, to the charge that the Jews murdered Jesus. For some it has come up in innocent ways, a casual observation made by a neighbor or fellow worker; for others it was the taunt of "Christ killer!" often encountered in childhood days. Even the 1965 declaration by the Vatican that the Jews as a group could not be held responsible for what occurred did not lay the matter to rest. Here, then, in brief, is what happened.

The trouble began when Jesus entered the Temple in Jerusalem three days before his death and drove out the vendors and money changers, predicted the destruction of the Temple, and attacked the Sadducean high priests. Followers of Jesus described him as a messiah or as "king of the Jews" and thus alarmed the Temple authorities. Fearful that such claims would bring the wrath of the Roman legions upon them (this had happened in the past with other messianic claimants), they paid one of Jesus' apostles, Judas Iscariot, to help them arrest Jesus. Why, as a loyal follower, Judas accepted the bribe is not known. In any case, Jesus was arrested at night and turned over to Pontius Pilate, the Roman procurator of Judea, who ordered him executed.

One misconception about these events is that it was the Jewish high court, known as the Sanhedrin, that ordered his execution. This is highly unlikely for several reasons. First, it was illegal for the court to meet at night, nor could it do so on the eve of a holiday, which in this instance was Passover. In fact, the court had no powers of arrest. Finally, according to the Gospels,

Jesus was tried at the palace of Caiaphas, the high priest. Yet the Sanhedrin never met anyplace but in their own court, known as the Chamber of Hewn Stone. For all of these reasons it seems far more likely that his arrest was arranged only by the aristocratic Sadducees, who were angered by his attacks upon them.

There is no evidence that the death sentence decreed by Pontius Pilate was instigated or supported by the Jews. In all likelihood the high priests merely wanted Jesus detained until after the Passover holiday. The Gospel according to John does say, however, that Pontius Pilate ordered Jesus' death because of pressure from the Jews. This seems rather improbable since Pontius Pilate was one of the most ruthless rulers in history and was, in any event, extremely unlikely to be afraid of an unarmed civilian population. This Gospel is, incidentally, the most pro-Roman, perhaps because, as the last Gospel, it was written at a time when the Christians had begun aiming their teachings at the Romans themselves. This last factor may account for the fact that it is the only Gospel to specifically blame the Jews for the crucifixion. Part of the problem here is that the Gospels are our only written record of these events and were only transcribed forty to ninety years after they occurred. They also contradict each other at various points.

Perhaps the greatest canard is the accusation that the Jews actually killed Jesus. To begin with, crucifixion was not permitted by Jewish law, even on the rare occasions when the Jewish courts sentenced someone to death. It was a Roman method of execution that was used on thousands of people, including many Jews. The flogging or scourging of Jesus prior to his crucifixion and forcing him to carry his own cross were also well-known Roman customs. In addition, executions were never carried out on Fridays by the Jews. Finally, according to Jewish law it was a requirement that as the accused was being led to his death a herald should walk before him and ask for any supporting witnesses to come forward and refute the charges. There is no record that this was done.

No one knows for certain what the Jewish population of Jerusalem was thinking as they watched Jesus being marched through the streets. Some may have felt his death justified because of his seemingly blasphemous messianic claims; others simply because the Temple priests were opposed to him. The majority, however, probably sympathized with him as just another Jewish victim of the Romans. It must be remembered that Jesus was a Jew, and his sect was only one of many Jewish groups. Moreover, he had never renounced the validity of Mosaic law. In fact, according to the Gospels it was the Jews, not the Romans, who wept at the crucifixion site. Will Durant sums up the event in *The Story of Civilization:* "Quite clearly the condemnation did not have the approval of the Jewish people."

In the face of all this, it is interesting that the charge should have survived for so long. In fact, even if it were true, why blame those not alive at the time? Apart from all the psychological and social reasons for stereotyping that have been mentioned in the first chapter, there is the seriousness of the charge of deicide. The Jews are accused of having killed the Son of God. The perception of the Jews as guilty is undoubtedly heightened by the fact that they continue to refuse to accept Jesus as the Savior, and have the nerve to regard him as a fake messiah. The Church's declaration that the Jews, past or present, could not be held accountable for his death prompted a suggestion by the humorist Harry Golden that the Jews issue a statement of their own clearing today's Christians from complicity in all the crusades and pogroms of the past two thousand years.

Smarter

It would not be accurate to say that Jews are smarter, but it would be correct to state that they are, as a group, more educated and intellectually oriented. As a result they may appear to be more intelligent. Although a positive attribute, this stereotype is considered valid even by those who dislike Jews.

In his book *Anti-Semite and Jew* Jean-Paul Sartre says the following:

"The anti-Semite readily admits that the Jew is intelligent and hardworking; he will even confess himself inferior in these respects . . . [for] the more virtues the Jew has, the more dangerous he will be."

A number of studies have shown that Jews are believed by many to be more intelligent than most people. For example, the sociologists Charles Glock and Rodney Stark found that about half of the Christians surveyed in a sample of people from various Protestant denominations agreed that "an unusual number of the world's greatest men have been Jews."

How accurate are these views? If we take Nobel Prize winners as a form of measurement, it becomes apparent that Jews are overrepresented. Throughout the world, from 1905 to 1970, sixty Jews have been awarded this coveted honor. Close to one third of American Nobel Prize winners have been Jews. Yet Jews make up less than 3 percent of the American population. This would seem to be more than chance occurrence. It is equally unusual that the three men with the greatest impact on the twentieth century were Jews: Karl Marx, Sigmund Freud, and Albert Einstein.

One factor is that Jews as a group are very highly educated. In 1968 less than 40 percent of the college-age population was in college. For Jews the figure was twice as high. Furthermore, among those in college Jews were considerably more likely than non-Jews to enter professions such as law, medicine, the physical sciences, dentistry, and psychology. They were also among those least likely to go into home economics, agriculture, nursing, and physical therapy. Since the fields selected by Jews include most of those in which Nobel Prizes can be won, and since Jews attend college out of proportion to their numbers, their capacity to produce outstanding scholars ought not to be so surprising.

This explanation falls short, however, in one significant respect. It does not explain *why* education is so important to the Jewish community. It only tells us that it is. To understand the reasons for this emphasis, we need to go back in history to biblical times. Even as citizens in their own independent kingdom of ancient Israel, the Jews placed great value on the written word. Their lives were lived in accordance with the precepts of the Bible or Torah, a book containing numerous references to the importance of study and the education of children in particular. Typical is the verse in Proverbs: "Train up a child in the way he should go, and even when he is old, he will not depart from it." With the destruction of the Temple in A.D. 70 and the loss of their country, the Torah became even more important—in fact, crucial. It was the most concrete symbol of their glorious past. By studying it and following the commandments, the Jews created a portable homeland. Since the laws were an essential part of community life, it followed that those who understood them best, namely, the rabbis, were among the most highly respected members of the community. In this way learning came to be seen as a supreme value. Through the centuries it was an important source of status. Jewish families of means took pride in being able to marry off their daughters to scholars, and Jewish communities gave financial support to Jewish institutions of learning. This was particularly true in Eastern Europe, the point of emigration for most of those who immigrated to America.

Many of those Jews who came to America abandoned their religious practices, but cultural values were much harder to shed. One of the most important was the attitude toward learning. Coincidentally, education was an avenue to success in the United States, and the Jew was able to adapt to it very well. Unlike other groups, he did not have to develop respect for education; it was already a part of his culture. It only remained for him to transfer the previous emphasis on religious knowledge to one that stressed secular learning. Jewish parents reinforced the education received in school by praising their children when they did well. By saying "What a smart boy you are" instead of "Look how well he hits the ball" the parent was telling his child what he needed to do in order to gain respect, admiration, and ultimately success.

Mary Antin, a Polish immigrant who came to America just before the turn of the century, is an excellent example of the passion for education that permeated the immigrant spirit. Unusual both as a woman and even by Jewish standards, she attended Barnard, had her first book published at eighteen, and eventually married a professor. Yet the dream she saw come true was shared, in varying degrees, by countless others. Listen to the words of the grocer in Antin's neighborhood as his daughter asks him

"Would you send me to high school, pa? . . . Would you really?"

"Sure as I'm a Jew," Mr. Rosenblum promptly replies, a look of aspiration in his deep eyes. "Only show yourself worthy and I'll keep you in school till you get to something. In America everybody can

get to something, if he only wants to. I would even send you farther
than high school—to be a teacher, maybe. Why not? In America everything is possible. But you have to work hard, Goldie, like Mary
Antin—study hard, put your mind to it." (*The Promised Land,* pp.
352–53)

Numbers have also played a role in the emphasis placed by
Jews upon intelligence. Wherever they lived, Jews were a small
minority. Unlike the Irish, who were sufficiently numerous to
have rebelled against their British oppressors, Jews were forced
to rely upon their wits when attacked or threatened. As a result,
they came to value intelligence highly. Jewish folklore is full of
stories where the Jews are saved from certain annihilation because of the cleverness of the local rabbi or community leader.
Sometimes, like the biblical Joseph, the duke or king demands
that the Jews interpret his dreams. On other occasions they must
answer a diabolically constructed riddle. Whatever the case, the
story ends with Jewish brainpower defeating the oppressor's evil
intentions.

So much for the cultural argument. There is also some basis
for a genetic argument, unpopular as that may be. During the
Middle Ages a popular avenue of upward mobility for intellectually gifted persons was the priesthood. In fact, for the sons
of peasants it was the *only* way to escape their impoverished status. It was also, as the social philosopher Ernest Van Den Haag
has pointed out in *The Jewish Mystique,* an attractive calling for
the intellectually oriented members of the upper classes. Unfortunately, the priesthood demanded celibacy, thus taking thousands of the brightest among the Christian population out of the
gene pool. The Jews, on the other hand, had no such problem.
Their shining lights, the rabbis, were encouraged to marry early,
and because their education enabled them to marry wealthy
girls, they were often able to afford and care for larger families.
Psychologists today agree, for the most part, that genetics and
culture both play a role in determining intelligence as it is usually measured. They differ primarily over how much importance
to give to each. Yet even if the genetic factor is important, it
must be remembered that there were married Protestant ministers hundreds of years ago and their presumably bright chil-

dren should have begun making up for this supposed deficiency.
Furthermore, this argument is not relevant to all the other non-
Christian cultures throughout the world that have produced
thousands of highly intelligent individuals.

Regardless of the merits of this argument, it no longer applies
today since intellectually gifted persons can and do gravitate to
many professions besides the clergy. While Jews generally do
better on I.Q. tests, this fact—given their cultural emphasis on
learning, reasoning ability, and the acquisition of knowledge—is
probably due far more to their environment than to inherited
traits. It should be noted that in addition to valuing learning, the
concentration of Jews in urban areas and among the middle
class are two other factors long associated with respect for education and a desire to attain it.

Cheap

This stereotype can perhaps best be answered with the following statement: Jews are more likely to be in business than any
other ethnic group. It is a fact of economic life that the lower
the cost of producing an item and the greater the sale price, the
larger the profit. Any businessman, be he Jewish or a member of
another group, seeks to maximize his profit. Since more Jews,
proportionately, are in business, they are more likely to be accused of what is, in fact, a basic feature of capitalism.

Another factor to consider is the image of the Jew in general.
As a member of a minority group about whom economic stereotypes are common, he is more apt to be accused of fulfilling
them than someone else. Thus, Abraham Lincoln is considered
thrifty because he saved his money, but Abraham Goldberg is
considered cheap for doing the same thing because he is a Jew.
A mere choice of a descriptive adjective tells the story. Another
example might be the description of a hardworking man of, shall
we say, Swedish origin as an individual "who wants to get ahead
and is willing to do something about it." On the other hand, the
Jew works hard because "he has a sweatshop mentality." These
cases portray the vicious cycle of prejudice. The person who
describes Jews in this manner is already biased and is actually

searching for examples to justify his opinion. He does not want to be confused by facts because his mind is already made up.

The type of business in which Jews have traditionally been engaged ought not to be overlooked either. Perhaps the majority of businesses in which Jews are to be found involve retail trade. Examples are clothing, food, and real estate. This means that they are likely to have greater personal contact with the public than, say, those in businesses such as utilities, oil, or steel. Consequently, they will bear the brunt of consumer antagonism even though such hostility is probably a natural by-product of customer/store or management/tenant relationships.

While there is no statistical evidence of the cheapness of Jews compared to that of other groups, it can be said that they are certainly not cheap in the area of philanthropy. Jews probably give more to both their own charities and those of nonsectarian organizations than any other nationality. In his book *Why They Give*, a study of Jewish philanthropy, Milton Goldin, a professional fund-raiser, wrote as follows:

I often spoke with colleagues who have also worked for both Jewish and nonsectarian organizations. Again and again we agreed that goals are higher . . . in Jewish organizations. Refusal to give is an affront . . . Where else are brochures largely unnecessary because contributors will give in any case?" (p. ix)

Control Wall Street and the banks

This stereotype was accurate around the turn of the century, when the major stock brokerage firms were both founded and run by Jews. As an example of their power, the financier Jacob Schiff was able to float a $200 million bond issue for the Japanese government on short notice. Jews are still well represented in Wall Street brokerage houses. A glance at the names listed in the *New York Stock Exchange Directory* indicates that perhaps a quarter of them are Jewish-sounding. In addition, important companies such as Goldman Sachs, Lehman Brothers, Kuhn Loeb, Bear Stearns, and Lazard Freres were started by Jews. On the other hand, some of the largest firms on Wall Street today, such as Merrill Lynch, The First Boston Corporation, and Blythe

Eastman Dillon are most definitely not "Jewish" firms. Furthermore, the so-called "Jewish houses" are often so in name only.
Many of the children of the early founders intermarried and
quite a few are, in fact, no longer Jewish. Finally, there are
probably no firms of any size in existence today on Wall Street
that are exclusively Jewish in terms of those who exercise power
within them.

Jewish influence in banking today is virtually nonexistent. Several banks such as Bank Leumi and Republic National Bank of
New York are under Jewish ownership, but the vast majority of
banks are not only controlled by non-Jews but do not, in fact,
employ Jews in high positions. For example, in New York City,
where two million Jews live, there are almost no Jews among the
top executives of the city's seven largest banks. Elsewhere in the
country the proportion is even smaller. A 1978 study by Professor Stephen Slavin of Brooklyn College of the City University
of New York found that schools with low Jewish enrollment
received far more visits from corporate recruiters than those with
large numbers of Jewish students.

IBM's recruiting manual, for example, lists hundreds of U.S. colleges
that the company visits annually, but the list doesn't include Brandeis
or Yeshiva. But the worst offenders, according to Slavin, were the
large New York City banks, which send recruiters all over the country
while ignoring the largely Jewish colleges in their own backyard.

> (Dan Rottenberg, "How to Succeed in Business Without
> Being Gentile."
> *Jewish Living*, December 1979: 41)

In recent years some banks have begun to make a more concerted effort to attract Jews. There are, however, two major obstacles. The first is that, notwithstanding the increased acceptance of Jews in general, there are still many people who are
simply not comfortable among Jews. American business has always been tied in with social connections, and many of these are
made in private clubs that still discriminate against Jews. As a
result, banks are often reluctant to hire or promote Jews because
they fear it will affect their business. Naturally, they may use
this argument as an excuse to perpetuate their own prejudices. A
second problem is that the word is already out among Jewish

graduates of business schools that advancement is very difficult for Jews who enter banking. This means that many graduates who are highly qualified do not even bother to try. Recognizing this, some banks have sponsored meetings and seminars focusing on recruiting more Jews, but thus far banking is still a very closed field to Jews.*

If there are so few Jews in banking, why and how did this stereotype emerge? It is here that we encounter the kernel of truth theory. Although the major role was probably played by the bankers of the Italian city-states, Jews became heavily involved in moneylending, which eventually became known as banking, in the late Middle Ages. During the nineteenth century their influence in banking increased with the rise of banking houses such as Rothschild, Marcus and Warburg, Salomons, Kuhn and Loeb, and others. In America there was the well-known case of Haym Salomon, who helped finance the American Revolution. In the mid-nineteenth century numerous important banking houses were established in this country by German-Jewish immigrants. Moreover, families such as the Schiffs, Seligmans, Loebs, and others often acted together to offset the financial influence of the much larger Gentile concerns. This contributed to the feeling that Jews, as a group, "controlled things." Fueled by Populist politics, anti-Semitism increased. This, combined with the rise of large impersonal corporations, served to virtually eliminate the influence of Jews in banking. A B'nai Brith study done in 1939 found that less than 1 percent of all bankers in the United States were Jewish.

Despite the fact that what was once true is no longer the case, the stereotype about Jewish control in these areas persists, all of which attests to the staying power of prejudice in general. Moreover, the perception of Jews as controlling Wall Street or the banks carries with it the belief that the Jew often acts to promote specific Jewish interests at the expense of those who do not belong to the faith. This is actually part of the anti-Semitic image of the Jew as a world conspirator. What better place to employ this stereotype than in money matters where Jews are,

---

* There are, incidentally, almost no Jews at the upper echelons of major industries such as insurance, oil, steel, and the utility companies.

for various reasons, heavily involved? The fact that the world of finance and the reasons for the ups and downs of the economy are so poorly understood by the average person makes this a very convenient area in which to target Jews as scapegoats.

Rich and ostentatious

Teaching a course on minority relations at City College of the City University of New York, I once spent an hour discussing the general view that "all Jews are rich." The class, predominantly Afro-American and Hispanic, had just seen a short film on the Holocaust when one Black student, a middle-aged man who had been an aide to former New York City Mayor John Lindsay, raised his hand and asked, "Why are we feeling so sorry for the Jews? Everyone knows that five years after the Holocaust they made all their money back." Others chimed in with comments such as, "Everybody knows that Jews are rich," "Money's in their blood," and so forth.

To what extent are such assertions true? On the one hand, only one of the ten wealthiest families in America is Jewish. They are the Pritzkers of Chicago, worth an estimated $850 million. Compared to the Mellons, worth between $3 and $5 *billion*, and the Gettys, whose wealth is well over $2 billion, the Pritzker fortune, large as it may be, does not put them into the category of the super-rich. On the other hand, a 1979 survey of American wealth by writer Dan Rottenberg found ten Jews among the seventy-four families in this country whose net worth was $200 million or more. Thus Jews, who constitute but 3 percent of the population, are indeed overrepresented among the nation's richest families.

The majority of Jews in this country are not millionaires, being both solidly middle-class and earning more, on the average, than the average American. Studies by the National Opinion Research Center and United States Census Bureau material reveal that the median income of Jews is significantly higher than that of non-Jews. Demographers have pointed out, however, that this is directly related to education. When Jews and others in the population with similar educational levels are compared, the differences are less than 10 percent.

All but overlooked by many is the existence of large numbers of poor Jews, mostly elderly folk living on pensions and social security. In an article called "The Invisible Jewish Poor," which appeared in the *Journal of Jewish Communal Service*, the number of American Jews living at or below the poverty level was estimated at between 700,000 and 800,000. The author, Ann Wolfe, a consultant to the American Jewish Committee, cited the case of a thirty-square-block area in "wealthy" Miami Beach's south shore, where the *average* annual income in 1968 was $2,460 and where thousands of Jews were subsisting on less than $28 a week for food and rent.

One major reason for the common perception of Jews as rich is their concentration in retail businesses ranging from grocery stores to large department stores. As a result, they must often deal directly with the poor and the working class, many of whom are apt to focus general resentment at their economic status on an easily identifiable scapegoat. The same is true in the housing area. It is much simpler to focus on the Jewish landlord (or slumlord) than on the impersonal gas or electric company, whose wealth is far greater. It makes little difference to a poverty-stricken ghetto dweller that his Jewish landlord is middle-class. Compared to his own economic plight, the Jew is rich. As long as Jews are heavily involved in highly visible occupations of this sort, such stereotypes are likely to persist.

As far as ostentatiousness goes, it is not clear that Jews are, in fact, more showy than other groups, but the stereotype, greatly popularized by the unforgettable wedding scene in Philip Roth's *Goodbye Columbus*, is well known. Puerto Ricans and Afro-Americans have also been accused of ostentatiousness, mostly in terms of loud clothing, fancy cars, and so forth. Behavior of this sort, where it exists, can perhaps be explained as a response by a minority group to perceived or actual rejection by the larger society. It is a way of saying, "You may think I'm a nobody but my material well-being proves that, at least in one way, I have made it." For the upwardly mobile Jew, motivated as he is by a strong work ethic and a general desire to succeed, conspicuous consumption can sometimes become a way of justifying one's efforts. Doing so is obviously easier if, as is true of many Jews, one has the financial means.

Acting in what has come to be called the style of the "nouveau
riche" can also be attributed to the insecurities of those who are
more recent arrivals to the United States. Writing in 1930 about
Jews who had immigrated to America and settled in the Bor-
ough Park section of Brooklyn, New York, the writer Michael
Gold gave the following description of one such family:

We came into a large gaudy room glowing with red wallpaper, and
stuffed like the show window of a furniture store with tables, chairs,
sofas, dressers, bric-a-brac. Mrs. Cohen wore a purple silk waist,
hung with yards of tapestry and lace. Diamonds shone from her
ears; diamond rings sparkled from every finger . . . typical wife of
a Jewish *nouveau riche.*" (*Jews Without Money,* p. 217)

It is interesting that today the Orthodox Jewish community,
whose members probably include the largest chunk of recent arrivals to this country among American Jews, seems most concerned about this issue. In an address given at the 1974 convention of the strictly Orthodox organization Agudath Israel of
America, Rabbi Chaim Dov Keller, a prominent leader in the
community, chastised his audience for such tendencies, saying,

Many of our people have suffered a warping of priorities, throwing
themselves headlong into the pursuit of materialism. Unbelievable
sums of money are spent for one night of a wedding celebration,
while yeshivas [Hebrew schools] pay their teachers coolie wages for
lack of funds. Plush carpets and ornate furnishings have become status symbols among a people whose aristocracy was always measured
in terms of . . . learning and righteousness. (*Jewish Observer,* January 1975: 10)

Generally speaking, as members of a group become more
Americanized they will lose their cultural distinctiveness. Often
this includes a conscious downplaying of certain traits associated
with the group. One respondent whom I interviewed in a study
of Jewish identity stated:

I am super-conscious of being Jewish. I will overtip in a restaurant
because I know people think Jews are cheap. I'll order in a soft
voice, and my taste in cars, clothes, and the furniture I buy for our
home is very conservative because I know what others think of Jews.

Pushy and aggressive

Writing about social discrimination against Jews in the *American Jewish Historical Quarterly,* the prominent historian John Higham once observed:

The Jew [who had immigrated to America] became identified as the quintessential parvenu . . . attracting attention by clamorous behavior, and always forcing his way into society that is above him. (pp. 9–10)

While it is difficult to scientifically verify whether or not Jews are physically pushier than other people, it can be said that they are, as a group, extremely ambitious and upwardly mobile. Moreover, in his book *The Jewish Mind* the well-known anthropologist Dr. Raphael Patai reports on numerous psychological studies—such as the Bell Adjustment Inventory and the Benreuter Personality Inventory—that suggest higher aggressiveness among Jews. Looked at in terms of level of education, types of occupations, value systems, and so forth, it is clear that Jews not only want to do well but are willing to go to considerable lengths to achieve success.

To some extent prejudice against Jews may bring about such behavior. Many Jews anticipate discrimination and are not surprised when it occurs. They need only reach back one or two generations for strong evidence of its existence, be it the American context, where Jews were systematically excluded from various occupations and barred from social clubs and other organizations, or in the much harsher European context, where they were victims of mass murder. As a result, they often feel the need to "do better" than the average person. This attitude can even affect the size of their families. As one Jewish parent said to me in an interview on the effects of anti-Semitism, "Jack and I stopped after our second child because we wanted to provide our children with the best opportunities possible. If you're Jewish you often start out with two strikes against you." Other studies that have focused on the very low birth rate of Jews have also confirmed the presence of such concerns. Such perceptions, when transmitted to children and when supported by actual dis-

crimination, can result in compensatory behavior such as com-
petitiveness and aggressiveness.

In some cases the emergence of such personality traits may
come about as a result of the stereotype itself. The individual
knows that certain people will see him as pushy simply because
he is Jewish. Feeling that he cannot negate this view, he decides
to act in accordance with it. This is, of course, known as the
"self-fulfilling prophecy." On the other hand, such stereotyping
is often completely false and may be employed to explain away
unpleasant truths or to rationalize failure. For example, the Jew
is promoted ahead of the Gentile in a company because he is
"manipulative" or "a rate-buster."

Naturally, when people are prejudiced against members of a
particular group they will be acutely sensitive toward efforts by
its members to win general acceptance, as in the previously
quoted statement "forcing his way into society. . . ." Still, it can
be speculated that Jews may sometimes deliberately test the
limits of tolerance by efforts to gain admission to certain clubs
or to obtain employment in firms known to have few Jews. Such
attempts may be accidental, but they may also be rooted in
Jewish-Christian relations. From the time most of the Jews were
dispersed from their homeland in A.D. 70, they became a mar-
ginal people subject to the whims and demands of their often reluctant hosts. They could be persecuted with impunity, exiled
with ease, and stripped of their rights on the slightest pretext.
They had no country of their own, they had not accepted Jesus
as their savior, and they were generally viewed as social
outcasts. Such a legacy does not die easily, and the insecurity of
this type of marginality can lead to efforts on the part of the Jew
to see how far he can go and whether or not he is truly accepted. Given the continued existence of prejudice, it is not surprising that at some point he will be confronted by rejection and
accusations of pushiness. Lest one blame the Jew for this, it
ought to be remembered that if society were truly open, such
efforts would not be necessary.

Over 95 percent of all Jews in the United States live in urban
areas; some have cited the pressures of urban living, including
crowds and high population density, as factors in aggressiveness.
If this is true, it ought not to be applied to Jews alone. Anyone

walking the streets of Port-au-Prince, Calcutta, East Berlin, or any of a hundred cities throughout the world where the Jewish population is rather low will find himself jostled, pushed, and confronted by aggressive behavior. Moreover, the cities, which are often magnets for those looking to get ahead, have opportunities for the ambitious that are pursued by members of all nations, races, and faiths. This is, therefore, not a significant factor in explaining the stereotype.

Control the media

Jews play an important role in media industries in the United States. Some examples are CBS, chaired by William Paley, and ABC, headed by Leonard Goldenson, both Jews. NBC was founded by another Jew, David Sarnoff, who also created RCA. Lester Bernstein, editor of *Newsweek,* and Henry Grunwald, who occupies the post of editor-in-chief at *Time* magazine, are both Jewish. The Newhouse chain of newspapers, which, with a combined daily circulation of close to 3.3 million in 1978, is the third largest in the United States, is owned by the Newhouse family. Then, of course, there is the New York *Times,* owned by the Sulzbergers.

At the same time, it would be an exaggeration to say that Jews dominate this field. The Newhouse group includes only 31 out of a total of 291 chain-operated newspapers. A survey by political scientist Stephen Isaacs revealed that only 3.1 percent of the 1,007 newspapers in this country were owned by Jews. Moreover, the magazines with the second and third largest circulation, *Reader's Digest* and *National Geographic,* have relatively few Jews in top posts, as do the two major news services, AP and UPI. Morton Yarmon, public relations director at the American Jewish Committee, found only about half a dozen Jewish-sounding names among 200 chief editorial writers of newspapers around the country—hardly a scientific approach but interesting nonetheless.

One area where Jews have always had a major impact is Hollywood. In fact, it was Jews, for the most part, who founded the filmmaking industry. Men such as William Fox, Samuel Goldwyn, Louis Mayer, Adolph Zukor, the Selznicks, and many others got their start around the beginning of the century running nickelodeons where customers saw movies for a nickel while seated on wooden chairs. These men, known as "moguls," gravitated to filmmaking and distribution because it offered opportunities to the new immigrants unavailable in more established fields. They remained typically Jewish, often had accents, and, as a result, became identified in the public mind with the media in general.

For the anti-Semite looking for a scapegoat, the media and the Jews are a perfect match. Many people have a deep suspicion of both what they read in the papers and what TV and radio commentators tell them. "You can't trust what you read in the paper" or "Don't believe everything you see on the news" are common expressions even among those not prejudiced against Jews. (Jews also hold such views.) But for the anti-Semite suspicion of the media in terms of credibility adds fuel to his feelings vis-à-vis Jews. It matters little that most news commentators are not Jewish. He may even see persons such as Walter Cronkite, Howard K. Smith, and John Chancellor as front people for the Jewish conspiracy he imagines must be behind the news.

Most studies have demonstrated that, notwithstanding the recent tilt to conservatism, Jews are generally liberal. The presence of substantial numbers of Jews in the media might be partially responsible for its seemingly liberal bias, but there is no evidence linking the two. In fact, the giant Newhouse chain is well known for its policy of not interfering with the positions taken by its newspapers, many of which are politically and ideologically conservative.

If Jews are well represented in the media, this does not mean that they work actively to promote Jewish interests. A good case in point is the State of Israel. The overwhelming majority of Jews in this country are pro-Israel. Yet the New York *Times* has certainly not been pro-Israel in its editorials over the years. At best it could be regarded as "even-handed." Columnists such as James Reston and Anthony Lewis, while occasionally sympathetic to Israel, have generally been highly critical of its policies. In a scathing article that appeared in *The Village Voice*, reporter Sol Stern charged:

Our most important newspaper [the New York *Times*] has turned its only page of outside opinion into an exclusive sounding board for the opposition to the democratically elected government of an allied country. This is unprecedented and scandalous. (*The Village Voice*, October 1–7, 1980: 13)

According to Stern, the Op-Ed page of the New York *Times* has carried about forty "guest" columns and articles on the Middle East since Menachem Begin's election in May 1977. Not one has appeared that supports the Begin government. Stern cites three pieces that were submitted and rejected, including one by Manhattan District Attorney Robert Morgenthau. Interestingly, the New York *Times* published an article favorable to Begin on its Op-Ed page several days after Stern's attack.

The two major news weeklies, *Time* magazine and *Newsweek*, have, over the years, published many stories favorable to the Arabs despite the involvement of Jews at the highest levels in both places. Surely it is possible for Jews to disagree with Israeli policies. The fact, however, that such disagreement or even neutrality is often expressed in the media indicates that there is a big difference between saying that many Jews work in the media and that they make a concerted effort to promote the interests of Jews as a whole. Why are so many Jews found in this field? The major reasons are probably: their generally high level of education; their interest in intellectual and literary affairs; the fact that so many Jews live in New York and Los Angeles, the communications nerve centers of the country; and the fact that Jews were able to enter this profession from the ground floor many years ago as immigrants.

Have big noses

Among the Ashkenazim [European Jews] one can pick out Palestinian types that could readily be drawn from the courts of Solomon and David; Nordics to delight the eye of Julius Streicher, if he were to see them without their passports; Alpines who could yodel in any Hofbrauhaus; and Dinarics who could be Tyrolese skiers or Parisian policemen. (p. 31)

These words were written by the noted anthropologist Dr. Carleton Coon in an essay called "Have the Jews a Racial Identity?" that appeared in 1942. Many people, however, including Jews, will swear that they can "more or less" tell who is Jewish by looking at the individual's physical features. Among those likely to be cited are: a large hooked nose; swarthy complexion; dark hair, usually curly; a weak chin and eyes; hairy body; and a shorter than average stature. In fact, Jews tend to resemble the peoples in whose countries they have lived. Thus Yemenite Jews look more like Yemenite Moslems and German Jews more like German Christians. (One indication of this reality was the Nazi party policy requiring all Jews in Germany and elsewhere to wear a Star of David or one sewn on an armband, an obviously unnecessary procedure if Jews were readily identifiable.) The reasons for this are geography, similarities in diet, and the degree of intermarriage that has occurred over a span of hundreds, or even thousands, of years.

Does this mean that anyone who claims the existence of a Jewish "look" is either an anti-Semite or a fool? Not at all. Through a phenomenon called "selective perception" we tend at times to see what we want to see. Thus, if one thinks there is such a thing as a Jewish nose, one may take special note of it when looking at a Jew who has one while conveniently ignoring other groups, such as Arabs, who do not. One social scientist actually did a study of Jewish noses in the early part of this century. Dr. Maurice Fishberg examined over four thousand noses in New York City. To the disappointment of many anti-Semites, especially cartoonists, and the surprise of quite a few Jews, he found that only 14 percent of those surveyed had aquiline or hooked noses. The rest had noses that were categorized as straight, snub, flat, or broad.

To be sure, there are probably hundreds of thousands of Jews with curly hair and larger than average noses who came from countries such as Poland, Germany, Holland, and elsewhere where such features are not that representative of the general population. There are, however, *millions* of non-Jews throughout the world with identical features. Nevertheless, to deny the existence of any genetic similarities among Jews would be too extreme a statement, for there have been studies suggesting certain commonalities. For instance, Dr. Patai observes in *The Myth of the Jewish Race* that an examination of the fingerprint whorls of Yemenite, Moroccan, and other Sephardic Jews demonstrates that they are more similar to those of European Jews than to non-Jews from their own native lands. This suggests, says Patai, that while Jews today differ greatly in physical features, they do have a certain residue of Mediterranean traits. Such features, when they appear among Jews, are likely to be traceable to the fact that the Jews originated in that part of western Asia Minor where Semitic people lived. Thus, the answer to whether or not there is a Jewish race or look must be yes and no, depending on which Jew you are looking at.

THREE

Italians

"Mangia! mangia!"

Food is important to Latin and Mediterranean people in general, but among Italians it appears to have special significance. This is no accident, being directly related to their culture and history.

Most Italians who came to America were from poverty-stricken backgrounds. In his memoir *The Other Side: Growing Up Italian in America* Vincent Panella notes that "the consistent custom of an Italian family is to feed its guests and overfeed itself. *'Mangia! Mangia!'* is an Italian joke with its measure of truth. [The Jewish equivalent is *'Ess! Ess!'*] A scarcity of food produces an obsession with eating. In America this obsession could be satisfied." Indeed, the Italian peasant was too poor to afford many of the dishes associated with contemporary Italian cuisine such as veal marsala, chicken cacciatore, or even spaghetti with meatballs, for meat was very expensive. The standard fare usually consisted of bread, pasta, rice, vegetables, beans, fruit, nuts, and cornmeal, with meat reserved for flavoring or special occasions.

Another important reason has to do with the central role of

the family in Italian life. As a result, anything that brings the family closer is of value. In his autobiographical account of life in an Italian family in Rochester, New York, Jerre Mangione writes:

There was a banquet for as many occasions as my father could imagine, and his imagination was fertile. He once gave a banquet for some relatives who were moving to California and, when they were suddenly obliged to change their plans, he gave another banquet to celebrate their staying . . . Like the rest of my relatives he believed implicitly in the goodness of food and liked to repeat the motto: "Food is the only thing you can take with you when you die." . . . The dinner usually closed with my Uncle Nino making a speech in pure Italian . . . He would . . . talk about the glories of Italy or the wonders of New York City, but always he remembered to finish up with Dante. (*Mount Allegro*, pp. 131–32, 141–42)

In short, food becomes a way of holding the family together, a setting for sharing common experiences and reinforcing common bonds. Moreover, the ethnic foods serve not only to reunite the family but to root it in a larger common culture and history.

The fact that Italian families tend to be male-dominated may also be a factor. The father/husband generally makes the decisions and is deferred to in any matters of importance. In such an environment the woman has a potential source of fulfillment in the preparation of food and uses it as a way of showing off to friends and family alike. This division of roles is perhaps best expressed by the southern Italian saying, "The father is the head of the family and the mother the center."

Lastly, Americans in general have contributed to this obsession by consuming vast amounts of Italian food. The existence of numerous franchised pizza parlors, many of them in locations where few Italians live, attest to the entry of Italian food into the average American's diet. More pizza is eaten in the United States than in Italy. Such widespread acceptance encourages the Italian-American community's focus in this area by telling it that its ethnic foods (e.g., broccoli, zucchini, ravioli, escarole) are as American as apple pie. Nevertheless, a good deal of cultural integration has occurred. In his classic study of Italian-Americans, *The Urban Villagers*, sociologist Herbert Gans reports that in many Italian families turkey is eaten on Thanksgiving but is preceded by antipastos and followed by spumoni. While such combinations are not unusual among a wide range of ethnic groups, they suggest that even among the ethnically conscious Italians a good deal of accommodation to American culture has taken place.

Even if it is granted that Italians consider food an important part of their culture, this stereotype, like all others, should be taken with a grain of salt, not to mention pepper. As Jerry Della Femina and Charles Sopkin observe in their bittersweet memoir *An Italian Grows in Brooklyn,* "There are one hell of a lot of Italian women out there who can't cook worth a damn." And, one might add, one hell of a lot of Italians who haven't had lasagna or chicken cacciatore in years.

Stupid, ignorant, suspicious of education

Why are Polish jokes so short?
So that Italians will understand them.

Most Italian-Americans come from southern Italy and Sicily, a traditional peasant culture that stressed strong family and community ties and nurtured extreme distrust of outsiders. Although Italy was unified in 1870, it has always been divided into at least two distinct societies—that of the North and that of the South. Northerners viewed the South as backward and only half-civilized, fit only for exporting agricultural produce to the wealthier and more developed North. The educational system in the South was controlled by the North, which, among other things, used literary Italian in the schools and held local culture in contempt.

Like all peasant societies, southern Italians considered education or knowledge to be the accumulated wisdom, moral codes, and experiences of the community and looked upon the schools as cultural wastelands. In southern Italy the term *buon educato* means that a person has learned how to act morally and properly within his community and not that he has gone to college. "Do not make your child better than you are" is a popular saying in southern Italy that typifies this attitude.

When southern Italians arrived in the United States, they brought with them these attitudes. They often moved into neighborhoods populated by relatives or friends from the old country. While Jews, with whom the Italians are often compared, came from a tradition that valued education, Italians saw it as valuable only if it helped the person "learn a trade." This was because in Italy one went to school beyond the fifth grade only to acquire a profession. Many Italians were unable to understand how a school could waste a young man's energy by teaching him sports or take up his time by giving him lessons in how the government worked. The important thing was practical learning.

Another problem was that Italians from the South were mostly laborers or small contract farmers prior to their arrival here around the turn of the century. They were unskilled laborers in an urban industrial society and worked very hard for little pay, all of which did not create an atmosphere that encouraged learning. Nor was it all the fault of the immigrants. The schools themselves quickly learned to expect little from Italian schoolchildren and stereotyped all of them as slow learners, truants, and troublemakers, which many of them rapidly and obligingly became.

The effects of a long peasant tradition that views education as unimportant are difficult to overcome. Italians are the largest Catholic ethnic group in America today. This is not reflected in higher education, where they are somewhat underrepresented. Still, the stereotype about Italians not valuing education is no longer true of today's younger generation. In fact, as early as 1960 the median number of school years completed among Italian-Americans over fourteen years of age was 10.9, compared to 11 for all second-generation Americans. The Italians have by no means been overachievers educationally, but they have performed about as well as the average American. Things are changing in southern Italy too, where more and more young persons of both sexes attend universities. Regarding I.Q., scores of Italians today approximate the national average, though at the turn of the century they were much lower.

Despite prejudice and discrimination, many individuals of Italian background have held, or hold, important positions in American life. They include: Joseph Califano, Pete Domenici,

John Pastore, Mario Biaggi, and John Volpe in government; Lee (Lido) Iacocca and Giovanni Buitoni in the corporate world; and Melvin Belli, Joseph Blasi, Paul Rao, and John Sirica (about whom Richard Nixon once said, "He's Italian and I don't deal with them. They're not like us") in the legal professions. They have also produced a fair share of outstanding intellectuals and scientists, among them Nobel Prize winner Enrico Fermi, Mario Pei, Max Ascoli, Richard Gambino, Gay Talese, and John Scali.

Family-oriented, clannish, distrustful of outsiders

Senator Alfonse D'Amato is a man who fully understands the importance of the family in Italian culture and history. This is why he featured his mother in advertisements that appeared in the 1980 New York State Senate campaign urging voters to elect him. In southern Italy the only community that mattered was *la famiglia*. In his excellent work *The Social Background of the Italo-American School Child* educator Leonard Covello shows how one immigrant distinguished between family and the American brand of friendship:

. . . friendship could not exist except with members of our own family. People outside the family, though good acquaintances, are not to be trusted. (p. 186)

Another immigrant, born in Apulia, Italy, explained these ties at greater length:

. . . a friend is a person who can help you when you are in trouble, a person in whom you can confide family matters . . . a friend must be able to render some service to you . . . to return a favor with a bigger favor . . . my people think that a person who is not a relative could not perform all these duties, and therefore, he could never make a real friend. For example one could never confide an intimate problem which involved the family to a non-relative. Nor could you be sure that a non-relative would help you since he is not obligated to do so. [A relative] is least apt to betray you since if he did that, then he would betray the whole family. (p. 190)

The above statement is an accurate reflection of the Italian attitude toward family, but it does not tell us how it developed.

For this we must first look at life in the southern Italian villages from which most Italian-Americans originally came. It was a peasant society where family and community were inseparable. The farming of small plots of land was a family enterprise. Formal education ended early, usually by age ten, with children expected to contribute to the economic well-being of the family. Those who worked outside the home were expected to turn over their earnings to the family. In addition, the celebration of holidays, responsibility for the aged and infirm, and the protection of individual rights were the responsibility of the family unit. While this created a strong sense of security and satisfaction among those who belonged, it also resulted in hostility and suspicion toward outsiders. It was felt that one owed nothing to those outside the family circle, a view that social scientists such as Edward Banfield called "amoral familism."

In such a system everyone had their place. Members of the immediate family came first, followed by extended family members, close friends, or respected elders. After this came acquaintances and, lastly, everyone else, known as *stranieri* or strangers. Included in this category might be a village merchant or a teacher in a local school. The primary consideration was the welfare of the family. A job was measured in terms of how it benefited the family, not simply the individual; an insult to one family member was an insult to all.

Of course, a family-centered life is typical of all peasant societies, be they of Polish, Spanish, French, or Italian origin. In Italy, however, there were other factors. Not only was formal education considered largely irrelevant but there was considerable antagonism toward the Church for a variety of reasons. The Church controlled a great deal of land and many priests were corrupt. Some observers have also suggested that celibacy was a problem in a society where children as well as sexual gratification were important values. With educational and religious institutions (though not religious practices and rituals) greatly weakened, a void was created and subsequently filled by the all-encompassing family.

In the larger context there was the historical experience of invasion and oppression. Through the centuries the region was conquered and occupied by various groups, including Cartha-

ginians, Greeks, Romans, Goths, Byzantines, Arabs, French, and
Spaniards. Exploitation by absentee landlords and cultural and
economic domination by northern Italy after unification also contributed mightily to both a sense of isolation and a lack of nationalistic feeling. As a result, the family became the center of
the life of the *contadini* (peasant class) largely because there
was no place else to turn.

The all-pervasive role of family life in southern Italy explains,
to some degree, why it was an important part of Italian culture
for the more than two million immigrants who arrived in the
United States between 1899 and 1910, but it does not fully explain why such values persisted—if indeed they did. Like other
groups, the Italian newcomers found the American environment
strange in a number of ways. They could not be farmers because
they lacked funds and were not, in any case, familiar with the
methods required for cultivating the typical large-scale American farm, which differed greatly from the small plots of land
typical in the old country. Turning instead to the cities, Italians
formed subcommunities made up of family and fellow villagers.
This, plus the belief that they were here only temporarily until
they could earn enough to return home helped keep the old
values, including that of *la famiglia,* alive. Another reason for
the family's strength in the early years was discrimination. One
newspaper called the immigrants "a horde of steerage slime" and
charged that almost all of them were criminals. A number of
states in the South did not allow Italian children to enroll in the
public schools, and in Tallulah, Louisiana, five immigrants who
befriended Black residents of the town were lynched by an
angry mob. Small wonder, then, that the Italians turned inward
to the protective confines of the family.

Despite strong prejudice against them, Italians gradually became Americanized. The children of immigrants attended
schools where they came into contact with non-Italians. Unlike
the villages of southern Italy, the Little Italys of America's cities
did not have the money or space to build recreation centers, and
these children turned instead to the streetcorner or the Irish-
dominated Catholic Church. During this period, which lasted
from about 1921 to the early 1940s, the Italian family entered

what Dr. Paul Campisi has called the "conflict stage." Many Italians married outside the community, thereby weakening the old ties to the family. Still, there was a great deal of ambivalence, as we see from the following account by Panella:

We were to favor our family first, other Italians next. This was our concept of loyalty, and one prescription for growing up. Our job was not so much to become Americans as it was to be "moxie" and successful, like the Jewish people. (p. 20)

Panella, however, was unable to accept this "prescription":

But I felt a special responsibility to break the pattern of living near family . . . A cousin once told me, "You were lucky, you escaped." Had I lived close to home I would have had to explain everything . . . from my taste in shoes to my taste in friends . . . Was I taking the subway downtown? Why not the bus? . . . And there was a blind impulse to chop, curb, or redirect any activity which I might do independently . . . I was torn between what I conceived as my responsibility toward my own growth and my responsibility toward my parents. (pp. 47–48)

Today, sixty years after the great wave of Italian immigration, the stereotype persists. Is it true? Yes and no. Many Italian-Americans still live as extended families. In New York City, for example, which has a large Italian population, a common form of housing in Italian neighborhoods is still the two-family house, with the parents or in-laws occupying one floor and the children another. Nevertheless, the majority of Italian-Americans, large numbers of whom are by now third generation, have become typical Americans, often indistinguishable in their lack of adherence to traditional family values, marked by life away from parents, a tendency toward smaller families, and less emphasis on family loyalty. As the years go by, this stereotype is therefore likely to die a slow death despite the sporadic attempts to revive it in the mass media. In southern Italy itself children are still quite respectful to their parents and the family still plays a significant role in the community, but it, too, is beginning to change somewhat under the impact of modernization and shifting values in the society as a whole.

Great singers

This is one stereotype that has a great deal of truth to it. While no research has established anything special about Italian vocal cords, and while there are millions of Italians who regularly sing off key, Italians have contributed far more than their share of outstanding vocalists.

Opera, as a musical art form, was born in Florence, Italy, at the onset of the seventeenth century. It was started by aristocrats who wanted to revive the stories of ancient Greek mythology. The first opera, so to speak, was *Dafne,* by Peri and Caccini. It was Peri who defined opera as music whose form was somewhere between speech and song, with the harmony changing only if the meaning of the words changed. The rest is history. Opera became one of the great art forms and has remained so to this very day. While originally the province of the Italian nobility, it became accessible to the masses as early as 1637, when the first public opera house opened in Venice, spreading soon to Naples, where it achieved even greater popularity.

Italian opera is generally believed to have made its American debut in 1825, when Manuel García's Italian Opera Company presented nine Italian operas to audiences in New York City. Cleofonte Campanini became the general director of the Chicago Opera Company in 1913 and had been one of two conductors of the Metropolitan Opera Company's first season in 1883. Since then persons of Italian extraction have dominated this field. Among the most famous opera singers then and now have been Enrico Caruso, Ezio Pinza, Anna Moffo, Renata Tebaldi, Rosa Ponselle, and Luciano Pavarotti. Some of the better known popular singers of Italian heritage include Frank Sinatra, Tony Bennett, Perry Como, Enzo Stuarti, Sergio Franchi, Mario Lanza, Vic Damone, Carol Lawrence, Julius La Rosa, Anna Maria Alberghetti, and many, many more. A large number of vocal coaches are Italian, and a significant number of members of the American Federation of Musicians are Italian-Americans. Italians have also had distinguished careers in other areas of music, including conducting, composing, as instrumentalists, and as bandleaders.

From the start, Italian immigrants to this country took great pride in their musical heritage, and both opera and music in general enjoyed considerable success. Just as Jewish immigrants flocked to the Yiddish theater, Italians crowded into the music halls to listen to their favorite performers, who both sang and danced. As a result, it was not surprising that music came to be seen as an avenue for moving up and out of the ghetto. It was not so much the talent of the Italians (though it was there) that enabled them to gain pre-eminence as it was a cultural predisposition to encourage the development of such abilities, as well as to appreciate them. In this sense, success begat success as Italian parents came to see those singers who had already made it as success symbols to be emulated by their children.

Talk with their hands

No one has, to my knowledge, done a study of how many Italian-Americans today talk with their hands, but such an investigation was indeed carried out in 1941 by David Efron, a political scientist, at Columbia University. In his book *Gesture and Environment* Efron presents an exhaustive analysis of the many gestures that are part of southern Italian culture and observes that Sicilians and especially Neapolitans are perfectly capable of carrying out a conversation without saying a single word. Contrary to Jews, Italians seem to leave a good deal of maneuvering space between each other, perhaps because, unlike Jews, they do not have a history of urban living in close quarters. Dr. Efron noted the existence of at least 125 separate gestures among his subjects.

Interestingly, many of the gestures employed by Italians have an ancient history dating back to Roman and Greek times. In his work on Roman gestures, the rhetorician Quintilian identified several oratorical gestures that are identical to those used by contemporary Italians. Other researchers, most notably Andrea de Jorio, pointed to the presence of such gestures on ancient statues.

Regardless of the tradition of gestural language among Italians, the practice would probably have died out were it not for the fact that it served a very important function throughout

Italy's history, especially that of the South. Oppressed and invaded over the centuries, gestures lived on as a language of clandestine communication in the same manner that secret societies or criminals may use them. The active use of gestures among Neapolitans and Sicilians not only helped them plan strategy and deceive the enemy but also gave them a feeling of solidarity in their struggles. One of the best known examples of this was the Sicilian Vespers rebellion of 1282, in which much of the revolt against the French was planned and discussed in the streets through the use of gestures.

Efron presents evidence that gestural behavior is a function of environment and not heredity. In his study he showed how the use of this expressive language disappeared as Italians became more assimilated. Nevertheless, to the extent that it is present, the gesture is as old as the Italian people themselves.

Belong to the Mafia

The beginnings of the Mafia go back at least as far as the thirteenth century, when the Sicilian Vespers tried to drive the French out of Sicily. The word itself is of uncertain origin. Some claim it is an acronym for *Morte alla Francia Italia anela* (Italy desires France's death). Others attribute it to a slogan used in the days when Giuseppe Mazzini was battling the Bourbons—*Mazzini Autorizza Furti, Incendi, Avvelenamenti* (Mazzini authorizes thievery, arson, and poisoning). Over the centuries numerous secret organizations were established to fight against foreign domination. Gradually these groups became a permanent feature of southern Italy. The term Mafia came into common use during the nineteenth century, when the organization—actually a loose confederation of many societies—greatly expanded its operations, particularly in western Sicily. Sometimes they were nothing more than extortionists and thieves, while at other times they were vanguard members of political movements fighting against either the landowners or the peasants. By the twentieth century, however, the Mafia in Italy had become synonymous with greed and corruption, as its members sought only to increase their power and maximize their profits.

The term mafia, when not capitalized, had a different connotation among Italians. It was an adjective used to describe someone who commanded respect, who knew how to "take care of things" without running to the authorities. It referred to an individual who had both power and dignity while also inspiring fear. He was, most importantly, a person whom one could approach when in need. Thus, such a term might be applied to a family patriarch who had no connection with the organization known as the Mafia. Such values were deeply rooted in the culture and heritage of southern Italian peasant society. All too often Americans who heard this term used by the newcomers when conversing among themselves confused the adjective with the noun.

Although they were only a small minority of the immigrant population, the stereotype that all Italian-Americans from southern Italy belonged to the Mafia was quite popular in this country around the turn of the century. Two incidents were highly instrumental in the development of this attitude. The first took place in 1890 in New Orleans, where eleven Italians were lynched by an angry mob after the police chief, David Henessey, was murdered. Although a court failed to find anyone guilty, the prevalent belief was that the Mafia had been behind it. (Henessey had been investigating extortion in the local Italian community.) The second incident concerned a New York City police lieutenant who was killed by a Mafia chieftain in Palermo, Sicily, where he had gone to look into possible connections between organized crime in America and Sicily. The attendant publicity greatly heightened the suspicion and hostility with which Americans viewed southern Italians.

When the fascists came to power in Italy during the 1920s and began a campaign against the Mafia, many came to the United States, hoping to get rich quickly. Their optimism was justified, for this was the era of Prohibition, when qualities such as ruthlessness, lust for power, and a tightly knit organization paid off. The Mafia established itself in American crime circles and has remained there ever since. True, the Jews and the Irish had their gangs too—actually, the Irish got started long before the Italians—but neither group had a history of criminal activity that stretched back for centuries. What all three groups did have in common was a willingness to use crime as a vehicle for economic betterment. The Irish were influential in politics and, of course, they had always controlled the Catholic Church hierarchy in the United States. As for the Jews, their strong belief in education, as well as their experience in commerce, helped them immeasurably in their efforts at raising their status. The Italian-Americans had none of these advantages, and subsequent to Prohibition many became involved in gambling, prostitution, contract murder, and loan-sharking. The majority, it should be added, were law-abiding citizens who were nonetheless stigmatized as criminals by the larger society.

While hardly anyone today would deny the existence of a Mafia organization made up almost solely of Italian-Americans (not to mention a very active one in Italy), relatively few Italian-Americans belong to it. In a 1967 article that appeared in *Life* magazine, writer Sandy Smith put the number of Mafia or Cosa Nostra (Our Thing or Our Affair, a synonym for Mafia) members at about five thousand. In *Blood of My Blood* author Richard Gambino estimated the membership at approximately five to six thousand, a small figure when one considers that there are over twenty million Italian-Americans in the United States. Why, then, has the stereotype survived? For one thing, the Mafia makes excellent copy and entertainment. With its Black Hand symbol, its code of *omertà* (requiring silence, which is actually part of Italian culture in general), and its unique customs and rituals, it has provided material for countless books, movies, and television programs. Take, for example, the following quote from Joseph Valachi's testimony before the McClellan committee of the U. S. Senate:

The boss picks up the gun and intones . . . . : Niatri reprentam La Cosa Nostra. Sta famigghia è La Cosa Nostra (We represent La Cosa Nostra. This family is Our Thing.) The sponsor then pricks his trigger finger and the trigger finger of the new member, holding both together to symbolize the mixing of blood. After swearing to hold the family above his religion, his country, and his wife and children, the inductee finished the ritual. A picture of a saint or a religious card is placed in his cupped hands and ignited. As the paper burns, the inductee, together with his sponsor, proclaims: "If I ever violate this oath, may I burn as this paper." (*Time*, August 22, 1969: 19)

Now, what screenwriter or novelist could resist copy based on real life experiences that sounds better than most fiction?

Helped by TV series such as "The Untouchables" and "The F.B.I.," plus movies like *The Godfather* and books such as *Honor Thy Father*, by Gay Talese, the term Mafia has become synonymous with crime of every sort. Thus people will talk about a "Mafia-type organization" that has no Italian members, or they will accuse someone of "Mafia tactics," which both perpetuates the stereotype and demonstrates how pervasive it is. The popularity of the term makes it harder to deal with the stereotype because whenever the word is uttered the speaker is almost always aware of its Italian origin.

Not to be overlooked is the Italian-American community's contribution. Notwithstanding his criminal activity, the Mafioso is perceived as having many characteristics generally respected by Italians. He is, first of all, a family man. This is driven home by the fact that the structure of the Mafia is based on kinship. In a recent study of the twenty leading "syndicate" families in a major midwestern city, the anthropologist Francis Ianni found that *all* twenty families had intermarried. Moreover, they had formed alliances through marriage with crime families in New York City, New Orleans, and Buffalo. Other valued traits associated with the Mafioso (in theory at least) are loyalty, courage, power, decisiveness, cunning, and a strong sense of honor. Thus, while the average Italian is likely to condemn the Mafia as well as fear it, he may also admire it. This point is clearly made by Della Femina and Sopkin:

Soon a flashy car would drive up, and the soldier of the family would emerge. He'd be dressed simply—white shirt, pair of dark slacks, jacket—and usually he would conduct his business very quietly near the candy store. All the gamblers, the bust-out guys, the hangers-on, the potential hoods, the kids desperately wanting to become connected were trying to stay cool and unconcerned but they were watching. *After all, this was our version of royalty.* [emphasis added] (*An Italian Grows in Brooklyn*, p. 40)

Exaggerations stemming from a desire to impress can also keep alive the stereotype that "all Italians either belong to the Mafia or know someone who does." An Italian acquaintance of mine has his co-workers believing that he is "Mafia-connected" despite the fact that he knows no one personally who belongs to the Mafia. "It makes them respect me more" he says without a trace of defensiveness.

The Mafia's days as a criminal organization are numbered despite its long though not so venerable history. The main factor is competition from Latins and Blacks, who have the same economic needs and lack of legitimate opportunities that faced their ethnic forbears of sixty years ago. In some cases actual wars have erupted, while in others, such as New York's East Harlem, the area has simply been "leased" to others, who then "work the neighborhood." Government efforts to destroy the syndicates have also sapped its strength. Finally, the increased opportunities for upward mobility that await young Italians means that fewer and fewer will see crime as an attractive alternative. The extinction of this stereotype will come as a great relief to most Italians, for never have so few been given credit for being so many.

Cowards in battle

The ancient Romans were, of course, great soldiers. The "coward" stereotype did not appear in the literature or in the popular mind until the 1940s. It owes its origins to World War II, in which the Italians performed poorly. The Italians were hardly enthusiastic about a campaign of aggression under the banner of fascism. Even Mussolini admitted that fascism had achieved its greatest popularity in 1937. One commentator at the time characterized the Italian Army as one predominantly made up of conscientious objectors. Italy entered World War II against a backdrop of having suffered reverses at the hands of antifascist forces during the Spanish Civil War. Nor had its reputation been enhanced by reports that it had liberally sprayed poison gases on Ethiopian villages. After some initial victories in North Africa, the Italians were decisively defeated by the British and driven out of Egypt, which they had briefly occupied. This was followed by humiliating defeats in Greece and Albania.

The failure of the Italian war effort in these areas was due not so much to incompetence as to poor preparedness and miscalculation. Mussolini's generals had told him that Italy's Army was not ready to go to war, but he ignored their advice. He had invaded Greece without informing Hitler and was subsequently forced to beg him for help. The Nazi leader obliged, but in the process Italy almost became a colony of Germany to be exploited at will. Throughout the war Italy was successful only when it fought alongside the Germans or with massive aid. By itself it lacked the firepower to successfully engage the Allies.

The American image of the Italian soldier was formed primarily by reports from the front, especially by newsreels in 1942, which showed soldiers surrendering by the thousands in North Africa. Some historians have noted that American attitudes toward the Italians were shaped by the line of invasion, which began in the impoverished and devastated South, where the people had been reduced to begging and stealing by the ravages of the war. The occupying forces did little to hide their contempt as they swept through the Italian countryside. Very few demonstrated the compassion shown by the officer in John Hersey's novel *A Bell for Adano*.

There is no doubt that the military record of the Italians during World War II was a poor one, but it is atypical. In fact, a standard work on the subject of military failure by individuals, *On the Psychology of Military Incompetence*, by Norman Dixon, does not even honor the Italian people with a footnote, though it records the foibles of other nations in great detail. The fact is that Italy's overall record of battlefield successes prior to World War II was not particularly bad or good. Despite this Americans are fond of telling jokes such as:

How does an Italian admiral review his fleet?
Through a glass-bottomed boat.

Perhaps it may be because of the traditional contempt that the victor has for the vanquished—especially when the latter loses badly. Nevertheless, the attitude is yet another instance of the phenomenon of selective perception, for these are the same people who are accused of inspiring fear through the Mafia, who are known for their violence, and in whose neighborhoods others fear to tread. Certainly this observer does not recall receiving the impression as a child that Italian boys were cowards. Quite the contrary. In the neighborhood where I was raised on Manhattan's West Side they were highly respected for their fighting prowess.

There is, furthermore, no evidence that Italians are genetically inferior as soldiers. The military record of Italian-Americans is a distinguished one. An estimated 250,000 fought in World War I; for World War II the figure is believed to have been over 500,000. Moreover, many distinguished themselves in battle. While polls taken in the United States were indicating that Americans thought the Italians faint of heart in combat, soldiers of Italian extraction were winning Congressional Medals of Honor—a dozen in all—while ten were awarded the Navy Cross. Perhaps the most famous soldier was pilot Donald Gentile, who flew 182 missions and downed 23 German warplanes.

Violent and quick-tempered

Such perceptions owe a good deal to the Mafia and the broader stereotype that Mediterranean/Latin people are hot tempered, but there were other factors as well that pertain to Italians in particular. The first was the attitude toward law and order that prevailed in the old country. The authorities in southern Italy tended to be corrupt and disinterested in settling local squabbles. As a result, the peasants often had no recourse but to take the law into their own hands, using violence if necessary. When they arrived here, their contempt for the law continued and was, in fact, reinforced by policemen who already viewed them rather negatively. Commenting on the Italians in general, one judge observed that it was well known "that Italians carry concealed weapons." And indeed, many did, if only for their own protection. To understand their perceptions of American society one need only recall the lynchings in Louisiana; the Sacco and Vanzetti trial, in which the defendants charged that they had been persecuted because of their nationality as well as their philosophy; and the thousands of other unreported cases of discrimination that confronted immigrants.

Another consideration was the Italian attitude toward certain types of crimes. While Americans might regard divorce as the solution to adultery, Italians felt compelled, within the context of their culture, to treat unfaithfulness as a grave affront to the honor of the family; this may have meant that as a matter of pride the individual had to take matters into his own hands. This did not only apply to adultery, promiscuity, and similar offenses but to anything where manhood was challenged. Any humiliation demanded a direct and, if necessary, violent response. If the community perceived that the individual had not been sufficiently assertive, his respect and standing within that community suffered greatly and he was often openly ridiculed. Yet, while a violent response to an insult was completely justified in the public eye, American law treated it rather harshly.

Differences in physical appearances had an effect too. Southern Italians were more swarthy than the average American. Moreover, they spoke a foreign language and had many strange customs that were unfamiliar to those already here. Their arrival in great numbers within a relatively short period of time made these differences even more noticeable. Coupled with their reputation for conducting vendettas against their own kind and their emphasis on *omertà*, the general impression that they were a "dark and sinister lot" gained wide acceptance.

Did Italian immigrants really commit violent crimes more often? As any police officer knows, crimes of passion are among the most easily discovered, with the perpetrator often making no attempt to deny his or her guilt. Even so, criminologist Donald Cressey reports that Italian immigrants committed fewer crimes than native born Americans. This is echoed by Professor Gambino, who cites statistical evidence from Boston and Providence indicating a lower crime rate among Italian arrivals than among other foreign-born peoples. Interestingly enough, there were even penologists who supported the exaggerated view of the Italian propensity for violence. In *Strangers in the Land* historian John Higham quotes one such expert: "The knife with which he cuts his bread he also uses to lop off another dago's finger or ear." Such stereotypes were often supported by the highest officials in the land. Long after the Italians had arrived here, President Franklin Delano Roosevelt made the following accusation regarding Italy's entry into World War II:

On this tenth day of June 1940 the hand that held the dagger has struck it into the back of its neighbor. (New York *World Telegram*, June 11, 1940)

If the President of the United States saw nothing wrong with making suggestive statements of this sort, what could one expect of the average American?

It is highly doubtful that a propensity for violent behavior exists among Italian-Americans today. In fact, there is no evidence to support it. Criminologists have not reported any tendency toward violent crime on the part of Italian-Americans except for the Mafia, which involves a statistically tiny minority. Nor does the behavior of contemporary Italians in their native land support such an assumption. A man walking down the street of a major Italian city may find his wallet filched by a pickpocket. If you are a woman, a passing male may stare at you with a frankness unusual in the United States. Violence, on the other hand, is not at all common. The incidence of armed robbery and homicide is quite low, relatively speaking. True, there are attacks by political terrorists as well as by organized crime figures, but there is little of the random violence that most Americans have become accustomed to in their own land. Thus, it would seem as though this stereotype may have been somewhat accurate in the past but is no longer so today.

Great shoemakers

In the early part of the twentieth century about two thirds of all shoemakers in New York City were of Italian origin. Today this percentage has declined as upward mobility continues to influence one's choice of occupation. Still, there are many neighborhoods throughout urban America where people go to their "Italian shoemaker" though Jews, Greeks, and other groups are, of course, also represented.

Part of the reason for this stereotype is that shoemaking was a highly respected craft in Italian village society for centuries. It required an apprenticeship to a master craftsman that generally began at an early age. The leather and style of shoe had to be selected according to individual specifications. Listen to Henry Tolino as he describes the art to which he devoted a lifetime:

I began to learn the shoemaking trade in Italy when I was 6 years old. The craft of shoemakers was learned from the bottom up. As an apprentice we would take shoes apart to learn how to make the shoe patterns for women, children, and men. Each aspect of shoe-making was a specialty in itself and bootmaking required still different techniques . . . I was about 12 or 13 when we came to this country and I had 7 or 8 years apprenticeship in shoemaking. (La Gumina [ed.], *The Immigrants Speak: The Italian Americans Tell Their Story*, p. 54)

Those who became shoemakers in Italy were usually guaranteed lifetime job security. This, plus the fact that education was considered unimportant, made shoemaking a respectable occupation within the community. Moreover, it meant that one could be independent. When economic conditions worsened around the turn of the century, even established artisans were forced to emigrate. Upon their arrival in the United States, they found that industrialization had created two problems for them. First, their work was regarded as fit only for persons with little ambition. The thing to do was to find employment in an expanding industry. Second, there was no need for individual shoemakers when shoe manufacturers were mass-producing boots, shoes, slippers, and so forth. As a result, the shoemaker turned to shoe *repairing*, though he was still called a shoemaker. Here his skills could be used in rehabilitating shoes. It is quite possible that his abilities in this area were, in fact, superior because of his background. Unlike the auto mechanic or TV repairman, an integral part of his training involved actually creating the product that he was now forced, by economic necessity, to repair.

To be sure, there were shoemakers in most of the other countries from which America's immigrants came, but additional factors also played a role in their decision to pursue this field. For example, the Jews may have come here as shoemakers, but their culturally determined attitudes toward education made them see it less as a craft than as something to be done until one's financial position improved. Other groups, such as the Irish, who were mostly small tenant farmers driven here by the potato famine, simply did not number many shoemakers in their midst.

While most shoemakers kept to their vocations, there were many exceptions. One of the most notable was that of Remigio

The things they say behind your back

Pane, who, after working as a shoemaker for a number of years, attended college in the evening, eventually obtaining a degree. Today he is a recently retired full professor of Italian at Rutgers University, which has a nationally acclaimed Department of Italian.

Today Italy has an international reputation for making quality shoes that are the height of fashion. The pride that the Italians take in the design, workmanship, and quality of their product is directly related to the historical importance of this craft in a country that, ironically, is shaped just like a boot.

FOUR

Blacks

Persisting to this day is an attitude, shared by black and white alike, that blacks are inferior. This belief permeates every facet of this country, and it is the etiological agent from which has developed the national sickness. (Grier and Cobbs, *Black Rage*, p. 25)

These words, written in 1969 by two prominent Black psychiatrists, summed up the prevailing perception of Blacks in this country. In the past ten years Black people have made significant gains in housing, employment, and politics. Despite this, an article based on a 1980 survey of five thousand Black Americans concluded that socially Blacks were no better off and that negative stereotyping by whites continued.

The greatest irony is that for all the economic and political progress we have made, we are ignored and held in greater disdain than ever before. White America's preferred portrait of us has not progressed a great deal from the stereotypes we have fought so long to bury. In fact, our image in film, television, and literature may be worse now than it was in 1970. (*Black Enterprise*, August 1980: 49)

No group in American society has suffered as much from discrimination as Afro-Americans. This fact is reflected in the paucity of positive stereotypes about them. The perceptions of Black people in this country are particularly vicious even when compared to other negatively viewed groups such as Hispanics and Jews, and it would seem doubtful that they will disappear in the near future.

Hypersensitive

Hypersensitivity is difficult to define. If a person imagines bigotry where none exists, he can, in the strict sense of the term, be accused of hypersensitivity. If, on the other hand, one considers the real insults and degradation that an individual has suffered because of membership in a certain group, his "hypersensitivity" might more aptly be called "high sensitivity." In Gordon W. Allport's *The Nature of Prejudice* the following incident is cited:

One day in the late 30's a recently arrived refugee couple went shopping in a village grocery store in New England. The husband ordered some oranges.

"For juice?" inquired the clerk.

"Did you hear that," the woman whispered to her husband, "for Jews? You see, it's beginning here too." (p. 141)

Members of any discriminated against group are apt to be very sensitive to comments by others about their national, religious, or racial characteristics. In the case of Blacks this is likely to be heightened by several factors. First, the Black movement of the 1960s was marked by the development of Black consciousness. Many Blacks became acutely aware of the centuries of discrimination to which their people had been subjected. Unable to lash out at plantation owners and slave traders, many directed their anger at whites in general, whether they were radical, liberal, or conservative in their attitudes toward Blacks. This included extreme sensitivity to comments made by whites about the Black race. The movement also reintroduced the concept of separatism. This idea, while popular in the 1920s under the influence of Marcus Garvey, had given way to an integrationist approach that lasted until about 1964. Separatism was largely justified on two grounds: the need to develop Black pride and the pervasiveness of white racism. The latter requirement made Blacks acutely conscious of statements by whites about them even when they were well-intentioned, as illustrated by the following incident.

In 1969, at the height of the movement's militant phase, I invited a sympathetic white to a Black power conference at which Imamu Amiri Baraka (a.k.a. LeRoi Jones) was the principal speaker. My own involvement stemmed from the fact that I was writing a book about a paramilitary Black organization that had sponsored the event and for which I was working as a liaison officer. We listened—the only whites in the audience of about two hundred persons—as Baraka denounced whites as "honkies, capitalist pigs, and bloodsucking racists" and implored Blacks to rise up in revolt against the "white oppressor." After the talk was over, my acquaintance—let us call him Bob—walked up to a general of the aforementioned paramilitary group and said to him, "You know, I really admire you people. I mean, you got it all together; you really know where it's at. The way you take pride in your culture is really beautiful." His well-meant observation was greeted with the following response: "Excuse me," said the general, "but would you mind telling me what nationality *you* are?" Bob seemed momentarily taken aback. An assimilated Jew, he regarded himself as an agnostic and did not identify himself ethnically. After some hesitation he blurted out, "Why . . . why—I'm Jewish." "Oh yeah," said the general in a slightly menacing tone, "then why are you here? You've got a culture. You've got a people and a history. What are you? Some kind of parasite, trying to get an identity offa my people? Why don't you go back where you belong, *honkie*?" And with that he turned on his heel and stalked off, leaving Bob alone with me and his bruised ego. "What did I do?" he asked me. In truth Bob had done nothing very wrong. His admiring remarks had simply been interpreted by the general as patronizing and condescending. Given the emotional climate between Blacks and whites at the time, this was entirely understandable.

Sensitivity of this sort has not diminished greatly in the past ten years. In fact, as Blacks move up the socioeconomic ladder, thereby both threatening white positions of power while at the same time coming into greater contact with them, misunderstandings are likely to increase.

Take, for example, the following account by a Black senior corporate director:

I was on a trip to Chicago with the chairman of my board of directors. In the morning I sat down in the hotel lobby and he said, "Hey, Williams, go up to my room and get my luggage." My first reaction was to say "Get your own luggage. What do I look like to you, a redcap?" But I swallowed my pride and got his bags. My jaws were tight for a week. Then I began to notice how the white vice presidents, senior vice presidents, knocked each other down to take care of the chairman's luggage, get him checked out of hotels and see that his limo was waiting . . . You can be a so-called "man" and work in the mailroom for the rest of your life, or you can take some crap and make $65,000 per year. Everybody in a corporation takes crap, and the higher you get, the more you have to take. They use it to test you. (*Black Enterprise*, November 1977: 34)

The problem is exacerbated by the fact that being sensitive to slights against one's own group does not mean that the individual will be sensitive to slights against others. This insensitivity to others was brought home to members of a class I taught in race relations.

We were discussing responses to minority status when one student offered the observation that Jews were more sensitive than any other group. Others supported this position and one student, who was Black, recalled the following incident that had taken place in her office at work. "I told this Jewish woman 'Why don't you go fly a kite?' and she said, 'Don't you call me a kike.'" Other remarks, some of which were openly hostile to Jews, were then made by numerous students in the class, which was predominantly Black with a scattering of Hispanics. I decided that an object lesson might be in order here. "You know, all this reminds me of a joke I heard the other day while I was walking on the City College campus down Convent Avenue. There were students walking ahead of me and I heard one say to the other, 'Wanna hear a good joke?' 'Yeah,' said the other. 'What's the easiest way to kill a Jew?' 'I give up,' he replied. 'Throw a nickel into the middle of the street.'" The entire class burst out laughing at this caricature of the Jew's stereotyped preoccupation with money. "Now let me tell you another joke," I said after the laughter had subsided somewhat. "I was in a store in Forest Hills, Queens, when I heard the following exchange: 'What's the easiest way to kill a *schvartzer*?' said one man. 'I don't know,' replied the other. 'Throw a bottle of Old Grand-Dad into the middle of 125th Street.'" This time there was no laughter, only dead silence. The class appeared stunned as I went on. "Why isn't anybody laughing? Why isn't this joke as funny as the other one? Is it because it's about your own people? Why is it that we fail to perceive that others have the same feelings that we do?" Eventually students began joining in the discussion, which then focused on how different groups could come to have a greater sense of appreciation for each other.

Hypersensitivity is not unique to Blacks. It is a feature of virtually any group that suffers and is oppressed by others. Since Blacks have suffered more than any other group in America, they may respond more quickly to slights, real or imagined. Sometimes hypersensitivity becomes a way of rationalizing failures. For instance, a Black person is fired from his job because he has performed poorly. Unwilling to recognize his own failings, he accuses his employer of racism. In another case a Black person is laid off from his job by an employer who has been known to make prejudiced comments about Blacks. The Black employee files a suit against the employer and is labeled hypersensitive. He wins his suit and is vindicated. Both patterns exist and are unavoidable in a multiracial society such as ours, where racism is part of the fabric of our culture.

Sexual prowess

Two workers at a steel mill in Pittsburgh are changing shifts. Don, who is Black, says to his white replacement, Gene, "You sure got a pretty wife."

"Maybe," says Gene, "but did you ever look at her when she wakes up in the morning?"

"No," replies Don. "She always makes me leave before you come back from the night shift."

This joke embodies both the potency stereotype and that of the Black who always wants white women. In addition, there is the view that Black members of both sexes are loose, promiscuous, and generally easygoing concerning sexual matters. One statistic often cited concerns the number of children born out of wedlock. The rate for Blacks is estimated to be between five and seven times as high as for whites. The reasons for this have nothing to do with inherent racial characteristics, being rooted in socioeconomic and cultural factors that stem from centuries of discrimination and oppression. Moreover, these figures do not always tell the whole story. Studies have shown, for example, that Blacks are less likely than whites to have abortions. This does not mean, however, that they are necessarily more *promiscuous* than whites. Whites are also more likely to be able to afford private hospital care, where it is far easier to avoid recording an illegitimate birth than in a public hospital.

The stereotype that Blacks have great sexual prowess is also highly questionable. In fact, psychologists Abram Kardiner and Lionel Ovesey suggest in their book *Mark of Oppression* that broken homes, lack of opportunity, and status anxieties often create impotence and passivity. Black psychologist Kenneth Clark observes in *Dark Ghetto* that

Negro males were [portrayed by whites as] animal-like and brutish in their appetites and hence to be feared and shunned by white women. The ironic fact has been that, given the inferiority of their racial status, Negro males have had to struggle simply to believe themselves men. It has long been an "inside" bit of bitter humor among Negroes to say that Negro men should bribe their wives to silence. (p. 68)

Dr. Clark goes on to state that Black women of status may often reject Black men as sexual partners simply because their social status is inferior. He also notes the irony of whites who connect this lack of status with uninhibited sexual lusts and high potency.

Dr. John Dollard's study of a town in the Deep South provides further evidence that all is not as it seems in this area. Most of the town's whites believed that interracial sexual contacts were almost always initiated by Blacks. Yet Dollard's exhaustive research proved that the opposite was the case. He explained this state of affairs as a feature of projection. Whites felt guilty about the sexual liberties they took with Blacks and tried to pin the blame on the Black partner for whatever happened. In this sense Blacks represented certain secret desires that no white Southerner of the thirties could admit to having. In the context of life in those times, Blacks were often powerless to resist sexual advances by whites.

In addition to accusing Blacks of "starting up with them," whites found theories of racial superiority very useful in the context of their own sexual desires. By viewing Blacks as inferior, they were now able to exploit them in good conscience. This ploy was, of course, used to justify not only sexual oppression but slavery and economic and social discrimination in a variety of areas.

Both foreign and domestic critics of American culture have noted that we are a sexually repressed nation in many ways. This was especially true of life in the small towns of the Deep South during the first half of this century, where religious and racial taboos were often inextricably intertwined. In *Killers of the Dream* writer Lillian Smith noted how these two topics were mixed together.

Now parts of your body are segregated areas which you must stay away from and keep others away from. These areas you touch only when necessary. In other words, you cannot associate freely with them any more than you can associate freely with colored children . . . your body is God's holy temple. (p. 73)

By putting white women on a pedestal of purity and chastity, Southern white men set into motion a vicious cycle from which it was almost impossible to escape. Having designated their wives as chaste, they often succeeded in making them frigid. In response, they sought out Black women whom their society had debased. Forced by their own code to deny having achieved satisfaction in this manner, they were compelled to deny having initiated or even taken part in such liaisons. And finally, they suspected their own white wives of similar entanglements, reasoning "If I can, then perhaps she can too." In this manner the white male was able to accuse the Black male of the "mongrelization" that was often his own doing.

The helpless and accessible Black became the solution for the white, who often equated sexual yearnings with racial prohibitions. But to appreciate the depth of such feelings we need to reach a bit further into history than the American experience with slavery. It is in the Bible that we find the first association of licentiousness with blackness when Ham is cursed for "looking upon his father's nakedness." As Dr. Winthrop Jordan points out in *White Over Black*, the expansionist policies of sixteenth-century England gave this story a new sense of relevance and immediacy. Displacing the African became acceptable, for were these not the descendants of Ham? It is no accident that Shakespeare's *Othello* weaves a narrative in which sex and race are treated as parts of a larger whole. Thus Iago says: "I hate the Moor;/And it is thought abroad that 'twixt my sheets/He has done my office . . ."

The English, upon seeing the attire that prevailed in Africa at the time, interpreted this as a further sign of free and easy attitudes toward sex. Also, as Dr. Jordan notes, there was a common notion in those times that there were bestial connections between Africans and apes, who, they believed, often attacked and copulated with Black women. Establishing such a link tremendously heightened the impression that Africans were lustful, wanton, and uninhibited in their sexual desires and appetites. Such opinions found their way into innumerable literary and scholarly works of Elizabethan England and became part of the cultural baggage brought over by whites to this country. Typical were the views of the writer John Atkins, as cited by Jordan:

At some places the *Negroes* have been suspected of Bestiality with them [apes and monkeys] . . . . from the near resemblances are sometimes met to the Human Species would tempt one to suspect the Fact. (*White Over Black*, p. 31)

Views such as these helped sustain racism on both the individual and group levels for centuries thereafter.

Physically powerful, great athletes

This stereotype owes its origin to a number of factors. First, lack of equal opportunity for many years restricted Blacks to unskilled work that often involved hard physical labor. As people grew accustomed to seeing Blacks working as sharecroppers, ditch diggers, and at other menial jobs, the idea grew that they must be especially capable in types of work requiring strenuous physical exertion when, in fact, Blacks often worked at whatever jobs they could get, namely, those whites didn't want.

To the degree that certain physical traits are inherited, a common notion has developed that those Blacks capable of doing backbreaking work on the plantations during slavery produced offspring who were equally strong. This may or may not be true, but it cannot be proven and conveniently ignores those Afro-Americans who are not so well endowed.

The prominence of Blacks in sports also enhances the image of strength. Until the 1950s racial prejudice greatly restricted Black participation in sports. By 1956, however, five out of six weight-class championships in boxing had been won by Blacks. In fact, for all but five years since 1937 Blacks have held the prestigious heavyweight championship. Blacks are represented in football, basketball, and baseball in far greater proportion than in the general population, and many are outstanding performers. It should be understood, however, that sports has traditionally been a way of "making it" for members of other minority groups too. In boxing, for example, the Jews had Benny Leonard and Barney Ross, the Irish Jack Dempsey and Jack Sharkey, and the Italians Rocky Marciano and Carmen Basilio, to name just a few. Because they are the most discriminated against group in American society, for Blacks sports as a way of advancing is perhaps even more important. Take the case of Michael "Campy" Russell, forward for the New York Knicks. One of ten children, Russell began playing basketball at age ten and was selected to the pros as a hardship case following his junior year in college.

Notice how he equates basketball with the Black experience in
the following quote from an interview he gave to the New York
Times.

We lived in a Black neighborhood and as soon as we came home
from school or church, everybody played basketball in the play-
ground near our home.

Some will note the relative absence of Blacks in tennis, golf,
and ice hockey. This is not, however, due to lack of ability.
Given the socioeconomic conditions prevailing in the Black community, finding both the time and the money for tennis was very
difficult. Unlike basketball, urban areas, where most Blacks live,
do not have tennis courts in every neighborhood. Finally, until
recently tennis tended to be regarded as a "gentleman's game,"
one that was played, for the most part, in private clubs from
which Blacks were almost always excluded. That Althea Gibson
and Arthur Ashe became standout tennis players (both won the
prestigious Wimbledon Tournament) is a tribute to both their
abilities and perseverance. Golf suffered from the same disadvantages. Those few athletes who became golf pros were able to
do so either because a parent was employed at a golf course or
because they themselves worked there as caddies. As for ice
hockey, it is a Canadian game and until recently there were, relatively speaking, few Blacks living in Canada. True, most major
American cities have hockey teams, but the Canadian influence
still predominates, as can be seen from the fact that the majority
of players on American teams are Canadian.

Most Black youths who dream of making it in professional
sports do not see that dream fulfilled. Nevertheless, well-known
Blacks in various sports have always been strong role models for
youngsters raised in circumstances characterized by poverty and
limited opportunities. The high salaries, glamorous life-styles,
and public recognition are often seen as a shortcut to success despite appeals by Arthur Ashe and other Black athletes, or by
parents, to stay in school as long as possible.

Notwithstanding the environmental factors that resulted in
Blacks working as laborers and their dominance in various sports
that depend on brute strength, many, including Blacks themselves, believe their pre-eminence in these areas is due to certain

innate abilities. Typical is the following statement, which appeared in 1966 in *The Negro Handbook*, a compendium of facts about Blacks published by the Black-owned Johnson Company:

Although noted for speed and strength *since slavery days,* the Negro has had to overcome many obstacles in order to earn a living in any field. [emphasis added] (p. 399)

Interestingly, there is evidence that Blacks are more athletic and stronger physically than whites. In his doctoral dissertation anthropologist Robert Malina studied the growth, maturation, and performance of a sample of Philadelphia schoolchildren between the ages of six and twelve. Black children of both sexes had greater strength values in four measures of static strength. In another study on the nutritional status of adult Black women, researchers found them to have greater grip strength than white women. Although there are studies reporting no significant differences, most research on this issue suggests that Blacks generally have better muscle development than whites. The same is true for studies of athletic ability. For example, Blacks outperform whites in gymnastic tests of jumping ability, running (except for long-distance running, where whites seem to do better), throwing, and other areas. Because of the unpopularity of research on racial differences, and because of methodological problems in doing such research, conclusions on this matter cannot be drawn. Still, the limited data that are available point to differences in physical prowess and related motor skills between Blacks and whites.

This stereotype, it should be understood, is one that the prejudiced white finds easier to accept because it fits in with the image of the Black as a subhuman brute. From who else is one to expect displays of extraordinary physical strength? In other words, the prejudiced white is willing to grant the Black man superiority in the ring as long as it can be established that he is inferior in other respects. Eldridge Cleaver makes this point very well in *Soul on Ice* in his discussion of what Muhammad Ali means to Blacks and whites.

. . . a black champion, as long as he is firmly fettered in his private life, is a fallen lion at every white man's feet . . . But when the ape breaks away from the leash, beats with deadly fists upon his massive

chest and starts talking to boot, proclaiming himself to be the
greatest, spouting poetry . . . a very serious slippage takes place in
the white man's self-image—*because that by which he defined himself no longer has a recognizable identity.* "If that black ape is a
man," the white man asks himself, "then what am I?" (pp. 93–94)

Dirty and slovenly

In cafeterias here you go around and collect your food, then niggers
paw over it and then you have to give them a tip to carry your tray.
Big, old dirty black paws pawing over your food and then you've
got to eat it.

                                        Paul A. Marlin, Inverness, Florida

It's the idea of rubbing up against them. It won't rub off, but it
doesn't feel right either.

                                        Claude Sanderson, Detroit

I don't like to touch them. It just makes me squeamish. I know I
shouldn't be that way, but it still bothers me.

                                        Neva Riggle, Washington, Pennsylvania
                                        (*Newsweek*, October 21, 1963: 48–50)

Although recent studies point to a steady decline in anti-Black
stereotypes, the depth of feelings expressed in this *Newsweek* article on prejudice indicates that association of Blacks with that
which is unclean is deeply embedded in the minds of many
whites. The color black has always had negative connotations in
the English language. Some examples are: black magic, black as
the night, a black day, black as the devil, and so forth. Con-
versely, white is seen as pure, clean, and chaste.

As Dr. Jordan has pointed out in *White Over Black*, blackness
as a synonym for dirt was transferred to the general perception
of Africans from the time Europeans first came into contact with
them. Indeed, even prior to that period the Oxford English Dictionary defined black as "foul, atrocious, baneful, deeply stained
with dirt, soiled," and so forth.

Interestingly, Europeans in those days rarely bathed, prefer-
ring instead to use perfumes and pomades to cover the odor
caused by their uncleanliness.

Such views continue to exist among whites today. In a study published in 1964, anthropologist Mary Ellen Goodman explored racial attitudes among 104 young children of both races. Her study demonstrated that most white children perceive Blacks as dirty, and therefore inferior, as early as age four. The question is: Why?

Here we must turn again to the concept of projection, which is basic to understanding prejudice. In the anal phase of psychological development the child develops strong negative feelings toward excrement. This comes at a crucial point in the child's life. As psychiatrist Joel Kovel explains in his *White Racism: A Psychohistory,*

. . . anality is the form of drive behavior which predominates . . . when a child is painfully detaching himself from his mother . . . [It] becomes symbolically associated with the ambivalent feelings a child has about separation from his mother . . . Dirt becomes, then, the recipient of his anger at separation. (p. 49)

The problem is that the child finds it too difficult to accept the fact that parts of his body are dirty, smelly, and bad. As a result, he or she unconsciously projects such feelings onto others.

All this may sound plausible in theory, but is there any concrete evidence for it? In a 1978 article that appeared in the *Journal of Nervous and Mental Diseases,* Dr. Seymour Fisher, who teaches in the Department of Psychiatry at the Upstate Medical Center in Syracuse, New York, presented the results of an effort to test this hypothesis. Eight samples of males and females were evaluated with respect to their attitudes toward anality and Black people. The results confirmed the hypothesis. Those who scored high in the dirt-anality dimension of the test also scored high in their negative views of Blacks.

To be sure, other groups have also been viewed in this manner. The English think the Irish are dirty; the Poles in Europe held the same view of Jews; in America poor whites are called "white trash"; there are Polish jokes about dirt, and so forth. Clearly, the anality theory can be applied to many groups. In the United States, the subordinate status of Blacks makes them the most likely target of such perceptions.

Environment and culture also play a role here. Poor people

often have problems with cleanliness because of the conditions of their poverty. It is well known that Blacks buy more household cleaning items than whites. This has, however, been directly correlated with socioeconomic class. Poor people, irrespective of their race, live in crowded, often dirty conditions that they do not like but are forced to endure. That they spend more money on cleansers, roach spray, and so forth, is clear evidence that they are concerned about them. Yet the white who is anxious to "prove" his projective assertion will take delight in driving through a Black ghetto and will cite its littered streets—these areas are last in line for garbage pickup—and shabbily dressed inhabitants as evidence of their ingrained slovenliness. "Look how they live," he will say, never inquiring seriously as to *why* they live that way.

Body odor is often associated with dirt in the way whites stereotype Blacks. This emerged in Europe during the period of exploration and maintained its primacy in the era of slavery. Even were there some truth to the assertion that slaves smelled bad, it would be perfectly understandable when one considers their living conditions. How many bathhouses did the plantation owner build for them? How much soap were they given? How clean were their living quarters? It is a fact that hard physical labor makes a person sweat. The harder you work, the more you sweat. Forced to do hard, menial labor, such as working as a cleaning lady, a busboy, or a dishwasher, people will sweat, whether they are Black or white.

The apocrine glands control the bacteriological agents that create offensive smells in the human body. One of the leading authorities in this field is Dr. William Montagna, who concludes in *The Structure and Function of the Skin,* standard text for dermatologists, that there is no definitive evidence that Blacks have more apocrine glands than members of other races, and that very little is understood about these glands. A study of consumer behavior done in the late sixties indicated that in eleven out of twelve possible income groupings Blacks used more deodorant, toothpaste, and mouthwash than comparable groups of whites. According to the authors of the study, the bulk of the differences, particularly among those with lower incomes, is related to family size. Nevertheless, it is clear that Blacks care at least as much about cleanliness as whites.

To sum up, there is no evidence that Blacks are any dirtier than whites. Moreover, research on this question reveals that this stereotype is probably held by whites because of certain very powerful psychological hangups that develop early in life.

Stupid

"Oh. You teach at City College. Tell me the truth. Don't the Black students do more poorly than the whites? I mean, are they really as smart as whites?"

Sometimes the questioner will throw in a comment about how intelligent Asian students are to reassure me (and perhaps himself) that he is not a racist but a person who deals in facts. Another line of questioning to which I am frequently exposed is:

"Now, as a social scientist, what do you think of the Jensen work about I.Q.? I mean, isn't it just political that you can't say that his work shows Blacks are not as smart as whites?"

Racism is, in part, an effort to explain the behavior and abilities of people on the basis of their color. One of the most common applications of this in the United States is the attempt to demonstrate that Black people are inherently inferior because of their genetic makeup. In terms of the history of civilization, it is a rather recent development, for ancient peoples generally distinguished among themselves on the basis of culture, not race. Race first became an important factor in the sixteenth century, when European explorers greatly increased their contacts with people of darker races whose culture differed from their own. As a result, many assumed there was a direct link between how people looked and how they behaved. In addition, part of the then emerging doctrine of imperialism claimed that enslaving foreign peoples was justified if it benefited the mother country. To rationalize what was morally wrong, theories of racial superiority emerged. In reality such views were already present in Western religion, for the Bible stated that Ham, the second son of Noah and the "father" of the Black race, had been cursed because he had looked upon his father's nakedness. Finally, nineteenth-century theories of evolution made it seem credible to some that mankind had gradually evolved and that certain physical differences were indicative of varying stages of development.

Clearly, then, the view that Blacks are not as intelligent as whites is deeply ingrained in white society. In recent years, however, increased attention has been devoted to the topic. Social scientists have presented data on this question based upon I.Q. tests. The best known social scientist is Arthur Jensen, a psychology professor at the University of California at Berkeley, who in 1969 published an article claiming that 80 percent of intelligence is inherited and that Blacks inherit less than whites. Moreover, Jensen asserted that his research proved that, on the average, Blacks were simply not as smart as whites. The ensuing uproar resulted, among other things, in Jensen's ostracism by the intellectual community.

Dr. Jensen argued that groups living in isolation from each other in different parts of the world have different gene pools that determine their physical and mental makeup. After examining more than 400 studies of I.Q. with respect to Blacks and whites, and after evaluating 81 different tests of mental functions, he concluded that there was an average difference of 10 to 20 points between the I.Q. scores of whites and Blacks. While acknowledging that the two groups showed no difference in rote learning and memory, he observed that Blacks did not perform as well on tests that measure abstract reasoning and problem solving. Moreover, Jensen discounted socioeconomic background as an important factor by pointing to studies comparing the children of low-income whites with those of high-income Blacks. On the average whites score higher.

The differences in I.Q. scores are an established fact, but there are many problems with what they really mean and how important they are. To begin with, there is considerable evidence that environment plays a major role in determining I.Q. and that Blacks, having suffered discrimination for hundreds of years, start out with many strikes against them. As Professor Thomas Sowell has observed, Italian, Polish, and Jewish immigrants did poorly on I.Q. tests in the early part of this century, scoring in the 80s, but they improved dramatically in their test perfor-

mance over several decades as their socioeconomic status rose.
Studies of children from poor white families as well as Oriental
immigrants to the United States show similar patterns, all of
which suggests that environment is a very important variable.
Even Jensen acknowledged that poor children tested in a clinic
where he worked achieved scores that were 8 to 10 points higher
once they felt comfortable with the tester and their surround-
ings, indicating that environment is of importance in assessing
performance on such tests. In response to this issue, Blacks have
developed I.Q. tests that are culturally biased to reflect their social environment. One of the best known of such tests is the
BITCH test (Black Intelligence Test of Cultural Homogeneity).
Developed by psychologist Robert L. Williams, it includes questions such as the following:

Blood:
   a. a vampire   *c.* an injured person   ans. *d*
   b. a dependent   *d.* a brother of color
      individual

CPT means a standard:
   a. time   *c.* tale   ans. *a*
   b. tune   *d.* twist

Who wrote the Negro National Anthem?
   a. Langston Hughes   *c.* James Weldon Johnson   ans. *c*
   b. Paul Laurence Dunbar   *d.* Frederick Douglass

Yawk:
   a. gun   *c.* high boat   ans. *a*
   b. fishing hook   *d.* heavy coat

I know you shame:
   a. you don't hear very   *c.* you don't mean what   ans. *c*
      well   you're saying
   b. you are a racist   *d.* you are guilty

A fascinating but rarely cited study by psychologist Otto
Klineberg seriously challenges the genetic argument. During
World War I Army recruiters found that Northern Blacks had
higher I.Q. scores than Southern Blacks, and in numerous instances they were higher than those of Southern whites. In-

trigued, Klineberg decided to find out whether this was due to environmental factors or whether it simply meant that smarter Blacks had migrated North. In looking at the records of over five hundred children from Birmingham, Charleston, and Nashville, he found no evidence to support the idea that smarter Blacks were more likely to leave the South.

Taking his assumption one step further, Dr. Klineberg tested over three thousand Harlem schoolchildren, all of them Southern-born. Among the tests given were the Stanford-Binet Intelligence Tests, National Intelligence Test, and Minnesota Form Board. The results demonstrated beyond any doubt that the longer the child had been living in New York City, the *higher* his or her I.Q. score was, with the most dramatic improvement taking place in the first five or six years. Klineberg's important research in this area shows that environment is a crucial factor in intelligence and deserves far greater attention than it has received until now.

There is other evidence challenging the notion that genetics is the main factor in intelligence. A study of National Merit Scholarship finalists showed that in families with five children *more than half* of the winners were the oldest children, while only 6 percent were drawn from the youngest members of the family. It would appear that environment played a major role in creating such a high disparity. Furthermore, studies of high-I.Q. Black children reveal that females are much more likely to attain high scores than males. Yet in the general population there is no great difference between males and females, though males tend to do somewhat better.

In his book *The I.Q. Argument* psychologist Hans Eysenck argues that Afro-Americans come from a less intelligent segment of the Black race. He theorizes that the more intelligent African tribesmen managed to elude the slave traders. Moreover, those slaves who rebelled and refused to play the "dull-submissive role" were killed, thus increasing the number of low-intelligence people in the gene pool.

Like Ernest Van Den Haag's argument concerning the Jews (see Chapter 2), this assumption cannot be proven. There is also no way of ascertaining how much of an opportunity the Africans actually had to evade capture. Certainly no one has argued that those Jews who were incarcerated in concentration camps or exterminated during World War II were less intelligent than those who were more fortunate.

Another researcher, Dr. Richard Herrnstein, has made the following argument: When all barriers to inequality are removed and everyone is treated the same, environmental factors will cease to be important. At that point genetics will become the crucial distinction. Thus, by making the environment more equal we ensure that heredity will play a more dominant role. It is highly questionable whether such equality of opportunity can be achieved in the foreseeable future, but if it can it is entirely possible that there will then be no differences in I.Q. among races or that Blacks will do even better than whites. Moreover, giving everyone the same chance to succeed does not mean they will take advantage of it. Factors such as personality, family wealth, or just plain luck are likely to continue to play significant roles regardless of equal opportunity.

Perhaps the greatest difficulty is that no way has yet been found to clearly separate genetic from environmental factors. A major problem in doing so is that so little is known about how the brain works. Neurobiologists now believe that certain types of intelligence are located in the right hemisphere while others are situated in the left hemisphere. Most importantly, a good number feel that genetic endowment in these hemispheres can be negated if people do not have the environmental opportunities to use it. They cite as an example parents who thwart the genetic inclination toward left-handedness on the part of their children and turn them into right-handers. Other research presently being conducted suggests that environment can affect the activity of RNA on the brain's molecular makeup.

It appears that both genetics and environment exercise considerable influence upon intelligence. Nevertheless, until tests are devised that are completely culture-free, until it is proven that the groups being tested are truly Black and white, and until there is complete equality, it will not be possible to fully assess whether or not one race is superior to the other in intellectual capabilities. Even if this were possible, it would only tell us about the *average* person within a group. Each individual would still have to be judged on his or her own merits.

What about achievement? There are those who argue that the accomplishments of white civilizations in literature, science, technology, philosophy, and the arts far exceed those of Blacks. Such an argument confuses performance with potential and also fails to take into account the fact that "civilization" as such is a relative term.

Under slavery in this country and under colonialism in Africa Black people were systematically exploited. In the United States they were often beaten, starved, treated like chattel, and given almost no opportunity to improve their lot. Despite these conditions, even before the twentieth century, they were able to produce leaders, inventors, and other individuals who distinguished themselves in a variety of areas. Two of the most noted abolitionists were Frederick Douglass and Sojourner Truth. Among the many prominent ministers were Henry Highland Garnet and Samuel Ringgold Ward. During this period sixteen Blacks received the Congressional Medal of Honor. Blanche Bruce of Mississippi and Hiram Revels of North Carolina, both Blacks, became U. S. Senators; another Black, Pinckney Pinchback, was elected lieutenant governor of Louisiana. In the field of science Blacks also achieved distinction. There was, of course, the well-known Benjamin Banneker, mathematician and astronomer, but there were others too, such as Elijah McCoy, responsible for over fifty mechanical inventions, and Granville Woods, whose inventions in the areas of automatic air brakes, electricity, and steam boilers were used by General Electric, Westinghouse, and Bell Telephone. Another prominent figure was Jan E. Matzeliger, whose shoe-lasting machine cut the cost of shoe manufacturing in half. Norbert Rillieu developed a process for sugar refining that had a profound impact upon the industry, and Lewis Latimer invented a sophisticated carbon-filament electric lamp. To say, as some have said, that these inventions cannot be compared to those of electricity, the telephone, the telegraph, the airplane, and so forth, is to ignore the tremendous disabilities created by centuries of slavery and general discrimination. Under these circumstances such achievements are truly remarkable. In fact, as opportunities increased in the twentieth century the contributions of Blacks to all fields of endeavor rose dramatically.

Our very definition of civilization is based on what *we* think important. Thus, while we may feel that scientific advances are of crucial significance, others may have different priorities. Were we to measure accomplishment by the absence of neuroses and psychoses, deference to the family and the aged, complexity of language, and physical conditioning, we might find other so-called primitive groups to be ahead of us in these areas. Even using our own criteria, it would appear that at various times in history Black civilization was on a "higher plane." Excavations at El Badari on the Nile and near Khartoum in the Sudan suggest that Blacks were among the earliest makers of pottery way back in the Stone Age. Other remains have been discovered in the Congo pointing to the use of an abacus among African tribes almost eight thousand years ago. The Egyptians, who built up a highly complex civilization, were a people of Negroid, Semitic, and Caucasian stock. Between the ninth and fifteenth centuries various societies flourished in Africa whose level of civilization was far higher than that of Western Europe—if we judge by Western standards. The kingdoms of Ghana, Mali, and Songhay supported large cities that included libraries, universities, and factories; they had systems of government in which banking, credit, and taxation played essential roles. In the schools people studied literature, law, medicine, and other subjects. All this was going on at a time when Europe was groping in the darkness of the Middle Ages.

What, then, caused the collapse of these centers? Christian and Moslem expansion into the continent, which brought in its wake the slave trade, was certainly partially responsible. Some have argued that the decadence of the African kingdoms in their later stages hastened their downfall. Whatever the case, those slaves who were brought to this country found it very difficult to maintain their traditions and culture. Worked to the bone, stripped of all dignity, often deliberately separated from their fellow tribesmen, forced to focus almost exclusively upon survival, many aspects of African culture disappeared. Perhaps no people on earth has been subjected to such a systematic form of humiliation and concentrated attack on its way of life over such a long period of time.

Perhaps the most discredited argument in scientific circles is the anatomical one. At one time scientists asserted that the Black man's physical characteristics were more similar to those of apes than whites, and that he was therefore of lower intelligence. Among the features cited were a flat nose, receding forehead, and a jaw that projected beyond the upper part of the face. Were it not for the fact that many whites, some educated and some not, continue to make statements such as "they look like apes," it would not be necessary to refute this argument. The fact is that in a number of ways whites actually resemble apes more closely. For instance, the thin lips, hair texture, as well as the body hair of whites is more similar to that of apes than Blacks. Furthermore, most members of the ape and monkey family have white skin beneath their fur. Thus, this is an argument that easily cuts both ways.

To sum up, there is no clear-cut evidence—either culturally, environmentally, genetically, or anatomically—to support the argument that Blacks are not as smart as whites.

Musically gifted, great rhythm, terrific entertainers

The origins of music in Black culture go back to the African heritage, where it occupied a central place in the lives of its peoples. There were hunting songs, drinking songs, work songs, funeral songs, lullabies, and love songs. When Africans came to the New World, those song styles that could most easily be adapted to the new environment survived. Among these were those songs that the slave sang while working. Clearly the slave could not sing, "If my harvest is bountiful, I will be rich." He could, however, sing the following song, one that not only helped to overcome the monotony of working on the plantation but also expressed his deepest yearnings:

> Dere's no rain to wet you
> Dere's no sun to burn you
> O push along believer
> I want to go home
> (W.E.B. DuBois, *The Souls of Black Folk*, pp. 211–12)

Since he could not practice his own religion in this country, the Afro-American eventually adopted Christianity as his faith.

It was in the rudimentary churches of the Deep South that the exile was able to express himself. Consequently music became an important medium there too. Song and dance had always been integral to African religion. As writer Imamu Amiri Baraka has written in *Blues People*, "gettin' the spirit" came from the African "spirit possession." As the slave rocked, shouted, and danced in his church, he fulfilled the ancient African dictum "The spirit will not descend without song." In this manner Afro-Americans found yet another way to preserve their culture.

A third important form was the use of lyrics and riddles to transmit folktales. In Africa songs had been one of the principal methods by which the young had been educated. In the United States they evolved into stories such as those told about Uncle Remus and Br'er Rabbit.

The use of rhythm was basic to African music, being most directly attributable to the use of drums as a means of communication. As Baraka explains, these drums were not some sort of primitive Morse code but "phonetic reproductions of the words themselves." As a result, the African's sense of rhythmic complexities was well developed. This became most obvious in the variations and subtleties of African music, which included the use of certain percussive techniques, harmonizing, singing in a call and response pattern, and a generally high level of rhythmic structure. Although the plantation owners were, in many cases, apprehensive about the use of drums—they had been employed with great success in Haiti to spread revolutionary messages among the Black population—these and such other instruments as guitars, xylophones, gourds, rattles, banjos, and mandolins were widely used by slaves.

Jazz, blues, spirituals, and modern rock music all have elements directly traceable to African music. This has been documented in countless books and articles. Dances such as the rhumba, mambo, conga, and Charleston had similar beginnings. What helped them survive was the fact that they served some very important purposes for Afro-American life and culture in terms of work, religion, and social life. As time passed they became established within the community regardless of their functionality. When white society's fascination with Blacks reached unprecedented heights during the Harlem renaissance period of the 1920s, music became a way in which Black people could move up the socioeconomic ladder, and it has remained one ever since.

Did Black people possess a certain talent in this area? Once it is established that music was an integral part of Black culture for hundreds of years, and that it survived in this country for very definite reasons, this becomes a rather difficult question to answer. Certainly the importance of musical expression among Afro-Americans meant that talented individuals were more likely to be recognized and encouraged. Literally thousands of Black men and women have achieved recognition as singers, dancers, and instrumentalists; probably no other nationality in America has so many people, proportionately speaking, in these areas.

If whites insist on believing that Blacks have more "natural rhythm"—it fits in well with the image of Blacks as "primitive"—it ought not to be assumed that Blacks will disagree with this stereotype. When the Black entertainer exhorts his Black audience to "clap your hands and show you got soul," he perpetuates both the belief and its crucial role in Black identity. A feeling of "being together" has as one of its main components an appreciation for musical sound and rhythm. The rejection of white music is not merely a question of its irrelevance to Black concerns but also whether it can be as good in quality as the music of Blacks. In his autobiography Malcolm X wrote:

With alcohol or marijuana lightening my head, and that wild music wailing away . . . it didn't take too long to loosen up the dancing instincts in my African heritage. (*The Autobiography of Malcolm X*, p. 56)

Motor coordination is obviously related to skill in dancing. In a 1969 review of the literature on motor development of Blacks and whites that appeared in *Clinical Pediatrics*, Dr. Malina cited twenty-one studies on the subject. The results point overwhelmingly to the existence of superior motor skills among Black people of all ages, including six studies done of children during the first three years of their lives. What percentage of such abilities are hereditary or environmental (e.g., these talents are often spotted early by parents and are positively reinforced) is not known, but it is clear that they exist.

Lazy and shiftless

Whites will often point to the number of unemployed Blacks to support this assertion. The ratio of unemployed Blacks to whites has been about 2 to 1 since 1954 and is even higher among Black teenagers. This is, however, due to complex developments in our society that have little to do with the willingness to work hard.

Automation and other technological improvements in industry have rendered many jobs obsolete. Those most affected have been unskilled workers, many of whom are Black. There has also been a movement by industry to relocate in areas outside the center of cities, where most Blacks live, because land there is cheaper. In addition, the increased use of the automobile and greater highway construction since World War II have made such areas more accessible. However, because of their generally lower socioeconomic status, Blacks find it difficult to commute to the outer areas of the city. With respect to teenagers, joblessness has increased partly because of a population explosion. Between 1960 and 1969 the number of Blacks in American cities between the ages of 16 and 19 increased by 75 percent, as compared to 14 percent for whites.

The result of all this has been that the only jobs left are often those that whites don't want. These are generally dirty, low-paying, uninteresting, and temporary by nature. As sociologist William J. Wilson has observed in *The Declining Significance of Race*,

Research on black employment problems has consistently shown that poor blacks tend not only to value work but also to feel that self-respect and employment are inseparable. Enduring lack of success in the labor market lowers their self-confidence and promotes feelings of resignation that can lead to abandoning the job search temporarily, if not permanently. (pp. 106–7)

Even in cases where an unskilled Black accepts a menial and undesirable job, he will, in many instances, either perform poorly or quit after a relatively short period of time. In a study of the attitudes held by liberal Northern employers toward

Black employees, sociologists Bernard Rosenberg and William Howton found that most employers viewed Blacks as lacking in dependability and willingness to work hard. Typical statements included:

Sometimes they just stay out and when you call them up they say they didn't like it or they have another job.

There are a lot of resignations. They don't stay too long.

The employers did not relate the type of job offered to reliability. In fact, one was quoted as saying, "Negroes gravitate to porter jobs. Why? They don't have the desire, from their home or their education." The authors note that employers favored whites in both hiring and promotions.

There is, incidentally, no evidence from this or any other study to indicate that Blacks employed in menial, low-paying jobs are more likely to quit work or "goof off" on the job than their white counterparts. In part the stereotype persists because Blacks are highly visible. In addition, as the group with the lowest esteem in American society they are a natural repository for the worst images which exist in the dominant culture.

What many whites do not realize is that working slowly, feigning illness or incompetence, or quitting entirely can be a passive form of aggression, whether it is used consciously or unconsciously. This method of "one-upping whitey" was used in slavery days as well. Numerous studies have shown that slaves frequently engaged in sabotage (e.g., destroying farm implements or driving animals very hard) and in general did as little work as possible. Some even cut off toes and hands to escape the often unbearable conditions of plantation labor. Today quitting a job without notice can be a way of expressing hostility, as is coming late or pretending not to understand instructions. Needless to say, it is also engaged in by whites who find themselves in dead-end jobs.

Another charge leveled by whites against Blacks is that they would rather be on welfare than work. That a disproportionate number of Blacks are on welfare is due to generations of prejudice that have affected both socioeconomic status as well as family structure. Many who make this accusation fail to realize that jobs that, when all is said and done, pay less than a family could receive from welfare are not much of an incentive especially when the work itself is often demeaning. Moreover, the popular notion among whites that the majority of Blacks in the United States are on welfare is simply false. Despite two very serious recessions, which are actually depressions in the Black community because of their socioeconomic status, less than 25 percent of all Black families today are on public assistance. In fact, in 1977 68 percent of all female-headed Black families and 91 percent among male-headed families depended on job income and not welfare.

In recent years it has become fashionable for politicians in quest of votes to talk of welfare cheats, a term which, given the strong association in the public mind of Blacks with welfare, further promotes the shiftlessness image. It is well-known, however, that far more people cheat on their income taxes than on welfare. Yet no politician has ever run on a platform that promises to rid the country of "income-tax cheats."

The "lazy and shiftless" stereotype is almost always directed at lower-class Blacks. Middle-class Blacks who work as business managers, teachers, lawyers, merchants, are rarely portrayed in this manner. Studies by various social scientists, including Franklin Frazier, Sidney Kronus, and Gunnar Myrdal, show that middle-class Blacks strongly resemble middle-class whites in their attitudes toward the work ethic and respectability in general. Between 1950 and 1970 the proportion of Black males employed in middle-class occupations more than doubled, as Blacks took advantage of opportunities for advancement that did not exist before. Still, the continued existence of large numbers of impoverished Blacks in this country suggests that much remains to be done in this area.

Big Cadillacs and flashy clothes

"Where do they get the money for all those fancy clothes?" a white person will ask. "If they're so oppressed, how can they afford to drive around in a Cadillac while I'm making do with a Dodge Dart?" asks another. In commenting upon Black ownership of cars, comedian Dick Gregory noted with at least a touch

of sarcasm that Blacks could more easily afford cars than whites
for the following reasons:

They won't let me in your country club, so that saves me $500 right
there. You know I'm not taking my family to Florida this winter, so
there's another $1,500 saved. I walk out and get hit by a truck, they
ain't taking me to no rich man's hospital. The city hospital is free,
which saves $2,500 more.

While the specific reasons given here ought perhaps not to be
taken seriously, there is a good deal of truth in the underlying
theme of Gregory's remarks, namely, that as a persecuted minority Blacks have limited options by which they can show off their
achievements.

Sociologists and psychologists refer to such behavior as "symbolic status striving." When people are blocked from advancement or denied social acceptance, they will seek other means to
attain their goals. Sociologist David Caplovitz calls this mecha-
nism "conspicuous compensation." The Black person who wears
expensive jewelry in an ostentatious manner, who buys a two-
hundred-dollar pair of shoes despite a modest income, or who
favors only expensive, showy automobiles is, in effect, compen-
sating for being denied the opportunity to, say, purchase a nice
home in a good (white) neighborhood. This pattern is not limited to Blacks, given the materialistic nature of American society; it has a high rate of occurrence among Jews, Italians, and
other discriminated against groups, especially if they are new arrivals to this country.

How much truth is there to the stereotype? A good deal, from
whatever evidence is available. According to D. Parke Gibson,
an authority on Black consumer behavior,

. . . being able to dress well carries some built-in status and he
[i.e., the Black man] knows that above almost anything else his
appearance as he moves about today must be smart.

Citing figures on consumer expenditures, Gibson observes that
the average Black spends 30 percent more on clothing than the
typical white.

Automobiles, long seen as both sex and power symbols, seem
to have a special appeal within the community—and not merely

to pimps and numbers racketeers. In a 1966 article by Ronald G. Shafer that appeared in the *Wall Street Journal*, Leroy Jeffries, then Midwest advertising manager for *Ebony*, noted that status considerations were the most important factor when a Black buyer selected a car. Others in Detroit's auto industry agree, and while no one knows precisely how many Blacks buy luxury autos, it is believed to be substantially higher than among whites. Among both Blacks and whites Chevy and Ford are still number one and two, respectively, but experts in the field claim that many Blacks of moderate income prefer used Cadillacs and Electras to new, lower-priced cars. Moreover, in 1966 3 percent of all Black car owners drove Cadillacs, the same percentage as among whites. The difference, however, is that white income is, on the average, considerably higher. Conversations with a number of Cadillac dealers in the New York metropolitan area confirm the continued popularity of the Cadillac in the Black community. Even in white neighborhoods a disproportionate number of customers are Black.

Besides status, there may be another factor. Tony Brown, a Black marketing consultant in Detroit, asserted

With a big car a Negro is saying I'm as good as you are. Also many Negroes don't own their own homes and they're more comfortable in a big, quiet car than where they live, in some crowded, noisy, urban neighborhood. (*Wall Street Journal*, December 2, 1966: 1)

Just how many Blacks who live in densely populated areas feel this way needs to be established, but it does seem like a reasonable possibility.

As the status of Blacks continues to improve, changes have been taking place in consumer tastes. New distinctions are being made. Writing in 1978, Gibson claimed that the Cadillac, or "hog," is coming to be seen by wealthier members of the community as typifying the "got-rich-quick Black," and there is now a shift toward Mercedes and other luxury cars. Given the experiences of other groups, it is entirely possible that as Blacks become more secure, the trend will be toward automobiles and other products that understate rather than emphasize power and affluence.

Violent criminals

This stereotype has some truth to it only with regard to one segment of the Black American population—young, Black, poor urban males. This is confirmed by almost every study of violent crime in the United States. Even allowing for the fact that Blacks are discriminated against by law enforcement authorities, the figures are quite high. According to The President's Commission on Law Enforcement and Administration of Justice, the Black arrest rate for murder in 1965 was 24.1, while the white rate was only 2.5 per 100,000 persons. Similarly, FBI statistics from the late seventies indicate that Blacks have much higher arrest rates for homicide, assault, rape, and robbery, though it should be noted that those who commit such crimes represent a small minority of the ghetto population. Significantly, Blacks are far more apt to be *victims* of crime than whites. A recent study of crime in New York City showed that a Black person's chances of being the victim of a crime was eight times as high as that of his white counterpart. Researchers have also found that whether the crime be rape or homicide, the race of the aggressor and the victim is most often the same. Thus, the stereotype of Blacks raping, robbing, and killing primarily whites is clearly not a valid one.

Most crimes of this sort are related to socioeconomic status. In studies of Chicago's slums done in the early part of the twentieth century, researchers found that delinquency occurred most often in low-income areas among all ethnic and racial groups. The culture of the gang, the glorification of pimps and hoodlums by youths who see no other way of "making it," the availability of weapons, drugs, and alcohol—all combine to provide a fertile breeding ground for crime and, in particular, violence.

Still, socioeconomic conditions are not in themselves a plausible explanation. In his book *Criminal Violence, Criminal Justice* writer Charles Silberman cites figures showing that in the period 1970–72, relative to population, Blacks in New York were arrested for violent crimes more than three times as often as were Hispanics. The disparities were equally great between Blacks and Hispanics in other parts of the country. The difference, according to Silberman, is that no group has suffered as much for so long—that the experience of Blacks has differed, especially as violent victims of slavery, "in kind, not just degree —from that of any other American group." Silberman also notes that the homicide rate in Black Africa is not much different from that of Western Europe and is considerably lower than that of the United States.

In recent times the violence stereotype has gained greater credibility because of the over four hundred riots that occurred in Black communities between 1964 and 1968. In addition to its actual occurrence, Black leaders discovered that threats of violence (e.g., "You better give us jobs or it's going to be a long, hot summer") and the popularization of slogans such as "Burn, baby, burn" were very useful in intimidating whites. As they were used more frequently in this fashion, the stereotype became more prevalent. When one considers that just thirty years ago the stereotype of the "docile, obedient nigra" was very prevalent, this turnabout is truly remarkable.

Among the chief causes of the riots cited by the Commission on Civil Disorders were the rising expectations created by the passage of the 1964 Civil Rights Act and other laws barring discrimination. The idea that frustration leads to aggression was first developed by John Dollard and has definite applicability to the question of why violence occurs in the Black community. Though it is difficult to directly connect the two, Blacks interviewed in the wake of the riots cited frustration as a cause, while also indicating that violence was justified to redress legitimate wrongs. In their work *Black Power* Black activist Stokely Carmichael and political scientist Charles V. Hamilton summed up the rationale for such feelings when they wrote:

If a nation fails to protect its citizens, then that nation cannot condemn those who take up the task themselves . . . White people must be made to understand that they must stop messing with black people, or the blacks *will* fight back. (pp. 52–53)

Social scientists have also argued that cultural factors in the lower-class Black community have played a role in the violence that often characterizes it. In this view, those living in the ghetto have distinct value systems that encourage violence (e.g., the ghetto youth values toughness and physical strength). The point is, however, that such cultural values develop largely because of a lack of other options for upward mobility.

Another argument is that the crowded conditions of ghetto life lead to violence. For this to be true it would have to be true everywhere. Many groups in America have lived in crowded ghettoes, but they have not all had the same rates of violent behavior. Moreover, crowded ghettoes elsewhere in the world (e.g., those in Port-au-Prince, Haiti) have lower rates of violence than ghettoes in the United States. No doubt physical discomfort can lead to aggression, but other factors need to be considered too.

Another possible explanation is that the South has, at least in terms of criminal statistics for violence, long been the most violent region in the country. Moreover, it is a region where owning a weapon is widely accepted and where feuds, lynchings, vigilante groups as exemplified by the Ku Klux Klan, and an emphasis on military training in general have been, or continue to be, an important part of the life-styles of its people. Therefore, it is argued, Blacks have absorbed and internalized some of these values. This is obviously difficult to prove, but like the Italians, who brought with them a tradition of violence, it may explain some of the behavior on the part of new Black migrants who came North in the twentieth century. Observers of the American scene have long commented on our fascination with violence. It would seem logical to assume that its greatest impact is upon those who have the least opportunity.

Finally, there is a biological school of thought whose proponents believe that certain individuals have a predisposition to crime. Some, such as sociologist Pierre Van den Berghe, believe that aggression is a natural instinct among human beings. One current theory has it that "criminal types" are more likely to have the abnormal XYY chromosome. (It was found in Richard Speck, for example.) What is interesting is the fact that the XYY chromosome is virtually nonexistent among Blacks. With the exception of those who link crime to low I.Q. and argue that Blacks have a heredity-based low I.Q.—a proposition that, as we saw earlier, is dubious, to say the least—no one has claimed that crime among Blacks is an inherited trait. There is, quite simply, no evidence to support it.

It would seem, then, from what we know to date, that the high rate of violent crime among Blacks has nothing to do with their race. Its existence is due primarily to the historical experiences of Blacks in this country and their present socioeconomic conditions. Regardless of the reasons, however, the prevalence of Black crime has Black leaders worried. Recently *Ebony* devoted an entire issue to the subject, and various groups, including the Black Leadership Forum and the National Black Police Association, have sponsored conferences or workshops on the subject. In a November 1980 New York *Times* article, the Reverend Wyatt Tee Walker, a prominent Harlem minister, was quoted as saying, "It's a matter of our community's physical survival. With the ravages of racism and high unemployment, we just can't afford to tolerate crime."

FIVE

Japanese

Chauvinistic

The Japanese cannot, may not, and will not provide desirable material for our citizenship. 1. The Japanese cannot assimilate and make good citizens because of their racial characteristics, heredity and religion. 2. The Japanese may not assimilate and make good citizens because their government claims all Japanese, no matter where born, as its citizens. 3. The Japanese will not assimilate and make good citizens. In the past when opportunity offered and even when born here, they have shown no disposition to do so. (V. S. McClatchy [publisher of the Sacramento Bee], *Annals of the American Academy of Political and Social Science*, January 1921: 29)

McClatchy later appeared before the U. S. Senate to denounce the Japanese as "dangerous" people who came here only "for the purpose of colonizing," concluding that they "never cease being Japanese." His views were typical of Americans at that time. Although his statements were basically false, as well as extremely misleading, they appeared accurate in the eyes of many ill-informed people. The origins of this stereotype are both historical and sociological.

One of the chief sources for the perception of the Japanese as chauvinistic was the reverence in which the emperor was held in Japan. According to Shintoism, the emperor was a divine figure who was believed to have been descended from the sun goddess Amaterasu. Thus, the leader of Japan was both a political and religious figure to whom loyalty was owed not simply because one was a citizen of the country but as a matter of religious faith. In some periods of Japanese history this was a strong feature of the religion; in others it was not.

The fears of Americans concerning the loyalties of the Japanese immigrants were also affected by several developments early in the twentieth century. There was, first of all, Japan's victory in the Russo-Japanese War (1904-5). This marked the first time in modern history that an Asian power had defeated a European one. When Japan turned Korea into a colony and invaded Manchuria, the United States began to view Japan more and more as an aggressive and expansionist power that might ultimately seek control over the Philippines, Guam, and Hawaii. Rumors about Japanese intentions and actions abounded during the early part of the century. These included a purported plan by Japan and Germany to destroy the Monroe Doctrine and a rumored military alliance with Indians on the West Coast. The accuracy of these stories was irrelevant. What mattered was that they gave added credence to the stereotype because large numbers of Americans believed them.

California politicians soon found that they could win elections quite easily by running on anti-Oriental platforms. Naturally, for those who were racists to begin with, spreading the idea that the Japanese were unassimilable chauvinists was very useful. Others felt threatened by the success of the Japanese in the economic sphere, particularly agriculture. In 1913 a law was passed in California that, in effect, made it illegal for foreign-born Japanese to own land. In 1922 the U. S. Supreme Court ruled that foreign-born Japanese could never become U.S. citizens. The 1924 Immigration Act, which severely limited immigration from all countries, was, however, seen by many here as aimed particularly at the Japanese and, in fact, Japan viewed it as an insult to its people.

Naturally, these restrictions probably caused many Japanese-

Americans to become more chauvinistic. After all, how could they feel loyal to a land that denied them citizenship? The sense of foreignness with which every new group was viewed by those already established here was heightened by physical differences. Their skin color, the shape of their eyes, and their short stature made them stand out.

The 1920–45 period in Japan was characterized by extreme nationalism, and even though emigration from Japan to the United States had slowed to a trickle, those living here were seen as sharing such views with their mother country. Even before Pearl Harbor was actually attacked, publisher William Randolph Hearst wrote in the Los Angeles *Examiner:*

Come out to California and see the myriads of little Japs peacefully raising fruits and flowers and vegetables on California sunshine, and saying hopefully and wistfully: "Someday I come with Japanese army and take all this. Yes, sir, thank you." Then the Colonel [Colonel Knox] should see the fleets of peaceful little Japanese fishing boats, plying up and down the California coast, catching fish and taking photographs. (Los Angeles *Examiner,* February 21, 1940)

The chief impetus for the chauvinistic stereotype was Pearl Harbor and the entry of Japan into World War II as America's enemy. While it is clear that the stereotype existed long before then, the war greatly reinforced and confirmed earlier apprehensions. Even liberal leaders and spokesmen began to depict Japanese-Americans in this fashion. For example, Earl Warren, famous as head of "the liberal Warren Court," who was then the California state attorney general, stated that "there is more potential danger among the group of Japanese who are born in this country than from the alien Japanese who were born in Japan." He went on to say that the country was threatened by "an invisible deadline of sabotage." In a similar vein the great liberal columnist Walter Lippmann, the originator of the concept of stereotypes and a man who believed that they were inaccurate and undesirable, wrote in support of mass evacuation of Japanese-Americans from the West Coast: "Nobody's constitutional rights include the right to reside and do business on a battlefield. And nobody ought to be on a battlefield who has no good reason for being there." The "battlefield," of course, was California.

Japanese conduct during the war fortified the chauvinistic image. They acquired a not undeserved reputation as fanatical fighters who were not afraid to die. As defeat loomed for Japan, the military command decided to send suicide planes whose pilots, known as *kamikaze* (divine wind), crash-dived their explosives-laden aircraft into enemy targets. In addition, there was the Japanese tradition of *hara-kiri*, a method of suicide involving disembowelment with the sword, begun by twelfth-century warriors (known as *samurai*) who were expected to show loyalty to their dead lords by accompanying them into the hereafter. Although the practice had been largely discontinued by the latter part of the seventeenth century, many Americans assumed it was quite common even in modern times.

One man's fanatical nationalism is another's wonderful patriotism, so one must be careful when making judgements in such matters. Still, Asian historians seem to feel that Japan has always been a highly chauvinistic society. Although influenced by Korean and Chinese culture, Japan has, as an island nation, always been relatively self-contained. Until the nineteenth century Japanese society was not especially prone to outside influences. Its people were a rather homogeneous grouping both racially and culturally. As a result they developed a strong sense of national identity. In historical accounts, for instance, Japan was often described by its chroniclers as a special land, located in the center of the universe, whose sun goddess was the ruler of the world.

Most immigrants tried very hard to adapt to American culture despite major differences in background and outlook. These efforts ranged from adopting American styles of dress and home furnishings to religious and social activities. Many of the immigrants became Christians, as did the majority of their children. They were law-abiding and accommodating almost to a fault. While they tried to keep alive their heritage to some extent, as evidenced by the establishment of Japanese language schools, they might have assimilated early in the twentieth century were it not for factors beyond their control.

Resentment against their success here, as well as prejudice and suspicion of a foreign culture, convinced many Japanese that America would never accept them. The last straw came when they were denied citizenship. There were, on the other hand, significant differences in attitude toward Japan between the Issei, or immigrants, and their children, often referred to as the Nisei. The Issei were more comfortable with and interested in Japanese culture. Their children, however, were much more apt to be interested in assimilating. Typical of the generation gap was the almost stereotypical Nisei response to their parents, "You wouldn't understand. Skip it."

With the outbreak of the war, agitation against Japanese-Americans reached a fever pitch, culminating in the by now infamous concentration camps set up in various parts of the West. More than 110,000 men, women, and children, three fourths of whom were citizens by birth, were incarcerated, prompting the bitter refrain, "born, raised, and captured in America." This was a first in American history and it reversed the judicial practice of assuming innocence to one of "guilty until proven innocent." Their treatment contrasted sharply with that of the Italian- and German-Americans, neither of whom were singled out in this manner. What was perhaps most interesting was the reaction of the Japanese themselves. Most co-operated with the authorities, hoping in this manner to prove their loyalty to America. Slightly more than 2 percent asked to be returned to Japan—a very low figure for a people stereotyped as extremely nationalistic. Moreover, those Japanese-Americans who were eventually cleared by the authorities and entered the Army compiled an exemplary record of service. A total of 33,000 (half from Hawaii) served, including two segregated units that fought in Europe and whose fame for bravery in battle reached epic proportions. One of these, the 442nd regiment, suffered 9,486 casualties, and individual members won 18,143 decorations. No other unit—white, yellow, or Black—did as well.

In the aftermath of the war stereotypes of Japanese-Americans underwent a radical change. They came to be viewed as exemplary American citizens participating actively in a variety of organizations, ranging from Christian churches to Rotary Clubs to Little League baseball. Although many maintained social ties with other Japanese, an equal number felt comfortable among Caucasians. With the passage of time, the stereotype of chauvinism has faded and has been replaced by other, more positive, attributes. As far as the accuracy of the stereotype goes, it can be said that historically chauvinism has been a strong feature of Japan, that it would probably have disappeared entirely in America were it not for white racism, and that even prejudice failed to halt the Americanization process of Japanese immigrants.

Hardworking, ambitious, and competitive

Some years ago Dr. Giovanni Agnelli, chairman of Fiat, was asked what he intended to do about Japanese competition. "I'm sorry to admit it," he said somewhat ruefully, "but they work harder than we do. It's quite a problem." Most foreigners who do business with Japan would agree with this assessment, but one distinction should be made before going any further: The Japanese concept of hard work is not the stereotypical American one of the rugged, driving individualist whose success story is frequently couched in Horatio Alger terms. Rather, it is one subordinated to the group. The typical Japanese employee is a company man first and an individual second. For instance, workers at the giant Matsushita Electric Corporation, which makes millions of TVs, radios, and other electronic products, begin each morning by singing the company song. Here is a stanza from it:

> We trust our strength together in harmony
> Finding happiness,
> MATSUSHITA DENKI.
> Animating joy everywhere,
> A world of dedication,
> Let us fulfill our hopes,
> Shining hopes,
> of a radiant dawning
> With Love, Light and a Dream.

Lest one think the masses are being brainwashed, it should be noted that the executives repeat the same jingle upon arriving half an hour later, as do the company's researchers and scientists.

Studies done by Harry Kitano, Mamoru Iga, and other social scientists demonstrate that conformity is very highly valued in

Japanese society. They have also commented on the Japanese ability to adapt to different cultures. This combination of values, together with high aspirations, helped the Japanese succeed in America because they were precisely the values considered important by American culture, which was, in turn, shaped by the Protestant work ethic. Anxious to please and eager to improve their status, the immigrants threw themselves into their work with a zeal and energy that was already a part of their culture in Japan. They bought as much property as possible, worked long hours, and sent their children to school in record numbers. They were also often highly competitive in their efforts to succeed.

As opposed to the feudal period, Japanese immigrants to the United States were no longer locked into the position of farmer, military man, or merchant. They could, more or less, pursue the American dream. Yet they were still, because of their history, very status conscious. Writing in *National Geographic*, Bart McDowell observed that when strangers are introduced, they study each other's professional affiliation, as indicated on their business cards, and then decide how to treat one another. Those on the boards of directors get the deepest bows and department heads the shallowest. In a society where status is so important, it is not surprising that people will work hard to attain it.

Another factor is the tolerance in Japan toward the coexistence of different religions. Dr. Kitano relates how he saw a pilgrim on his way to a Shinto shrine in Japan carrying a Protestant Bible and wearing a crucifix. In fact, the average Japanese will probably be blessed by a Shinto priest shortly after birth and buried in a Buddhist cemetery. When St. Francis Xavier sought to proselytize in Japan four hundred years ago, he had no problems gaining permission to do so. The generally open attitude toward different faiths—many Japanese will admit that they "like to touch all bases"—has led some to refer to Japan as a "museum of religions."

In such an atmosphere it became possible, whenever it suited Japan's rulers, to use religion to fulfill a variety of goals, some of which had little to do with religion itself. In the Tokugawa period, which lasted from the sixteenth to the mid-nineteenth centuries, power was in the hands of the *shōgun*, or military dictator. To consolidate his hold and that of his feudal lords, a renewed emphasis was placed on Confucianism. In Chinese culture this had always meant stressing loyalty to one's parents, but under the Tokugawas, Confucianism was reinterpreted to mean loyalty to one's lord.

This period also saw the rise to prominence of the Shingaku movement in Buddhism, which, like Protestantism, stressed the work ethic. Generally, Buddhist values had always encouraged people to not give up when frustrated. In fact, the contemporary Japanese expressions *gambatte* and *gaman*, loosely translated as "don't give up" and "don't let it bother you," stem from the Buddhist approach to life.

Eventually, as social and economic conditions in the country deteriorated, the Tokugawas were overthrown and in 1868 a new era began under Meiji leadership. Shintoism, which demanded, among other things, absolute loyalty to the emperor, self-sacrifice, and devotion, became popular again. At the same time, Japan had become convinced of the need to modernize. Given the fact that Shintoism and Confucianism embodied values conducive to modernization, and given the willingness of the Japanese to adapt to new religious forms, it became relatively simple to combine politics and economics with religious principles.

Japan's tremendous economic growth in itself supports the truth of this overachiever stereotype, for it is only through hard work and ambition that such a relatively small country could have become one of the industrial giants of the world. Yet even among Japanese-Americans there is ample evidence that these patterns have been maintained in the United States. Most studies indicate that the Japanese are not only ambitious but are very highly thought of by their employers. One such survey of seventy-nine firms by sociologists Lee Rainwater and Alan Jacobson revealed that more than two thirds rated their Japanese-American employees very favorably—this despite the fact that the study took place in the early 1950s, a time when anti-Japanese feelings were still quite common. Another sociologist, William Petersen, cites data that shows that Japanese-Americans are upper-middle-class in far greater numbers than their proportion in the population as a whole would suggest.

Highly educated and intelligent

We always knew you had to watch out for those Orientals. They were really smart, studied hard, but were very quiet in class. So they fooled you.

a Princeton University coed

Asians love to study. It's in our blood.

Seiji Ozawa, conductor

The only way for the superior man to civilize the people and establish good social customs is through education . . . Just as one cannot know the taste of good food without eating it, however excellent it may be, so without education one cannot come to know the excellence of a great body of knowledge.

Confucius

As we have already seen, a desire for learning and other similar characteristics are culturally and not biologically determined. Orientals in general, and Japanese in particular, are often stereotyped in this regard. Before looking at how Japanese culture shaped such attitudes, however, we ought to first establish that the stereotype has some truth to it. Here it would seem we are on pretty solid ground, for almost all research on this question supports the notion that the Japanese are rather well schooled and intelligent as a group.

The Issei, most of whom came here as adults, actively encouraged their children to gain as much education as possible, with excellent results. In Los Angeles, where large numbers of Japanese-Americans lived, in terms of college education Nisei (second-generation) males over twenty-five surpassed whites as early as 1940 despite their relative cultural deprivation. When one considers that most Nisei encountered serious discrimination in the job market, their persistence is truly remarkable. Moreover, they often surpassed whites in achievement too. In a well-known study Dr. Reginald Bell examined twenty thousand grade scores of Japanese-American high school students in Los Angeles in 1928 and compared them to other groups. He concluded that, overall, Japanese performance exceeded that of all other groups tested. I.Q. tests conducted during this period indicated that Oriental and white scores were about equal. Considering the fact that tests in those days did not allow sufficiently for cultural differences, these results reflect rather well on the Japanese-Americans.

After World War II the high level of educational attainment continued. Victor Boesen, in a 1948 article that appeared in *The New Republic*, observed that more Nisei were college graduates than any other racial group in the United States. A 1966 article by Dr. Petersen stated:

. . . among persons aged 14 years or over in 1960, the median years of schooling completed by Japanese were 12.2 compared with 11.1 years by Chinese, 11.0 by whites, 9.2 by Filipinos, 8.6 by Negroes and 8.4 by Indians. (The New York *Times Magazine*, January 9, 1966)

The reasons for such success in this area are often not understood by members of the group themselves. In a study of ethnic indentification among Sansei (third-generation) Japanese-Americans, sociologist Fumiko Hosokawa quoted one student who explained his having attended college as follows: "It was just kind of something that was expected . . . It's kind of odd. It's hard to explain." Others justified their decision in terms of professional aspirations. Said one, "If we didn't go to college, we would end up gardeners."

Notwithstanding the vagueness of such comments, the importance of education among the Japanese is traceable to their culture and history. Confucian philosophy emphasized the value of learning, and although it remained the province of the aristocracy in early times, it was always looked up to by the masses as an ideal. Education first became popular in the fourteenth century during the Ashikaga period. Many schools were built and significant numbers of *samurai* and well-off peasants sent their children to them. By the time of the Tokugawas, who also looked favorably upon education, there were between ten and fifteen thousand local schools administered by temples. Class size averaged from twenty to thirty students.

In the Meiji period Japan embarked on its most ambitious program yet, declaring education to be compulsory for four years and optional for another four. There was a very practical reason for this. Having decided that modernization was imperative for Japan's well-being, the Meiji undertook mass education in order to speed up the process. The structure of the educational system was based on the French model and the curriculum was American-inspired. When, in the 1880s, Japan became more conservative in outlook, it turned to the Germans for help in this area. In short, by 1925 Japan was probably the most literate nation in the world. Ninety-nine percent of its children attended school and in 1927 all but 7 percent of the population could read.

The Issei who migrated here left during the Meiji period; they therefore transplanted positive attitudes toward education onto American soil. These were combined with such other traditional Japanese attitudes as respect for authority, conformity, and hard work. Thus children were told by their parents, "The teacher is always right and you must listen to him." Because they were taught to respect authority at an early age, children were sensitive to what their parents expected and tried hard to please them. Their overall success drive helped them too as they competed with each other in their studies. Thus we see that general Japanese values were highly compatible with the requirements for success in school.

There is evidence from more recent studies that educational attainment has slowed somewhat among those in the third generation, though it is still quite high. Dr. Kitano found that grade scores in school had decreased somewhat among the Sansei and attributed this to greater Americanization. Typically, the American idea of a good student as one who also participates in extracurricular activities is being increasingly adopted by Sansei students, with grades suffering somewhat in the process.

Japanese women are servile and obedient

Ancient Japan was actually a matriarchal society. Religion was centered around the sun goddess Amaterasu and the country was often ruled by empresses. In the second half of the eighth century, however, the country, influenced by Chinese culture and Buddhist teachings, began to adopt the patriarchal model.

Buddhism held that women were more likely to sin than men and that they should be subservient to them.

By the nineteenth century a double standard was the rule. For example, women could be executed for adultery whereas men were free to engage in extramarital affairs without fear of retribution. The Meiji period saw many changes as the country implemented Western ways, but the status of women did not improve significantly. They needed the husband's permission to enter into legal agreements; in the event of divorce, the husband was awarded custody of the children.

It was only in 1911, when the Seito Society, a women's literary organization, was founded, that women started to assert themselves. The world recognition accorded stage personalities such as Miura Tamaki, the opera singer best known for her role in *Madama Butterfly,* and actress Matsui Samako began to affect attitudes toward women. In the 1920s women greatly increased their efforts at gaining equal rights in both the politicial and economic spheres.

After World War II the treatment of women in Japan improved considerably. They were allowed to vote and even elected a good number of representatives to the national Diet. They attended college in greater numbers and the media paid more attention to them and their concerns as time went on. Nevertheless, as Jack Seward wrote in 1972 in *The Japanese,* most husbands today do not feel obligated to let their wives know if they are coming home late and, according to one study, almost two thirds of them stop off "somewhere" before getting there. Seward told a fascinating story about former Prime Minister Eisaku Sato that would seem to indicate that though Japanese women may have certain inalienable rights, their status is still very unequal by Western standards. In an interview with a national magazine, Mrs. Sato remarked, in response to a reporter's query, that her husband had run around in his younger days, never sought her advice, and that he beat her. The Premier confirmed these assertions, observing, however, that he had stopped inflicting corporal punishment on her because "times have changed." He then asked the reporters whether *they* still beat their wives and half of them admitted—somewhat embarrassedly, that they did.

The Issei who came here left Japan at a time when women were still very much second-class citizens. Moreover, when many of them, after deciding to remain permanently in the United States, married women from Japan, these values were reinforced. Known as "picture-brides," many had been chosen by the men on the basis of a photo and background information supplied by a matchmaker, an old tradition in Japan. Having been brought here in this fashion, Japanese women were in no position to assert themselves even had there been no cultural restraints against doing so.

Throughout the twentieth century Americans have perceived Japanese women as submissive, lovely, and graceful, as can be seen from films such as *The Barbarian and the Geisha, Teahouse of the August Moon,* and *My Favorite Geisha.* She was often portrayed as a dainty and cultured person who performed the tea ceremony, arranged flowers, and existed only to please her man, both sexually and otherwise. Research on this question reveals that such images, if somewhat exaggerated, have some truth, though each succeeding generation of Japanese women acts more like its American counterpart. A comparative study of Japanese-American and Caucasian-American personality traits done in the 1960s by psychologists Gerald and Connie Meredith revealed that Japanese-American females are more affected by feeling, more obedient, and less self-assured. However, in another study of Japanese-Americans in Hawaii researchers found that while third-generation Japanese-American males approve of male-dominated marriages, their opinions are not shared by female Japanese-Americans. Based on this and other recent research, it is safe to conclude that things are changing and that those men who expect to find in the average Japanese-American woman the fulfillment of their fantasies, namely, a pliant, yielding, and delicate little thing, are likely to be disappointed.

The sneaky Jap

Most people assume that this stereotype originated with the surprise attack by the Japanese on Pearl Harbor. While the attack no doubt heightened such perceptions, they were already well entrenched in the mind of the American public long before then. Consider, for example, the following song that appeared in the July 23, 1916, edition of the New York *American:*

LOOK OUT CALIFORNIA, BEWARE
They've battleships, they say,
On Magdalena Bay!
Uncle Sam, won't you listen when we warn you?
They meet us with a smile
But they're working all the while,
And they're waiting just to steal our California!
So just keep your eyes on Togo,
With his pockets full of maps,
For we've found out we can't trust the Japs!

The reference to Magdalena Bay had to do with a rumor that Japan was about to acquire a naval base there from Mexico, from which it would seek to attack the United States. This and other similar stories were largely due to American fears that the Japanese, after having defeated the Russians in the Russo-Japanese War, might try to extend their power to the Western Hemisphere. An article in the November 3, 1907, issue of the San Francisco *Examiner* accusing the Japanese of preparing for war with the United States claimed that they were "the most secretive people in the world."

In the aftermath of Pearl Harbor, Americans pointed to the fact that many Japanese-Americans lived in strategically important areas. Therefore, they must be spying for Japan. Yet, as Allan Bosworth has pointed out in his book *America's Concentration Camps,* they lived there for reasons related to economic conditions and their history. They settled near the railroads because, having laid the tracks for them, they were often paid in the form of land grants along the right of way. Needless to say, such land was cheap and undesirable because of the noise made by passing freight trains. The same was true of land near the airports. Signal Hill had been farmed by the Japanese long before oil was discovered there. Despite this the Japanese were often portrayed as sneaky saboteurs by the media and public figures in government.

One explanation for the popularity of this stereotype may be the success of the Japanese-Americans. Like the Jew, who has also been stereotyped as sneaky, Japanese-Americans did very well in this country, quickly establishing themselves as efficient, reliable, ambitious, and hardworking. In his work *The Economics and Politics of Racial Accommodation* Dr. John Modell observes that Japanese fruit stands and floral businesses proliferated in Los Angeles because many whites believed that the produce and flowers of the Japanese were superior to those of their white competitors. The problem for prejudiced whites was how to explain the general success of this group of relatively new immigrants. Since their own bigotry prevented them from thinking of the Japanese as equal, whites were compelled to resort to other rationalizations, among them the idea that the Japanese had, by guile and deceit, managed to outwit their white counterparts. Americans, of course, would never stoop to such low levels. In addition, such charges often played into the hands of unscrupulous politicians, many of whom built entire careers by stirring up anti-Japanese (as well as anti-Chinese) sentiments on the West Coast.

Differences in culture also contribute to suspicions and apprehensions of this sort. This is no one's fault, yet it must be taken into account. For example, the Japanese smile not only when pleased or amused but also when they wish to indicate that a line of inquiry should not be pursued any further. The same smile can also be used to hide shame or anger. When misunderstood by foreigners it can sometimes lead to charges of deception. There is the well-known story of the Japanese *samurai* who, upon being scolded by his European boss, smiled broadly. This so angered his employer that he physically assaulted him. To atone for this insult the *samurai* committed suicide. The European was simply unaware that the smile in Oriental culture can be a way in which a person tries to minimize the discomfort or anger of the other person. This practice first became popular in the beginning of the seventeenth century under shōgun Iyeyasu, who felt it was a sign of disrespect to show any feeling of pain or sadness to one's superior.

In perhaps no area are misreadings of signals so common as in business, which is what prompted Frank Gibney, the vice-president of New Product and Development at the *Encyclopaedia Britannica,* to write an article for *Publishers Weekly* about cultural differences between Americans and Japanese. In it he gives numerous examples of how the Japanese will say no when they mean yes and vice versa, often expecting Americans to understand. According to Gibney, "In principle I am all for it," translated from polite Japanese, almost unfailingly means "We have a lot of problems." This is part of a general community pattern of deference and hesitancy in embarrassing others, known by insiders as *enryo*.

To be sure, the Japanese are not the only out-group to have been perceived as two-faced and deceitful. Yet because of a need to explain their success—and the usefulness of the accusation for opportunistic politicians—as well as certain historical developments, the stereotype has long been associated with them. There is no evidence that the Japanese are more sly and treacherous than the rest of us, although the reasons previously given, plus certain cultural differences, might lead people to think so.

Strong family ties

How can one be disrespectful toward one's wife since she is the center of the home? And how can one be disrespectful toward one's children since the children perpetuate the family? How dare he [a gentleman] be disrespectful or have no pious regard for himself since the self is a branch of the family line? (*Confucius*)

Many centuries have passed since these lines were uttered, but the twentieth-century Japanese family still adheres, to a large extent, to the values embodied in them. Like the Chinese, with whom they share many cultural similarities, the Japanese have one of the lowest divorce rates of any American subgroup. In both 1960 and 1970 it was 1.6 percent, including both the immigrant (Issei) and the second (Nisei) generation, as well as some members of the third (Sansei) generation.

The Japanese-American family system is characterized by mutual obligations and responsibilities between parents and children, with the parents sacrificing for the children's sake while at the same time expecting unquestioned obedience from their offspring. In his book *Japanese Americans* Dr. Kitano gives the following example to illustrate how the Japanese-American family differs from the American family:

. . . an Issei would say: "Here are your eggs; eat them," in contrast to the more typical American motivational question . . . "Johnny, do you want eggs? How do you want them? Oh, please, you know eggs are good for you. If you love me you'll eat eggs." (pp. 72–73)

In addition to unswerving familial loyalty and respect for parents, children are taught that they represent the family name in everything they do. If they fail in school or at work, the entire family is shamed. Upon marriage, children are expected to take up residence near their families. This is part of a feeling of mutual dependence that is fostered by the Sunday outings, family dinners, and other activities centered around the family unit.

The closeness of the family is due to several factors. First, both Buddhism and Confucianism emphasized the importance of family life, influencing, in turn, Shintoism, the religion native to Japan. Drawing upon religious values, the political system within Japan was founded on the concept that all Japanese belonged to one large family, the head or "father" of which was the emperor. By intertwining family with politics and religion, the importance of the familial unit increased to the point where it was seen as embodying such basic values of the society as discipline, self-sacrifice, loyalty, and unity.

The majority of Japanese immigrated to America between 1890 and 1924. They came here seeking to improve their economic status. Upon their arrival they encountered considerable prejudice and discrimination that was heightened because of racial differences and economic factors. As a result they drew inward and formed a strong community structure that stressed the old values, including the primacy of the family. Evidence that these values survived can be seen from the fact that the second generation attempted to transmit them to their own children.

As we saw in our discussion of the Black family, extreme poverty often has disastrous effects on the family structure. The Japanese were able to avoid this situation in part because of a system that provided help for the indigent. A poverty-stricken individual was expected to ask members of his extended family for assistance. If this failed he could approach friends. When all informal appeals had been exhausted, he could appeal to the *kenjinkai*. These were associations whose members came from the same province in Japan, similar to the Jewish *Landsmanschaften* (immigrant societies). Their desire to help stemmed largely from the fact that it was considered a disgrace for a community to be unable to provide help for its own members. Such help, which usually consisted of either money or job assistance, enabled the Japanese to attain a near-perfect record of family stability and a corresponding lack of deviant behavior in the community.

According to informed observers in the community, there are signs that as the Japanese become more and more Americanized, family values are changing. Parents are more apt to complain that their children are ungrateful and do not respect them. Evidence of increased erosion in the future comes from statistics concerning Japanese-American marriages to outsiders. For example, in 1948 12 percent of Japanese marriages in Los Angeles were to non-Japanese. By 1959 the figure had risen to 23 percent, and by 1972 it was 49 percent. Information from other cities with large Japanese-American populations confirms this trend. Clearly, any community where almost half or more than half of its members marry outside the group will have difficulty maintaining its cultural uniqueness.

In a study of Japanese youth some years ago, psychologist Robert Jay Lifton remarked that many Japanese youths felt "a break in their sense of connection." As is true in many societies, the younger generation in Japan finds many of the old values irrelevant to their world. Traditional patterns of deference and respect toward parents are no longer as widely adhered to, and the overwhelming majority of young couples do not live with their parents, as opposed to past generations. The rejection of parental authority is often part of a larger perspective that sees the previous generation as responsible for the ills of present-day Japan. It is most apparent in the violence that occurred in the universities in the past two decades and the confrontations between radical students and academic administrators and professors. While family values were deeply embedded in Japanese society, the traumatic experiences of World War II, combined with an exceptionally rapid pace of technological change, virtually guaranteed that the young would challenge and question the motives and outlook of those responsible for these events.

Great imitators

"Did you hear about the Japanese admiral who raised a sunken battleship during the war and copied it to a T, right down to the hole that made it sink?" This joke was popular in the years following World War II. Today, what with all the new discoveries and fine products made by Japan in virtually every field, such humor sounds more like sour grapes than anything else.

The Japanese themselves are not likely to be offended by charges of imitativeness, for such an approach was a matter of historical necessity as well as policy. Ironically, it was a Westerner, Commodore Matthew Perry, who helped bring it about. In 1853 Perry anchored his heavily armed, steam-powered fleet off the Japanese coast and demanded that Japan open up her borders to trade with the West. Such gunboat diplomacy came at a time when the Tokugawa dynasty, which had kept the country isolated from the world for two hundred and fifty years in semifeudal conditions, was already in an advanced state of decay.

Perry's arrival was the beginning of the end for the Tokugawas. In 1868 the Meiji era was proclaimed, and the new government, having realized how much it lagged behind the rest of the civilized world, embarked on an ambitious policy of modernization. Perry and others had impressed upon Japan the fact that there was much to learn from the West. To accomplish this, Japanese leaders from every walk of life were sent to Europe and America to learn how things were done there. From the Americans they discovered new methods of farming and educational approaches; from the British they learned how to develop a navy and a system of currency; and from the French and the Germans they gained insight into the workings of a modern legal system and the military machine. Thus we see that for Japan imitation was a conscious policy determined by its own lack of contact with the outside world and a desire to catch up with that world.

Japan also brought in outsiders to help it advance. These people taught the Japanese the latest techniques in a wide range of areas, including construction, railroads, postal service, and education. For example, in 1877 twenty-seven of the thirty-nine professors at the University of Tokyo were Westerners. The West was amused—in fact, flattered—that the Japanese wanted to copy everything they did. At first their products were shoddy and inferior to those made in the West. The term "cheap Japanese imports" gained wide popularity. About the best that could be said was "not bad, considering the price."

In recent years, however, all this has changed. One no longer hears such talk about Japanese products. SONY, Panasonic, and Sanyo are respected names. No one sneers at Minolta or Canon cameras. Often overlooked in the past was the fact that in addition to imitating the West, the hardworking and ambitious Japanese also altered and improved many techniques and products. In the seventies only the United States and the Soviet Union have spent more on research. A good example is the automobile industry. After World War II Japan produced imitations of Western cars similar in all but name, such as Skyline, Debonair, and Contessa. When Toyota, Datsun, and Honda began flooding the American market with their cars, Detroit turned up its nose, calling them "cheap Japanese imports." Americans (and now Europeans too) were not fooled, however. They knew a good deal when they saw one, and by 1980 Japan owned 29 percent of the U.S. market. The big three—Ford, GM, and Chrysler—have belatedly come to the realization that Japan has what America wants. Moreover, in terms of mileage, efficiency, design, and repair incidence, the imports more than hold their own. As X cars, K cars, Escorts, and Lynx are rushed into production, it becomes clear who is imitating whom. Will there come a day when our cars are called "cheaply made American imitations" by others?

Law-abiding

Statistically the chances of being mugged, robbed, raped, or murdered by someone who is a Japanese-American are very small. According to FBI figures, Japanese-American arrest rates are lower than those of any group surveyed. Statistics in cities around the country confirm this pattern; in 1960 arrest rates for non-Japanese-Americans in Los Angeles were more than *thirteen* times higher than for Japanese-Americans. Moreover, those crimes for which Japanese are charged tend to be minor offenses, usually drunkenness or gambling, both of which are viewed more tolerantly in Japanese society than in American society.

One group that has shown a slight increase in criminal behavior in the past ten or fifteen years has been the Sansei, or third generation, who have a higher rate of adolescent delinquency than previous generations. Studies done of the Sansei reveal that those who get in trouble with the law are more likely to come from broken families and suffer from psychological disorders.

Most of the standard theories put forth by criminologists to explain why members of certain groups commit crimes more often than those of others do not seem to apply to Japanese-Americans. They certainly experienced a great deal of discrimination and were often frustrated in their efforts to get ahead. In the early period of their arrival here, the Japanese often lived in high-crime ghettoes, yet they were rarely involved in criminal behavior. In Seattle, for instance, only 3 out of 710 boys in a reformatory there between 1919 and 1930 were Japanese, and they came from families that had little contact with the Japanese-American community as a whole. In a similar vein, sociologists have observed that the conflict between the immigrants and their children often leads to a general rejection of authority by children who are ashamed of their parents' "strange" ways. The gap in the Japanese-American community between Issei and Nisei was a wide one, especially since the parents could not become citizens. Despite this and the other factors, the Japanese are, in fact, among the most law-abiding nationalities in the United States. Why?

The answer to this question lies, quite simply, in the Japanese value system, particularly that which prevailed in the period when most of the Japanese came to America. The family was authoritarian, with the father as the dominant figure, but it did not inspire rebellion among the young because the community at large emphasized conformity, an internalization of hostility, and a high degree of tolerance for frustration. Unlike other arriving groups, the Japanese were better equipped to deal with prejudice. Having always valued education, they were in a better position to take advantage of opportunities when they arose. True, a Japanese-American engineer might find himself working as a busboy upon first graduating, but the inner discipline characteristic of all Oriental cultures enabled them to be patient and persevering.

The stress on personal as well as familial honor provided a further impetus toward conformity. Because of discrimination and attachment to the old ways, the immigrants of the late nineteenth and early twentieth centuries were quick to set up community organizations that reinforced traditional values. Sometimes these organizations acted as judge, jury, and executioner for those who violated the norms. In his book Dr. Kitano discusses one such case told to him by a second-generation Japanese.

I knew these two brothers who were pretty wild. They would get drunk . . . were always fighting, always in trouble and were uncontrollable. Finally their father came to talk to my father and other Japanese families in the neighborhood . . . all agreed that these boys would hurt the reputation of the other Japanese and provide poor models for the younger boys . . . so even though the brothers were already young adults and out of high school, they were sent back to Japan in 1937. As far as I know, they never came back to the United States. (Japanese Americans, p. 73)

This excerpt demonstrates quite a few of the values we have been talking about. The honor of both family and community is considered very important. Training the young to conform to societal norms is a matter of high priority. Moreover, we see the power of the community to deal with those who challenge its sense of stability. One can only guess at the effect an action of this sort had on the youths, but it must have been considerable.

In Japan respect for authority and a sense of honor are still strong components of the culture. The overall crime rate in Tokyo is quite low for a city of that size. On the other hand, the strains affecting many industrialized societies around the world are apparently affecting Japan too. There has been a significant increase in white-collar as well as organized crime in recent years, and if it is not kept under control basic values are likely to be threatened.

SIX

Chinese

Sly, sinister, and deceitful

A Chinaman is cold, cunning and distrustful; always ready to take advantage of those he has to deal with; extremely covetous and deceitful. ("China," *Encyclopaedia Britannica,* 7th ed., vol. 6 [1842])

There is no scientific evidence that the Chinese are any more cunning, sly, or dishonest than the rest of us. Moreover, this stereotype appears to be dying out. A study of Princeton undergraduates in 1933 revealed that 29 percent thought the Chinese were sly and 14 percent felt they were deceitful. In 1967 another group of Princeton undergraduates were asked the same questions. The results: 6 percent believed the Chinese were sly and only 5 percent perceived them as deceitful. Still, since this stereotype was so prevalent among older Americans who grew up either before or shortly after the turn of the century, it is worth examining. Moreover, it provides an excellent example of how propaganda can play a major role in the development of such attitudes.

The first recorded instances of such views came from American traders who traveled to China in the late eighteenth and early nineteenth centuries. Historian Stuart Miller examined the records of fifty such traders and found that thirty-seven of them characterized the Chinese as dishonest. Typical were comments such as "[An American had] to be up very early to get the windward of a Chinaman," and "Barrington men never picked a pocket with such ingenuity." Obviously traders all over the world have been defrauded, and it is impossible to tell how accurate or even truthful these assertions were. Nevertheless, these traders were taken seriously by Americans back home because, if for no other reason, they had actually been to China.

In 1839 England started a war with China because it was looking for a market where it could sell opium, a trade that it gained control over through its conquest of India. Many Americans supported the British, and the media increasingly began to portray the Chinese in unflattering terms. Dr. Miller cites the following example from a book by Samuel Goodrich entitled *The Tales of Peter Parley About Asia for Children* that appeared in 1859:

The men [Chinese] are servile, deceitful and utterly regardless of the truth. From the emperor to the beggar through every rank of society, through every grade of office, there is a system of cheating, and hypocrisy, practiced without remorse. (*The Unwelcome Immigrant*, pp. 57–58)

One incident in particular crystallized this image. Representatives of England, the United States, and France arrived at Tientsin to present peace treaties and found new barriers in the Gulf of Pei-ho to replace those destroyed by the British a year earlier. Annoyed, they attempted to blow them up. To their surprise the Chinese ambushed them and inflicted heavy casualties. Caught by surprise, the British cried foul and accused the Chinese of treachery because, in the words of one editor, "The sinister Chinese showed no guns or soldiers in the forts." The Americans supported the British. In fact, American Commodore Josiah Tattnall rushed to the aid of the English with the by now famous slogan, "Blood is thicker than water." Some have questioned whether Tattnall originated this slogan, but it matters little in terms of our discussion, for the American press used the incident to strengthen the stereotype of trickery and cunning.

Within the United States the immigration of Chinese to these shores and the economic threat they seemed to pose to the white unions, small farmers, and businessmen created a need to justify the discriminatory acts that were now being contemplated against them. Thus legislators, journalists, and others seized upon this stereotype (as well as such others as immoral, unassimilable, cruel, and so forth). Its spread was aided by several other factors. To begin with, as historian Gunther Barth has argued, the fact that the Chinese regarded themselves as sojourners, here only temporarily to make some money, threatened a society that wanted all immigrants to become part of "the melting pot" and that was highly nationalistic. The Chinese were also suspect because they looked different. In fact, their appearance was often combined with this stereotype. In his work *Alien Americans* Bertram Schrieke notes how "every aspect of the invaders became unpleasant; their slant eyes bespoke slyness."

Cultural differences made such accusations sound more valid, for it became easier to condemn those whose habits, language, dress, and beliefs were not like those of other Americans. Despite the dislike that existed for the Japanese, the Chinese were often contrasted with them, with the former praised for their interest in and willingness to adopt Western culture and to modernize their country. In the background was the Boxer Rebellion. The Boxers (their name was actually the Society of Righteous and Harmonious Fists) attempted to violently expel foreigners and remove their influences from China. They were ultimately defeated by a coalition of soldiers that included Russians, Japanese, British, French, Germans, and Americans. Naturally, American sympathies lay with the "foreigners," and this, too, affected attitudes toward the Chinese in the United States.

The Exclusion Act of 1882, forbidding the Chinese to come here, marked the beginning of an era during which prejudice against the Chinese came to be increasingly sanctioned by the U. S. Government. From 1882 to 1902 Congress passed twelve more laws that specifically discriminated against the Chinese. By legalizing prejudice Congress encouraged greater open hostility against the Chinese. It was therefore not surprising that during those years there were anti-Chinese riots in scores of American communities in which people were beaten and killed, their homes burned, and their property taken away or destroyed by vicious mobs whose actions were often sanctioned by local authorities.

The role of the media in fostering such hatred was considerable. The New York *Times* ran an article in its April 30, 1905, edition about the efforts of female missionaries to rescue white slave girls held in captivity by Chinese "opium fiends." The title was "Rescuing Angel of the Little Slaves of Chinatown." Such articles routinely appeared in hundreds of newspapers throughout the country, with reporters occasionally admitting to exaggeration simply to get "some good copy" about "the yellow peril" into their editors' hands.

With the advent of the movies, the imagery became far more powerful. Millions saw Boris Karloff play the evil Dr. Fu Manchu, the sinister character created by the writer Sax Rohmer, as well as the equally notorious Mr. Wu, as portrayed by Lon Chaney. In her work *The Portrayal of China and India on the American Screen, 1896–1955* Dorothy Jones reminds us of how stereotyped their roles were. Fu Manchu was billed as a man with "menace in every twitch of his finger, a threat in every twitch of his eyebrow, terror in each split-second of his slanted eyes." Chinatown was depicted as a place of sin, with brothels and opium dens on every corner and sinister figures lurking in every shadow, waiting to corrupt the morals of the innocent and unwary.

As is so often the case, there was a kernel of truth to these assertions. There was crime in Chinatown in the form of tong warfare, for instance. The tongs, unlike the clan and district associations that were formed for mutual aid and reinforcement of common origin, were secret societies that preyed upon man's vices. They controlled the gambling, opium, and brothels that often existed in the community. They were similar to and, in some cases, descended from the secret organizations of southeast China called the Triad, or Heaven and Earth Society, which had fought against the various Chinese dynasties. Rival groups often battled each other, and those who carried out assassinations were referred to as highbinders. All this made great copy for screenwriters and dime-store novelists, who paid no attention to the fact that the majority of Chinese did not act in this fashion.

Another favorite was the smoke-filled opium den with its "mustachioed figures of the night." The Chinese may have introduced opium smoking into the United States, but it should not be forgotten that it was the British who made opium consumption a popular pastime in China. Besides, middle-class Americans were already using opium in various forms, such as laudanum, prior to the arrival of the Chinese. No one knows for certain how prevalent it was in the Chinese community, but reliable estimates fix the percentage of opium users in New York in 1897 at no more than 25 percent. One researcher notes that it was common practice to hire Chinese to pose as addicts for the benefit of the tourists visiting Chinatown. Others point out that many opium dens turned out, upon closer investigation, to contain as many Americans as Chinese. Like gambling and prostitution, which also existed in the early Chinatowns of America, opium fulfilled a very important function not unrelated to American racism. Because of the restrictive laws against the Chinese, many Chinese men found themselves stuck in America by laws which forbade their return. Unlike the Japanese, they were unable to send for brides from the old country. These activities provided much-needed recreation for a predominantly male population that was lonely and trapped here by circumstances beyond its control. It was ironic that such a numerically small group—they amounted to less than 1 percent of the population —could be so widely portrayed as a powerful force for evil and destruction.

By the mid twenties attitudes toward the Chinese began to change. After all, China had been on the side of the Allies in World War I. Moreover, American sympathy for the Chinese increased when they were attacked in 1931 by the Japanese in a war that was to last for fifteen years before a cease fire was signed. Pearl Buck's *The Good Earth* appeared in 1931 and was an instant, smashing success, eventually selling over two million copies. Twenty-three million Americans also saw the film in which Paul Muni starred. This story of how a Chinese peasant couple struggled against the elements to eke out an existence did much to change the image Americans held of the Chinese. Still, it is a testament to the tenacity of at least some stereotypes that another popular figure containing certain elements of earlier caricatures also became part of the American scene at this time, namely, Charlie Chan, the always polite detective-hero. In the new climate the adjective "sly" was replaced by the more subtle "damn clever." Charlie Chan was wily and shrewd but not deceitful. He was, as opposed to Dr. Fu Manchu, on the right side of the law and hence became acceptable, starring in no fewer than forty-eight films. In what was a not-so-subtle effort to lampoon Chinese culture, he was seen mouthing aphorisms often falsely attributed to Confucius. The white masses enjoyed hearing such pearls of wisdom as, "Theory, like mist on eyeglasses, obscures fact," though the Chinese in China and in this country protested in vain against them. The recent banning in San Francisco's Chinatown of a movie company that was planning to film yet another Charlie Chan episode is a measure of the community's resentment of this stereotype and of its increasing militancy.

Today, with the arrival of large numbers of immigrants from China, attention is again being focused on crime in the Chinese community, mostly in connection with its youth gangs. But this is a new era and the old stereotypes no longer spring forth so readily. Moreover, developments in U.S. policy toward China are likely to continue to influence such perceptions. If we move closer to China and further away from the Soviet Union, there will most likely be other shifts in our views of the Chinese (as well as the Soviets), the moral being that old stereotypes neither die nor fade away; they just change.

No tickee, no washee

In her book *Mountain of Gold* sociologist Betty Lee Sung tells the story of the first Chinese delegate to the United Nations who had gone to visit a friend in a Manhattan hotel. By mistake he rang the wrong doorbell. The woman who answered it took one look at him, thrust a bundle of laundry at him and, before he could say a word, slammed the door in his face.

Many Chinese can tell similar tales of how they were mistaken for laundrymen by their fellow American citizens. While there are many Chinese-owned laundries, they do not possess any innate abilities in this area; nor is it an especially popular occupation in China. In fact, there is a saying in China that "There were no 'Chinese' laundries in China. There were only laundries for the Chinese." Is it then a mistake to assume that the Chinese predominate in this area? Not really, because the Chinese in America did enter the laundry business in large numbers. In 1920 almost 1 out of every 3 Chinese workers in the United States were laundry workers. In a study done 30 years later of Chicago businesses, sociologist Rose Hum Lee noted that 430 out of 669 businesses operated by the Chinese in that city were laundries. Ten years later, in 1960, figures released in New York City by the Chinese-American Restaurant Association indicated that the laundry business was still a very likely source of employment for thousands of Chinese. Of the 3,295 Chinese-owned businesses in New York, 2,646 were laundries.

Since they were not historically or culturally inclined to do such work, how do we account for these statistics? The answer lies in their experiences upon immigrating to America. Substantial numbers of Chinese began coming here in 1849. At first they were accepted, but their ever-increasing numbers made them a threat to whites and they were forced out. Subsequently they turned to farming and railroad building, but there, too, they faced discrimination and open hostility from labor unions who agitated against them. Forbidden to own land by California law and denied entry into the unions, many became laundrymen, having discovered that the high ratio of men to women made this a relatively lucrative field. Operating a laundry required little capital investment beyond an iron, an ironing board, and a scrub board. It also demanded little knowledge of English and could be carried out in an inexpensive location, since the custom then was to pick up and deliver the clothing at the individual's home. In addition, whites did not object to the Chinese being laundrymen because washing clothes was "women's work."

Over a period of several decades there was a sort of snowball effect as new immigrants went into the laundry businesses already operated by their kinsfolk, who had often paid for their passage to the United States. For all the advantages that laundry work provided, it was hardly a choice occupation. In a doctoral dissertation entitled "The Chinese Laundryman: A Study in Social Isolation" Paul Siu describes the boredom, lack of contact with others, drudgery, long hours, and repetitive tasks that characterize laundry work. Maxine Hong Kingston, winner of the 1977 National Book Critics Circle Award for *The Woman Warrior,* grew up in a family that owned and operated a small laundry. The following poem of "The Laundry Song" by Wen I-to of Chicago appears in her newest book, *China Men:*

> Years pass and I let drop but one homesick tear.
> A laundry lamp burns at midnight.
> The laundry business is low, you say,
> Washing out blood that stinks like brass—
> Only a Chinaman can debase himself so.
> But who else wants to do it? Do you want it?
> Ask for the Chinaman. Ask the Chinaman. (p. 63)

Today Chinese laundries have declined to the point of extinction. The tremendous influx of Chinese immigrants since the quota laws were liberalized in 1965 means that there will be a large pool of unskilled laborers in the community for some time to come. Nevertheless, they are not likely to open up small laundries, as they had done in the past, because of the tremendous increase in self-service laundromats and the popularity of permanent-press clothing.

As for the stereotype itself, it is still part of the American scene, encouraged in some measure by media portrayals of the Chinese. Take, for example, the advertisement for a popular laundry detergent in which a Chinese person claims to be able to clean clothes better than other people because of an "ancient Chinese secret." Such portrayals both reflect and perpetuate stereotypes.

Inscrutable

The answer to whether or not this stereotype (usually directed at Orientals in general) has some basis in fact would have to be a qualified yes. Among the Chinese there seem to be certain cultural restraints vis-à-vis emotional expression, and there is some empirical evidence of it as well. On the other hand, there are some very good reasons why the Chinese, and Orientals in general, would have wanted to appear inscrutable when in contact with Occidentals.

The perception of Orientals as inscrutable, unfathomable, and suspicious is widespread among Americans. In a 1954 study of attitudes toward the Chinese, political scientist Harold Isaacs cited the following statements as typical of those made by a variety of respondents:

I think of Chinese pretending ignorance but understanding perfectly well. Pretended passivity and resistance, apt at concealing what they think.

A congressman

The Chinese officials here in Washington are pretty unfathomable. I have never met a Chinaman that I felt I could know, always a barrier.

Another congressman

I have always found the Chinese difficult, never felt that I really understood them. Maybe it is a stereotype I've had since childhood of the Chinese as mysterious people. I couldn't have got it in my home, where we almost made a fetish of tolerance of other people. The fact is I did have the experience of dealing with Chinese and never knowing what they really had in mind.

A foundation official
Scratches on Our Minds, p. 84

This association of the Chinese with inscrutability is a part of the everyday conversation of many Americans. One person will say, "Well, he's inscrutable; you know how the Chinese are," to which the other will nod sagely and understandingly. The term is used almost innocently in the media. Rather than being offensive, it is simply viewed as a descriptive adjective. Typical is the title of a 1971 article in *New York* Magazine by Pete Axthelm about the Chinese, "An Inscrutable Passion for Gambling."

One of the most common reasons given for this stereotype is that the Chinese concealed their emotions when in contact with Americans in the United States both because of the hostility with which they were regarded and because they often felt endangered by whites. One professional who teaches in a major American university explained to me some of the circumstances that might have given rise to such forms of interaction:

You see, my parents were here illegally. Many Chinese came here illegally because the Chinese Exclusion Acts limited our numbers greatly, and as a practical matter we couldn't afford to let the whites know about that. So I always heard in my home, "Don't trust the white devils."

If this is the basis for inscrutability, then why is it not a perceived characteristic among the millions of Hispanic illegal aliens presently in this country?

Western travelers to the Orient make similar claims of inscrutability in their encounters with natives, who would seem to have less to fear. One American businessman described his experiences while visiting Japan as follows:

. . . my first-ever live contact with really Oriental Orientals at Haneda Airport backed up the inscrutable warnings. I didn't know when the health man looked at my vaccination book whether everything was OK or whether I was going to be forcibly carried away for another smallpox shot. Even people in restaurants who were saying "Welcome" to me in Japanese when I entered looked like they were really saying "Get out." (Don Maloney, *Japan: It's Not All Raw Fish*, p. 198)

Maloney's last comment raises an interesting point that explains, to some extent, the prevalence of this stereotype among Westerners. Mention has already been made of how smiles can mean different things to Japanese (and Chinese, for that matter) as well as to Americans, but there are other instances too. A Chinese mother addressing her child, for example, will rub her finger against her cheek instead of saying "Shame on you!" or will push the child's head back with her forefinger to indicate displeasure with his or her behavior. Among the Chinese, opening one's eyes wide is often a sign of anger, while among Westerners it is more apt to reflect astonishment. Naturally, those unfamiliar with the culture are likely to be confused by or ignorant of such expressions.

In a similar vein, restraint in emotional expressiveness is also a part of Chinese culture. Its origins can be found in Confucian philosophy, in which attention to form and proper manners was regarded as a sign of the civilized man. This resulted in a good deal of concern about not losing face. As a result of their efforts to avoid embarrassing others, the Chinese developed an aversion to bluntness. Kenneth Latourette, the Yale historian and an authority on Chinese history, gives numerous examples of how this was achieved in Chinese society. One example he presents is that of the Chinese guest at a dinner who deliberately spoke in halting Chinese to his dinner companion so as not to embarrass him. Another is of the head of a household who told his servant "that the sugar under his charge was disappearing more rapidly than it ought." The servant, realizing he was being indirectly accused, suggested a method of safeguarding it against theft by strangers even though both men knew that, under the circumstances, only the servant could have taken the sugar.

There has been at least one scientific attempt to measure inscrutability. Otto Klineberg, the well-known social psychologist and authority on race, described such an experiment in his textbook *Social Psychology*. Chinese and American subjects were shown photographs of a group of Chinese and Americans whose facial expressions were supposed to demonstrate a variety of emotions. Both groups had an easier time identifying the expressions of the Americans. Klineberg admits, however, that since the situation was an artificial one, this single study cannot be regarded as conclusive. Still, it is suggestive.

It ought not to be assumed that the Chinese are *incapable* of revealing their emotions. *The Book of Rites*, or *Li Chi*, one of the five honored classics in Confucian thought, describes in great detail how grief and mourning should be expressed and states that it should be done openly and publicly. Rather, it is simply that for a variety of reasons the Chinese tend to discourage open emotional displays when interacting socially with others, especially outsiders and strangers.

Finally, there is even some evidence that this stereotype may have emerged because of some physical characteristics possessed by Orientals. Anatomical experts have noted that one of the facial muscles, the quadratus labii superioris, is pretty much fused together in the Oriental face, whereas among whites it is divided into three distinct parts, each of which can, to a large degree, be independently controlled. What this means is that whites are probably capable of a wider range of emotional expression than Orientals. There are other differences too. The muscle surrounding the eye is larger and flatter among Orientals and the platysma muscle in the neck is also different, but these have little to do with facial expression. Since all these muscles are very small, it is difficult to draw conclusions about their significance. Moreover, the cultural differences cited are probably far more important than the anatomical ones in explaining the origins of this stereotype.

The best food in the world

The Chinese have long been synonymous with restaurants in this country. In fact, while laundries, as an occupation, have been diminishing in popularity among the Chinese, the number of restaurants has grown by leaps and bounds in recent years. In 1960 there were, according to one estimate, more than six thousand Chinese eating establishments in the United States. By now the number is at least twice as high, with new ones opening up every day. They range in quality from David K's in New York City, one of the most luxurious in the world, to the ubiquitous take-out places found in almost every part of the country. Chinese food is even popular among groups that ordinarily have little contact with outsiders, such as Orthodox Jews. There are at least a half dozen strictly kosher Chinese restaurants in New York City bearing such names as Shang-Chai, Moshe Peking, Can Taam, and Bernstein's on Essex. Although dietary adjustments have to be made (e.g., no pork in your wonton and beef spareribs only), their staffs of chefs and waiters are often Chinese and their cuisine unmistakably Oriental.

Whether or not Chinese food is the best in the world is, of course, open to debate, but it is certainly extremely popular. There are more Chinese restaurants in the United States than of any other ethnic group, with the exception of Italians, who have made spaghetti (which the Chinese invented) and pizza into a national food. Chinese cooking was first brought here by the early immigrants to California, who discovered that their dishes were popular among the miners. Professor Betty Lee Sung recounts one version of how chop suey (which is not served in China since it is a native American dish) originated. Late one night a group of hungry miners were served by a Chinese proprietor who concocted it from leftovers of meat and vegetables. The miners loved it and asked him what it was called. "Chop suey," he replied, and the name stuck.

Actually, the interest of the Chinese in fine food goes back to ancient times. Writing in *The Story of Civilization. Part I: Our Oriental Heritage,* Will Durant noted:

The Chinese loved to eat; it was not unusual for a rich man's dinner to have forty courses, and to require three or four hours of gentlemanly absorption. (p. 775)

Among the rich, the favorite food was duck. The most pretentious of Peking's wealthy class, reports Durant, were known to have dinners consisting of "a hundred courses of duck." The virtues of food were even celebrated in Chinese prose and poetry.

Not only were the Chinese lovers of cuisine since ancient times, but the area of China from which most immigrants came, namely, southern China, is considered, according to Sung, "the culinary capital of China"—no small feat for a country of that size. There is, in fact, a popular saying in China that goes: "Live in Suchow, eat in Kwangchow (Canton), die in Wu-chow." Suchow is famed for its climate and natural beauty, Wu-chow is known for producing excellent lumber for coffins, and Canton is famous for its food.

Besides history and the American palate, there were other considerations. Like the Italians, the Chinese are family-oriented. In such cultures food serves the double function of filling both the stomach and the need for getting together with kinsfolk. Moreover, by serving traditional dishes members of the family emphasize their allegiance to each other and to a common value system, with food serving as the vehicle by means of which this is accomplished. With respect to the restaurant business itself, discrimination against the Chinese, particularly in the pre–World War II period, prevented many from moving into other fields, and there are numerous studies that show that even in later years many Chinese professionals, including teachers, accountants, and even doctors, have, at least temporarily, worked as waiters, busboys, and cooks. As for the population as a whole, 1970 U. S. Census figures show that at the time one out of every six Chinese workers was employed in eating or drinking establishments.

In conclusion, it can be said that the Chinese are disproportionately represented in this area and that the reasons for this are to be found in Chinese culture as well as in their experiences upon coming to the United States.

Learned and wise

The origins of this stereotype go back 3,500 years to the Shang dynasty, which ruled China from 1766 to 1122 B.C. Archeological discoveries of that period reveal that those who lived then addressed written questions to their gods, laboriously carving Chinese characters onto dried bones. According to noted historian Kenneth Latourette, it is entirely possible that schools existed in those days and that, if not, they had definitely been established by the time of the Chou dynasty (1122–256 B.C.).

Much of the credit for the esteem in which learning was held in China must go to Confucius, who wrote in *The Book of Great Learning*, "The aim of higher education is to illuminate or illustrate the illustrious virtue, to renew or renovate the man, and to press on to the supreme good from which all others are derived." China's rulers incorporated Confucian principles into their system of government. Candidates for civil service positions were required to take examinations that tested their knowledge of Confucian writings. Thus book learning became a means of upward mobility.

Of course, the majority of people never learned to read until well into the twentieth century, but the respect accorded men of learning was never in doubt. Even during the rule of the Mongols education never ceased. Those who could afford it (education in China was a private matter) sent their children to schools, about which Durant has written:

Hours were long and discipline was severe in these modest schoolhouses: the children reported to the teacher at sunrise, studied with him till ten, had breakfast, resumed their studies till five, and then

were free for the day. The chief instruments of instruction were the
writings of Confucius, the poetry of the T'ang, and a whip of clinging bamboo. (pp. 799–800)

In such an environment it was perhaps only natural that China
contributed numerous inventions that facilitated literary expression, among them the world's first paper (made from bark,
fishing nets, and flax) and movable type. Today the emphasis on
education continues in China, although it was considered of sec-
ondary importance during the Cultural Revolution under Mao
Zedong.

The Chinese immigrants to America, most of whom came
from the villages of southeastern China, were largely uneducated. Yet they valued learning and sought to give their children
an education. Other Americans also associated the Chinese with
knowledge. In Dr. Harold Isaacs' study of American perceptions
of the Chinese, respondents were asked to list favorable and unfavorable characteristics attributed to the group. Of eleven such
categories, the most often mentioned was "high intellectual quality." Whether this was derived from the popularization of Confucius via the Charlie Chan movies or from a general awareness
of Chinese culture and history is not known.

Available demographic data supports this stereotype. The
1960 U. S. Census showed that Chinese-Americans were more
than twice as likely to have completed college than whites. In
the 1970 U. S. Census more Chinese males had completed four
or more years of college than any other ethnic group. This is,
however, only one side of the picture. At the other end of the
scale the Chinese are overrepresented in service occupations.
Closer examination, however, reveals that most of those employed in this area are older and foreign-born.

Part of the education stereotype is the notion that Chinese-
Americans gravitate toward professions in the sciences and related areas. This is true. In 1960 more than half of all Chinese-
American professionals were employed in the following fields:
drafting, engineering, accounting, the natural sciences, and college teaching. Moreover, less than one quarter of those teaching
at the college level were in the humanities or social sciences.
The rest were either in the physical and natural sciences or in
medicine. There are several possible reasons for this. First,

Chinese-American professionals chose these fields in the early 1940s and thereby established a pattern to be followed by others in the community. Second, these areas did not require as much proficiency in English as, say, law or management. Third, Chinese-Americans felt that skills in these areas were more easily measured by objective standards, thus enabling them to avoid discrimination. Whatever the reasons, a number of Chinese-Americans have achieved world renown in the sciences, including Samuel Ting, Chen Ning Yang, and Tsung-Dao Lee, all of whom won Nobel Prizes in physics.

Love to gamble

There is a subway in New York City that pulls out of the station at Aqueduct Racetrack shortly after the daily double. To those who frequent the track it is known as the "Shanghai Express," named after the many Chinese, most of them elderly, who ride it back to their homes in Chinatown. For many Chinese who place their bets at Aqueduct or Belmont, horse racing is a serious business, worth taking off a few hours from work but not an entire day. As Pete Axthelm put it in his article on gambling,

. . . the double is quick. It provides the kind of speedy win-or-lose verdict that the Chinese appreciate in all their varied card games, lotteries, or games of chance—and it is over soon enough to allow a workingman to be on his job by midafternoon. ("An Inscrutable Passion for Gambling," New York Magazine, September 27, 1971: 55)

Perhaps the races are less of a social event, but this is not the case with other games of chance popular in Chinatown, such as card games, dominoes, and Mah-Jongg, where older men are apt to sit and talk for hours over steaming cups of strong black coffee. These patterns reflect the origins of gambling in the community, an activity created to relieve the boredom and loneliness of single life in the early Chinatowns of America. In *China Men* Maxine Hong Kingston describes some of the social aspects of a gambling house run by her father, who became its manager after his partners cheated him out of his laundry business.

We were getting the gambling house ready. Tonight the gamblers would come here from the towns and fields; they would sail from San Francisco all the way up the river through the Delta to Stockton, which had more gambling than any other city on the coast. It would be a party tonight. The gamblers would eat free food and drink free whiskey, and if times were bad, only tea. They'd laugh and exclaim over the poems they made, which were plain and very beautiful: "Shiny water, bright moon." They'd cheer when they won. (p. 241)

Kingston also describes the other side, namely, what it was like for her father as an employee:

. . . my mother keeps saying those were dismal years. "He worked twelve hours a day, no holidays," she said. "Even on New Year's day, no day off. He couldn't come home until two in the morning. He stood on his feet gambling twelve hours a day." (p. 244)

Besides serving as a gathering place, the gambling houses provided hope for a quick killing for those who regarded the United States as a temporary home until they could make enough money to return to China. Stanford Lyman, a sociologist familiar with the Chinese community, has suggested that the Chinese were attracted to gambling for this reason, and that they were not inhibited "by a Protestant ethic linking meritoriously earned rewards to hard labor."

How widespread an activity is gambling? In 1936 the average take among fifty gambling houses in New York City was thought to be at least one hundred thousand dollars. Portland, Oregon had three hundred such establishments. Today, however, gambling is largely confined to the older generation. Interestingly, Chinese ministers will, out of deference to their elderly parishioners' sensibilities, avoid preaching about the evils of gambling, recognizing that many see absolutely nothing wrong with it. The younger generation eschews this activity for the most part, but there have been problems in recent years with youth gangs extorting the proprietors of the gambling establishments that still do business in America's Chinatowns.

Summing up, there is no indication that Chinese-Americans as a whole are any more involved in gambling today than the average American, though it once played a major role in the community. In fact, as the older generation dies out, this stereotype will almost surely disappear.

Cruel

. . . cruel, savage, ruthless, barbaric, ferocious, violent, brutal; have no regard for human life or suffering; life is cheap; they butcher large numbers of people; beheadings; tortures; would save a hat in a river but not a man; are insensible to soldiers' lives; are cruel and brutal to animals. (Harold Isaacs, *Scratches on Our Minds*, p. 105)

These descriptions of the Chinese were attributed to American respondents interviewed by Dr. Isaacs in his study. They came mostly from persons who grew up in the first quarter of the twentieth century. No nation or people has a monopoly on cruelty, and the excesses of the Chinese throughout their history would probably compare favorably with the atrocities committed during the days of the Roman Empire, the Crusades, and the Nazi era. Yet the Chinese have frequently been perceived in this country as exceptionally cruel. Why?

The source of this stereotype can be traced to our relations with China. When they were strained such stereotypes increased, and when they improved the stereotypes lay dormant. Early American traders, who tended to view all non-Western cultures with contempt, included "refined in cruelty," "bloodthirsty," and "vicious" in their portrayals of the Chinese. Their perceptions were probably formed, in part, by Europe's experiences in the thirteenth century with Genghis Khan, who united China under Mongol rule and whose name was uttered with fear and awe throughout the Western world. For the traders the sight of large numbers of Asians must have conjured up images of wild hordes destroying everything in their path. In fact, as Stuart Miller tells us in *The Unwelcome Immigrant,* the media described China in just such terms in those days. A series of articles that appeared in *Gentleman's Quarterly* in 1753 called China "the fourth beast of Daniel" and warned that it would "devour the whole earth and . . . trample it down, and tear it in pieces." The writings of diplomatic historians generally echoed such views.

Perhaps the most vivid accounts came from nineteenth century Protestant missionaries, who had a vested interest in portraying the Chinese as godless barbarians in need of salvation. They emphasized and exaggerated the Chinese practice of infanticide, citing unsubstantiated claims that "dogs and swine" were set loose upon babies (mostly female) discarded by unfeeling parents. Articles in religious publications of the time were often accompanied by lurid drawings of parents leaving their children to die. The practice of infanticide did exist and was sanctioned in Chinese society. But it was not nearly as widespread as the missionary accounts claimed. It was, as a rule, limited to the impoverished classes and was employed only as a last resort when the family was faced with starvation. Moreover it did not, as the Church often asserted, have anything to do with paganism.

Accounts of Chinese conduct during the Opium Wars also helped fix the association of cruelty with the Chinese in the mind of nineteenth-century America. Almost without fail British actions, such as the bombardment of Canton, were regarded as just and Chinese retaliation as barbarous and inhuman. In 1851 one of the greatest peasant revolutions in the history of the world took place. The T'ai-P'ing rebellion, led by Hung Hsiuch'üan, who believed he was the younger brother of Jesus Christ, was a revolt against both foreign domination and the Manchu dynasty. It lasted for fourteen years, during which an estimated thirty to forty million people died. Journalists wrote about "savage cruelties" and "ruthless acts of destruction," omitting mention that both sides were guilty of them. The most widely publicized of these was the Tientsin massacre, in which the French consul, ten nuns, one priest, and several other persons were killed. Miller reports one horror story accusing the Chinese of drugging Christian children and removing their eyes and "private parts for the preparation of mysterious drugs." It was the same sort of rumor that had been responsible, in part, for the attack of the Chinese upon the nuns and priest. Not surprisingly perhaps, the American press had far less to say when twenty-eight Chinese were murdered in Rock Springs, Wyoming, in 1885, with many of their bodies mangled and left to decompose and be eaten by dogs and pigs. Some were burned alive beyond recognition. Their crime: dissenting in a strike vote taken by miners.

Like the sinister and sly stereotypes, that of the cruel Chinese gained greater impetus with the appearance on the screen of Dr. Fu Manchu and Mr. Wu, along with films recounting the tong wars. The crueler the acts of violence, the greater credence they seemed to have for a public whose fears and apprehensions about "the yellow peril" had been nurtured for decades. The "Chinese water torture" was probably no worse than that which prevailed in dozens of countries at the time, but it was the one that impressed itself upon the American consciousness.

Is there evidence of the extent to which the American frame of reference was shaped by historical events in China? A survey conducted by the political scientist Hadley Cantril in 1942 seems to bear out such an assumption. An opinion poll taken then showed that while only 3 percent described the Chinese, then our allies, as cruel, 56 percent applied the term to the Japanese, with whom America was then at war. Yet after the war, when the communists gained control of China, the stereotype began to be applied again to the Chinese, who had until then been characterized as wise, polite, cultured, self-effacing, honest, and peace loving. Thus a respondent in Isaacs' book could state,

I remember that when we heard of Japanese cruelties in China (at the time of the Sino-Japanese war) a friend of mine who had lived in China at the time told me that when it comes to cruelty, the Chinese don't have to take lessons from anybody. We are seeing some of this now in the Communist regime. [emphasis added] (*Scratches on Our Minds,* p. 105)

The era of communist rule saw the return of the stereotype in the form of brainwashing, which was heightened by the Korean War. No attempt is made here to deny that the Chinese often treated Americans with cruelty. Rather, we are dealing with how such perceptions waxed and waned in direct proportion to our relations with China.

Even by objective standards the struggles during the civil wars in China between 1927 and 1949 were both extended and vicious. An estimated fifty million persons died during those years. Still, it should be remembered that internal warfare often tends to be particularly brutal, as witnessed by the conflicts in Biafra, Burundi, Cambodia, Bangladesh, the Soviet Union, El Salvador, Ireland, and scores of other lands.

Given the fact that nations at war are almost always apt to depict the enemy as cruel and barbaric, it is impossible to objectively assess the validity of such claims. What about the United States' treatment of Indians and Blacks? the actions of Spain and Portugal in the days of the conquistadores? What shall we say about the behavior of the English and the French in Africa and Asia during the period of colonization, not to mention the Belgians and the Dutch? The list, it would seem, is rather long. Therefore, all that can be said about the Chinese is that our relations with China have been a major factor in coloring our views of it and its people.

Strong family ties

To understand the Chinese attitude toward the family we need to first know a little bit about Confucianism, one of the great religions or philosophies of China. Confucius (c. 551–479 B.C.) grew up in a period of great suffering and conflict. Wishing to become, as he put it, "a man of perfect virtue," he gained a reputation for great wisdom and attracted pupils from all over the country. His books, in which he set forth both his philosophy and his interpretations of Chinese history and its ancient works, were known as the "classics." Over a period of time they became the basis for much of Chinese life, especially the daily conduct of its people. Although Confucius was not a religious teacher, his approach eventually became so firmly entrenched that he acquired the status of a god. Shrines were built in his name and incense was burned to honor him.

One of Confucius' main concerns was the family, which he viewed as the logical starting point for moral development. By applying the principles of morality, kindness, and respect for others, man could learn to apply them to the community at large, thus resulting in a happy and just society. The home was seen as a model for general human conduct, with filial piety its

central goal. Filial piety can be divided into three areas: respect
for one's ancestors; honoring one's parents; and living properly
so as to bring honor upon the family as a whole.

It is in his observations on the status of women that Confucius
has been most severely criticized and condemned. Two of his
best known thoughts on this subject were: "Of the three acts of
unfiliality the lack of heir or successor to the land is the greatest"
and "that it is hard to deal with women and the immature because intimacy breeds lack of respect and remoteness causes
resentment." In the *Book of Poetry* Confucius wrote, "Sons of a
king, they will have scepters to play with." [Daughters] "They
will have only tiles to play with." Throughout Chinese history
and up until the twentieth century, women were considered inferior to men. A man's wife might be his other half, but she was
definitely not his better half. Today young Chinese militants have
castigated Confucius because of such views. For example, in a
review of children's books published in 1976, members of the
Asian American Children's Book Project wrote,

. . . the books [which they reviewed] put undue emphasis on the
Confucian cultural tradition . . . Confucianism was an elitist social
philosophy . . . based on the concept that a hierarchy should determine how the mass of Chinese should live. In specifying higher status
for men than for women, Confucianism sanctioned forced marriage,
female slavery, educational underdevelopment for women, and concubinage. ("How Children's Books Distort the Asian American
Image," *Interracial Books for Children Bulletin,* vol. 7, no. 2, 1976,
p. 3)

Much of this criticism is valid, but it should be borne in mind
that Confucius lived twenty-five centuries ago at a time when
women were treated as less than equal throughout the world,
not just in China. The system survived for thousands of years,
however, in part because the generally conservative approach of
Confucius helped justify the authority of the various dynasties
that ruled China until the Manchus were overthrown in 1911. In
1931 the Kuomintang party, led by Chiang Kai-shek, promul-
gated a new "Code of the Family" that, among other rights, allowed women to inherit property, outlawed concubinage, and

granted women the right of divorce. Social customs that have lasted for centuries change slowly, however, and these laws were not taken seriously by the masses until the communists passed a new law, called The Marriage Act, granting women equal status. At first the communists moved too quickly, forcibly removing concubines from their homes and driving some to suicide. The number of divorces increased dramatically as women took their liberation to heart (there were almost four hundred thousand in 1952), and the law soon became known as "The Divorce Act." In response the communists slowed down the process somewhat. Today their efforts in this area rank as one of the most significant achievements of their rule.

Notwithstanding the status of women in Chinese society, the closeness of family ties was a fact of life among the Chinese. For the peasant masses, tied as they were to the land, the extended family was crucial to its economic well-being. More than a wife and children were needed to till the land, and as a result the family came to include uncles, aunts, and cousins. True, other cultures had similar systems, but China remained an agricultural society far longer than many other countries. Besides, respect for the family was a basic feature of Chinese tradition for thousands of years. A son was required to be obedient to his father and all had to be respectful toward their elders. The extent to which family and country were intertwined can be seen from the following passage in Jade Snow Wong's *Fifth Chinese Daughter,* a novel in which a Chinese father who immigrated to the United States early in the twentieth century addresses his young daughter:

"Confucius said, 'He who is filial toward elders and fraternal toward brothers and is fond of offending his superiors is rare indeed; he who is not fond of offending his superiors and is fond of making revolutions has never been known.'

"So you see, the peace and stability of a nation depend upon the proper relationships established in the home; and to a great extent, the maintenance of proper relationships within the home depends on intelligent mothers. Now I do not want you to ever question why you should study Chinese," finished daddy. (p. 15)

Although China was ruled as one country throughout much of
its history, the mountainous terrain, frequently divided by major
rivers, helped create distinct cultures with separate dialects,
customs, and values. Violent conflict among warring groups was
common in many parts of the country. Under these circumstances, the family assumed even greater importance as a source
of security and strength.

Most of the early Chinese arrivals to this country were males.
Their intentions were to earn money quickly and return to
China. Thus, even those with families back home did not send
for them. In 1924 the Immigration Act effectively closed off all
emigration from China and the proportion of women to men
remained very small. After World War II, however, the government gave permission to Chinese-American males to bring their
wives into the United States as nonquota immigrants.

These women, dependent on their more acculturated American husbands, were not likely to assert themselves. With the passage of time this has changed, and relations between husbands
and wives are more apt to approximate those of the larger society. One indication of Chinese-American assimilation is the intermarriage rate. In 1970 30 percent of the men and 22 percent
of the women in California were married to non-Chinese, and
the number has risen since then. Although there is no information available on the nature of their relationships, it seems safe
to assume that there has been some diffusion of American
values. U. S. Census data show that Chinese-American women
today are more likely to have full-time jobs and obtain a college
education than they were twenty years ago.

With respect to attitudes toward parents and deference toward
elders, Chinese-Americans are probably somewhat more traditional than Americans in general. There has, nonetheless, been a
marked shift in this area in recent years due to a growing generation gap and the heavy influx of immigrants from China since
1965. In many families both husband and wife work. Their children go to American schools and adopt cultural values that often
conflict with those of their immigrant parents, a not unfamiliar
pattern in American history. Lacking encouragement and guid-

ance from parents, many children, especially the older ones, drop out. Being teenagers without skills, they are often unemployed and become ready recruits for the gangs that have proliferated in Chinatown during the last decade.

In the past few years the media has widely publicized gang warfare and the extortion of local merchants by gang members. Such activities are in and of themselves an indication of the breakdown of parental authority. Editorials have appeared in Chinese papers urging parents to reassert their positions in the family by giving moral guidance to their children. At the same time, they have urged the government to provide jobs for the teenage population that has left school and set up programs offering remedial courses, bilingual education, and precollege assistance for those who want to stay in school. Given the history of other groups in this country, the chances are that, in the long run, the Chinese immigrants will eventually overcome these problems.

Quiet, polite, and deferential

"You know, this Chinese couple moved in recently down the block."

"Yes, I heard. What are they like?"

"Oh, you know. They're very quiet. They seem nice."

This exchange might be heard in almost any neighborhood of middle-class America today. It points up a view whites hold of Chinese that, while difficult to prove, is nonetheless quite prevalent. Studies of stereotypes confirm the existence of such perceptions about the Chinese as well as other Orientals.

One possibility is the context in which Americans have come to know the Chinese. In terms of occupations, most Chinese immigrants went into service occupations such as laborers, laundrymen, busboys, and waiters. Such jobs almost demand politeness and encourage obsequiousness. On the other hand, no one has ever accused French waiters or Hispanic busboys of excessive politeness. It would seem, then, that we must look further.

The position in which the Chinese found themselves in the

United States must also have played a role in encouraging such behavior. The immigrants were a numerically small minority and as such were in no position to challenge authority even when wrongfully exercised. Not only the people, who often felt economically threatened by their presence, but the media and authorities were often against them. Moreover, the strict regulations against immigration to this country caused many to circumvent the law, especially those who wished to be reunited with their families. Fearful of being caught or discriminated against or both, the Chinese were unlikely to attract attention by protesting their lot. In adopting this mode of behavior the Chinese were not alone. It was a common response by Blacks during slavery and is used by the powerless around the world as a means of survival.

In the post–World War II period conditions for Chinese-Americans improved dramatically, and while the stereotype still exists, it is undergoing some changes as the Americanization process takes hold. Orientals have become more militant and aggressive, as can be seen from the founding of various organizations to protect their rights. Phrases such as "banana" (yellow on the outside, white inside) and "Uncle Tong" have found their way into the everyday language of the younger generation. The following quote from editor Cheng-tsu Wu's book *Chink!* certainly does not sound deferential:

You call me "Ching Chong Chinaman" sometimes? Hell, evil bull-jive asshole DEVIL is the only name I have for you—the only name I've ever been *taught*. ("Foreword," p. xi)

These explanations can be applied to the American context, but what about the Asian one? Travelers to the Orient have frequently noted the good grace and courteousness with which they have been received by their hosts in China, as well as in Japan, Korea, and elsewhere. This is traceable to the Confucian tradition that urged people to show respect for one another by putting oneself in the other's position and stated that self-improvement required the practice of virtue. In addition, Buddhist philosophy also exhorted individuals to show kindness and compassion toward others, as well as self-discipline. These attitudes, supported as they were by China's ruling classes for thousands of years, were deeply ingrained in the consciousness of the population and, as such, were an important part of the cultural heritage brought to these shores by the immigrants.

SEVEN

Irish

Heavy drinkers

McCloskey was stopped by a Boston policeman in the days of prohibition: "What's that you got in that bag?" "Oh, it's just a bottle of holy water," he replied. The officer removed the cap from the bottle and sniffed it for a second.

"Aha—just as I suspected. A bottle of gin!"

"The Lord be praised," exclaimed the man. "Another miracle!"

There are literally hundreds of jokes about the fondness of the Irish for "The Creature." Excessive drinking has, of course, been a problem for mankind in general for thousands of years. According to archeologists specializing in the Middle East, the ancient Egyptians and Babylonians were greatly concerned about it, as were the Greeks and Romans of later times. In China laws regarding the consumption, sale, and manufacture of alcohol were passed and repealed more than forty times during the reign of the fourth emperor of the Yüan dynasty in the fourteenth century. Yet it is the Irish who seem to be regarded as the champion tipplers among the nationalities of the world, a distinction they have alternately joked about and been ashamed of down through the years.

References to Irish drunkenness appear in the records of travelers to the Emerald Isle during the sixteenth, seventeenth, and eighteenth centuries, but the problem seems to have become especially severe in the nineteenth century, when famine and British oppression compelled millions to leave their ancestral homes in the hope of finding a better life elsewhere—often America and Canada. Their arrival in the United States was often greeted with hostility and violence by a population whose bigotry focused upon the Catholic loyalties and extreme poverty of the Irish, as well as their drinking habits. The historian Oscar Handlin observed that

Nothing the Irish found in Boston altered their tradition of alcoholic indulgence. Instead, crowded conditions drove men out of their homes into bars where they could meet friends, relax, and forget their anguish in the promised land. . . . Frequently drunk and often jailed for inebriety, the Irish "arrested and turned back" the short-lived temperance movement which had made promising progress up to their arrival. Other nationalities, particularly the Germans, were also fond of the glass, but neither their habits nor environment encouraged or even tolerated excessive drinking. (*Boston's Immigrants,* p. 121)

Handlin reports that the majority of taverns in Boston during this period were owned by Irishmen. The same was true in New York City, according to an article that appeared in a 1954 issue of the New York *Tribune.* Detailed studies of alcoholism among the Irish were first done in the twentieth century, and they indicated what the average man in the street had long known: Drinking was a severe problem among the Irish. In a 1947 article published in the respected *Quarterly Journal of Studies on Alcohol,* Dr. Donald Glad cited the following hospital admission figures for alcohol psychosis per 100,000 population:

Irish	25.6
Scandinavian	7.6
Italian	4.8
English	4.3
German	3.8
Jews	0.5

Another article published four years later in the same journal noted that 44 percent of the whites then on the Bowery, New York City's skid row, were Irish. During World War II more Irish were probably rejected for wartime service because of alcoholism than any other group.

Drinking is still a problem in the Irish community today, though it is less so as the Irish become more and more assimilated into the American mainstream. According to studies conducted in the mid sixties by Dr. Andrew Greeley at the National Opinion Research Center in Chicago, the Irish are still, as he puts it, "fond of 'the jar.'" Among his findings: They are least likely to be abstainers; most likely to report drinking at least twice a week; and most apt to have three or more drinks of hard liquor at a single sitting. They are also more likely to drink than WASPs. Nor is the tendency restricted to men. Although there is no hard data available, Greeley, a sociologist and priest and one of the most knowledgeable observers of the contemporary Irish scene, asserts in his book *That Most Distressful Nation,*

The suburban [Irish] matron quietly sipping martinis alone in her parlor or with her cronies on the country club veranda is becoming a frequent figure on the Irish suburban scene. Her husband and children do their best to pretend, frequently to themselves, that the good woman is just "nervous," but it doesn't take long for everyone in the community to learn that she is a lush. (p. 139)

Nor is the clergy exempt from such temptations. Dr. Greeley states that many priests drink enormous amounts of alcohol and notes that in one see not long ago all three bishops were alcoholics. Indeed, such assumptions are well supported in both Irish humor and song. Take, for example, the following lyrics in a ballad by the Clancy Brothers called "The Juice of the Barley," about a drunk who becomes a priest when told to mend his ways by a man of the cloth:

> So the very next morning as the dawn it did break
> I went down to the vestry the pledge for to take
> And there in the room sat the priests in a bunch
> Round a big roaring fire drinking tumblers of punch.
>
> (Arranged and adapted by Liam Clancy,
> Tiparm Music Publishers, Inc., 1963)

The visitor to Ireland today can easily see for himself that alcoholic consumption, especially in the convivial atmosphere of the public house, is a favorite pastime. True, the Irish drink less, per capita, than the British or Germans and are less likely to suffer from cirrhosis of the liver than the French. Moreover, almost one sixth of the population has pledged not to drink alcohol, often joining the Pioneers, an organization devoted to abstinence. And there are, no doubt, millions of Irish in Ireland and in the United States who either do not drink or who drink socially without any difficulties. Still, the zeal of the abstainers and their high degree of organization exist because there is a problem. And there are, after all, an estimated 14,000 pubs in Ireland. That works out to 1 for every 320 people.

Having established that linking the Irish (though by no means all or even most of them) to a tendency to drink heavily does not constitute a slanderous lie, how are we to account for it? Some have claimed that the Irishman's propensity toward sociability and his hard life made the saloon an attractive place. This is true to some extent, but it does not explain why he reacted in this particular fashion. After all, the Italians also came from a close-knit peasant culture characterized by extreme poverty and oppression. Yet they did not gain notoriety in this area. There is also the fact that Ireland's soil and climate were particularly conducive to the growth of certain crops required for alcohol production. However, this could be said of many countries. Others, in their effort to explain why so many immigrants opened taverns and liquor stores, have pointed out that it was a business requiring little capital, but, as we have already seen, this was equally true of Chinese laundries, not to mention tailor shops run by Jews and the Hispanic grocery stores of later times. To understand how the Irish became heavy drinkers we need to look at life in Ireland a bit more closely.

Beginning with the end of the sixteenth century, England, under the rule of Queen Elizabeth, made a determined effort to bring the often unruly Irish under her control. The English succeeded, after a century of struggle, in establishing their dominance and set into motion a series of discriminatory laws that incurred great resentment and hatred among the local inhabitants. A Catholic could not buy land from a Protestant unless he converted; he could not send his children abroad to study; and he was not permitted to lease land for longer than thirty-one years —a serious restriction in a predominantly agricultural society. He was also forbidden to vote, bear arms, or maintain religious schools. As a result, an entire nation was humiliated and degraded. True, the Irish rebelled frequently and displayed great courage in battle, but they also developed a strong sense of insecurity.

After the Napoleonic wars ended in 1815, the conditions of the Irish worsened. Grain prices collapsed and the landlords made efforts to transform the land from small farming plots to grazing land. In addition, the population was steadily increasing. As a result, the Irish were either driven off the land or found their plots so small that it became impossible to earn a living from them. To drown their sorrows they often turned to drink, finding in the public drinking establishment a place where they could meet with friends and temporarily escape from their troubles. Sociologists William and Joan McCord, in their well-known study of alcoholism in the Boston area, found that male alcoholics often came from backgrounds in which their masculine identity was not clearly defined and caused them considerable anxiety. As adults such people are, in the McCords' view, most likely to drink when their masculinity is threatened and when a social environment defines drinking as acceptable and enjoyable. Clearly, centuries of British domination threatened Irish manhood, but what about the acceptability of drinking? Was this also true of Ireland and, if so, why?

Prior to the famine years of the 1840s, a family's land was divided equally among all the adult males. The famine, however, so greatly impoverished the Irish that it was no longer feasible to have more than one heir, namely, the oldest son. There was simply not enough land to go around. As a result, marriage was either delayed or postponed indefinitely, with the unmarried and unpaid sons either working on the land for the married son or emigrating. This created an entire society of bachelors whose single status encouraged a life-style of hard drinking, exaggerated feats of bravado, violent behavior, and lack of responsibility. In his book *The Hair of a Dog* Richard Stivers points out how the bachelor groups became an important part of Irish society, often initiating young men into a life-style in which drinking played a significant role. In addition, Irish culture was characterized by a puritanical Catholic Church that exalted chastity and encouraged sexual repression. As evidence that booze became a substitute for sex, there exists an abundance of jokes in the popular culture, such as, "A Dublin queer is a man who prefers women to drink." Of course, men have been known to indulge in both sex and liquor simultaneously. Still, as Max Caulfield remarked in 1973 in *The Irish Mystique,*

There is something suspicious about a society that combines heavy drinking, late marriages (Ireland still tops the world in this), and a low rate of illegitimacy in a country where contraceptives are not on sale. (p. 214)

With this sort of historical backdrop it becomes easier to understand why the immigrant Irish, who, as a rule, comprised the most oppressed and poverty-stricken of the mother country, found the bottle such a source of comfort. Their history in a sense created it, their economic conditions sustained it, and their culture encouraged and perpetuated it. Not surprisingly, the Irish adapted their recreational life-styles to conform to the demands of American society. The bar became a transfer point from the rural, close-knit communities they had come from to the anonymity of urban life. It also became a focal point for political activity, a function it had also served in the old country.

Good at politics

The overrepresentation of the Irish in politics hardly requires extensive documentation. Not only have there been such well-known persons as Richard Daley, the Kennedy brothers, Joseph McCarthy, and Daniel Patrick Moynihan, but the Irish have made their mark at all levels of politics, from the lowest patronage positions to those of mayor, governor, senator, and president. Although their influence is waning now, the Irish controlled cities such as New York, Chicago, Philadelphia, and Boston as early as the mid and late nineteenth century. Do the Irish have, as many claim, a certain affinity for politics? Were they simply in the right place at the right time? What are the factors that have made the term "Irish politician" a descriptive adjective in the English language as it is used in the United States?

To begin with, it is worth mentioning two important advantages possessed by the Irish who came here. The first was their relatively early arrival. They came at a time when America was rapidly expanding and were therefore able to get into politics on the ground floor. More significantly, English was one of their native languages (the other, of course, was Gaelic), an important edge given the many difficulties faced by almost all immigrant groups who entered this country. It would seem, however, that this could not fully explain the love of and enthusiasm for politics that characterized so many of the immigrants. Edward Levine has raised this question in his study *The Irish and Irish Politicians:*

Why . . . had the Irish remained in urban politics for generations when, according to the academic literature dealing with the sociological functions of politics, the Irish ought to have abandoned politics for middle-class occupations once it had brought them middle-class status? (p. 3)

The answer, as suggested by Levine and others, has a great deal to do with Irish history and culture. Simply put, the Irish were intimately familiar with the nature and form of Anglo-Saxon politics as a result of the English occupation of Ireland. The Irish were exploited and persecuted politically by government officials who viewed the political process as a way of oppressing them and who were often corrupt and excessively harsh. Whenever the Irishman sought redress for his grievances, he found himself faced either with Protestants who were contemptuous of him or Catholics who had sold out to the occupiers. In order to survive they were often forced to become adept, cunning, and manipulative, as well as extremely knowledgeable in the basics of political infighting. As part of their efforts they sometimes formed political organizations, one of the most important of which was the Catholic Association, led by Daniel O'Connell. Through these organizations the Irish learned about political consciousness, the need to sacrifice for the common good, and the importance of group solidarity. It was to serve them well when the famine years precipitated the departure of millions of Irish for America. In addition, their negative experiences with the Anglican Church in England turned them into enthusiastic supporters of the separation of Church and State that prevailed in America.

As a result of their experiences in Ireland, the Irish had come to see politics as equivalent to power. This aspect was of far greater importance to them than the moral issues that often propelled members of the American Protestant establishment into the political sphere. They had seen bribery, violence, and every possible form of chicanery employed against them in the old country, and when they were greeted here by more of the same bigotry and suspicion they resolved to use the system for their own ends. There were, in all likelihood, many who derived a great deal of satisfaction from gaining control of the very institutions that had been used in the past to keep them down. Jokes such as the following probably had more than a bit of truth to them:

"Listen," said Mulligan to O'Grady as the two met in a saloon, "I'm no party man. I always vote for the best candidate."

"Oh yeah," responded O'Grady. "And how can you tell who that is until the votes are counted?"

What about other immigrant groups who had been mistreated in their countries of origin? Had not the southern Italians been oppressed by those in the North? And were not the Jews persecuted in czarist Russia? But the Irish were different. British policy toward the Irish was far more brutal than that of northern Italy toward the South. Rome refused to help the Neapolitans and Sicilians, but it did not invade and colonize them. The Jews, on the other hand, came from a tradition that emphasized education and commerce, and it was these power bases to which they gravitated. For the Irish—limited as they were by the anti-Catholicism of the intellectual class in America, and with no capital resources to speak of—politics was one of the few alternatives available that had practical benefits, for it provided power and jobs, both of which meant security in a hostile society.

As time passed the Irish were able to consolidate their hold on politics. They gained full control of the Democratic party in urban America, which they proclaimed as "the party of all the people." They used their skills in this area to win over the loyalty of the masses of East Europeans and southerners who had followed them to the new land. As cities continued to expand, the need for municipal services increased tremendously, making control of patronage a crucial variable in city power politics. The Irish, entrenched as they were in the system, made the most of it, as portrayed by the novelist Edwin O'Connor in the following two excerpts from *The Last Hurrah*. In the first Governor Frank Skeffington is talking about an Italian-American politician:

And while we're at it, let's count Camaratta out too. For good. I'm tired of him. He's a double-crosser we've put up with for years because he controlled that longshoreman vote. I've never liked him personally, but more important, I don't think he's as strong as he used to be. (p. 49)

We see here the stress on politics as power. Without that it loses its significance. In the next selection one of Skeffington's political sidekicks makes a play for the Polish vote to a Polish tire dealer:

"A grand people, the Poles," Ditto said, smiling at him. "A grand, grand people. They make grand citizens. I have always said that the Poles were some of our grandest citizens and always very loyal to the Governor. Every spring the Governor and I go down to the river and the Governor personally throws a beautiful wreath on the water in honor of that grand Polish hero Pilsudski." (p. 55)

Senator Daniel Patrick Moynihan has observed in *Beyond the Melting Pot* (with Nathan Glazer) that "instead of letting politics transform them, the Irish transformed politics, establishing a political system that, from a distance, seems like the social system of an Irish village writ large." Chief among its values was the idea of stability. The Irish village, as Moynihan notes, was a place where "almost everyone had a role to play" and where one's "position was likely to improve with the passage of time." This became the leitmotif of the political system that was fashioned in this country. Patience and waiting one's turn was rewarded with a job, a lucrative contract, money, or, at the very least, a favor of some sort.

There were other parallels too between rural Irish values and those that became part of the political infrastructure here. Irish politicians were characterized by a gift for words as well as a highly personal approach to politics. They were more interested in people as individuals than in larger issues. Levine cites one councilman who put it this way:

I get more satisfaction out of individuals getting—helping individuals [rather] than getting some big idea across in the city council or awakening the political conscience. (p. 157)

Levine cites one Irish politician who said, "Republicans are more fakers, so-called do-gooders, reformers. They insult the intelligence of the average man and woman." Attention to the individual was one of the most important features of life in the villages from which most of the Irish came. Moreover, friendships often superseded questions of political ethics. There is the well-known story of Irish-born Congressman Timothy J. Campbell, who made a request of President Grover Cleveland that the latter rejected because it was unconstitutional. "Ah, Mr. President," said Campbell, "what is the Constitution between friends?"

Another aspect was loyalty, an important commodity in a land where the Irish could depend only on themselves for trust. The weakness of the Irish when pitted against the British might have made this an absolute necessity for survival. Thus, it was hardly surprising that it became a hallmark of the Irish-American politician, especially among his own constituents.

Finally, there was power. As already noted, this was of primary importance in Ireland, where power was ruthlessly exercised by the English. When pondering the question of why the Irish stayed in politics for so long, it is useful to remember that, given their historical experiences, power meant far more than money. This is well illustrated in Mike Royko's book about former Mayor Richard Daley of Chicago, in which Daley is quoted as having said,

. . . the party permits ordinary people to get ahead. Without the party I couldn't be mayor. The rich guys can get elected on their money, but somebody like me, an ordinary person, needs the party. Without the party, only the rich would be elected to office. (*Boss: Richard J. Daley of Chicago*, p. 84)

In fact, power was probably the lure that attracted so many Irish to the police department, though the fact that it was a municipal job also helped. Here the immigrant or his children could be on the right side of the law. Moreover, as with any civil service position, he had security as well.

Today the Irish, though still prominent in politics, are no longer nearly as dominant as they were in the past. If they are, it is as national figures à la Moynihan that they have made it, not as party machine politicians, and their status has far more to do with individual capabilities than with ethnic background. This is in sharp contrast to Ireland, where politics is still a very serious business, with voter turnout one of the highest among all democratic nations. Choices are often based on ancestral cleavages, particularly what one's daddy did in 1916. Moynihan attributes much of the loss of influence to the fact that as the Irish have moved up the socioeconomic ladder they have left the cities and become dispersed throughout the suburbs, where they no longer vote in blocs but as individuals. To this can be added the fact that as government has grown in complexity it has become less responsive to the personal approach, and that technological advances have caused many of the patronage jobs on which the little fellow, the backbone of the party, depended to disappear.

Moynihan is critical of the Irish politicians of the past, charging that they "did not know what to do with power once they got it." He argues that power was their primary goal rather than working for social change, and that as society changed they were left behind. Today the Irish hold on politics is no more, and we will never know if things could have been different. Considering the nature of the Irish, they probably wouldn't have wanted it any other way.

Sexually repressed

Not long ago a young Frenchwoman living in Dublin wrote, "When the *History of Great Irish Lovers* is written, it will be the thinnest book in the library." Clearly, accurate information about sexual repression is difficult to obtain, for individuals are often likely to either not discuss it at all or defensively exaggerate their sexual prowess. Moreover, there is (perhaps for these reasons) little empirical research on the subject. As a result, we are forced to turn to knowledgeable observers of the Irish scene whose intuitive knowledge is, one hopes, reliable.

Andrew Greeley has written,

. . . many, if not most, Irish-Americans get rather little enjoyment out of sex and are not very skillful in the art of lovemaking . . . The Irish male, particularly in his cups, may spin out romantic poetry extolling the beauty of his true love, but he becomes awkward and tongue-tied in her presence and clumsy, if not rough, in his attempts at intimacy. (*That Most Distressful Nation*, p. 114)

Perhaps most appalling is the lack of knowledge about sex in Ireland, a fact widely reported in the literature by both researchers and popular writers. In his book *The Irish* Donald Connery writes of a "modern" Irish girl who asks a magazine columnist, "Can French kissing lead to pregnancy?" According to Alan Bestic, who used to work for the *Irish Press*,

Many [women] enter marriage knowing that "babies are made in Mammy's tummy," but with only the flimsiest knowledge of how they [the babies] can escape from it . . . A hospital Sister told me of one woman who learned the full facts when she woke up too soon from the anaesthetic . . . An English girl, living in Dublin, told me that she was shocked by the number of Irish girls who believed that babies came out via the navel. (*The Importance of Being Irish*, p. 109)

Both Connery and Bestic described Irish life during the 1960s. Since then, however, significant changes have occurred. With the increase in TV shows from Britain and the United States, attitudes have begun to change. More people are aware of the women's liberation movement and many support it; the use of contraceptives, now legal, is widespread; and sex is now discussed far more openly in the media as well as in private. For many in the older generation, however, these changes may be too late. Moreover, they have raised an entire generation of children who have been affected by the old values even as they seek to break away from them.

Those who came to this country frequently transmitted their straitlaced attitudes about sex to their offspring. In James T. Farrell's classic *Young Lonigan*, Studs describes how these attitudes were also inculcated in school:

At school, he'd been taught it [sex] was the terriblest sin you could commit . . . he remembered Sister Bertha saying that God tested you with temptations of sins of the flesh, and if you were able to withstand them you needn't worry about not getting into Heaven. Ninety-nine per cent of all the souls in Hell were there because of sins of the flesh. (p. 151)

Greeley asserts that things have not changed much since 1932, when *Young Lonigan* was first published, and he argues that "children who grow up in an atmosphere of sexual tension . . . are not likely to have too strong a grip on their own sexual identity."

How true this is today among Irish-Americans is hard to say since it is a little studied subject. Dr. Greeley, however, reports on a National Opinion Research Center [NORC] study done in the mid sixties that asked questions about sexual permissiveness. Surprisingly, the findings suggest that Irish men are somewhere in the middle, less permissive than WASPs and Slavic Catholics but more liberal then German and Italian Catholics. The same is true of their attitudes toward sexual permissiveness for women. They are less permissive than Jews and Scandinavians but more so than Italians. There are several problems with the study, including the small size of the sample and the fact that it runs counter to the assumptions of nearly all social scientists familiar with the Irish-American community. Greeley notes that when he showed the data to sociologists, several simply refused to believe them. Perhaps such inquiries are too personal for a questionnaire. On the other hand, it may simply be that the Irish are rapidly acculturating in this area. In any case, there is no recent evidence to prove that what was probably true long ago is still the case today, and the stereotype is therefore of questionable validity.

If the Irish were sexually repressed in the past, what factors could account for it? The Catholic Church probably played a major role by virtue of its teachings. Then again, the Catholic Church was pre-eminent in a number of countries, such as France and Italy, where sexual repression was not commonly associated with the citizens of those nations. Perhaps the difference was that the Irish church was influenced by Jansenism, a puritanical doctrine that emphasized the sinfulness of sex, among other teachings. It was brought to Maynooth College in Ireland around 1795 by French theologians who had fled France during the Revolution.

It would, nonetheless, be simplistic and unfair to lay the entire blame at the doorstep of the Church. The truth is that sexual repression probably flourished in Ireland because socioeconomic conditions were receptive to it. The bachelor societies, created by extreme poverty that made marriage unrealistic, required a rationale for the lack of sexual activity, particularly since their members emphasized a machismo approach to life in general. The Church provided them with one. It may be noted that before the famine the Irish typically married early. There is, in addition, the question of how greatly British oppression affected the masculine self-image. By being deprived of his land, the Irish male was, in effect, emasculated, and this may have affected his relations with women. Certainly, more research needs to be done on this question. Given the economic misery of Ireland at the time, the drinking culture that flourished, and the strong sense of inferiority brought about by centuries of foreign domination, it would seem that the Church found Ireland extremely fertile ground for its teachings on this topic. Had this not been the case, however, one wonders whether the Irish would have been any different from other peoples in their views about sex.

One final factor needs to be considered, namely, the Irish mother. Donald Connery has portrayed her as follows:

I have seen the elderly Irish mother described as just about "the most jealous and unreasoning female on the face of the earth." Harsh words, and yet by pampering and then clinging desperately to her dear boy she makes him a victim of her possessiveness and he turns out to be something less than a full man. (*The Irish*, pp. 199–200)

Late marriage, combined with a father who was, in many cases, a heavy drinker, chronically underemployed, and chauvinistic in his attitudes toward his wife, probably had much to do with the attention and affection lavished by Irish mothers on their sons. Some writers believe that the Irish male so treated tries to marry a substitute mother, a wife who, according to one marriage counselor, "is a king size water bottle." The problem is: How do you have sex with your mother? Moreover, the guilt that the mother may inspire in her son for "deserting her on account of some scheming girl" can cause him to develop a highly ambivalent attitude toward his wife in many areas, including sexual relations.

This may seem like a strong indictment to some, but it is echoed by nearly every social scientist who has written about the Irish family, as well as by popular chroniclers of Irish life. Jewish and Italian mothers also form close relationships with their sons, but perhaps they do not threaten their self-confidence as much. Moreover, the Jewish and Italian male egos have developed in cultures that differ in other important ways from that of the Irish. A comparative study of Italian, Jewish, and Irish mothers would probably be fascinating. Doubtless there are millions of Irish males who are perfectly well adjusted sexually and countless millions of other males belonging to different nationalities who are not. Nevertheless, the stress placed on this issue by knowledgeable persons suggests that it is—or, until recently, has been—a problem.

As for Ireland, it is difficult to say what the future holds. On December 28, 1980, about ten thousand persons marched through the streets of Dublin protesting against the legalization of abortion. On the other hand, British statistics show that at least three thousand Irishwomen had abortions in England last year. Perhaps the most significant harbinger of change is the marriage rate. The number of married people in 1979 was 20 percent higher than in 1971, and the population has increased by slightly more than 13 percent. It would seem, therefore, that the bachelor society and all its attendant problems are disappearing, and that the Ireland of the future may not be much different socially from its English neighbor.

Very religious

Before dealing with this stereotype we should perhaps note that anyone making such a claim in Ireland during the Middle Ages would probably have been laughed out of the Church. Divorce was more common in those days and could be granted for practically anything, ranging from childlessness to simply "being a troublemaker," whatever that meant. Illegitimacy and concubinage was not unusual either, and many men of the cloth were married and had children. It was only after the Reformation that things began to change.

Ironically perhaps, the English deserve a great deal of credit for bringing the Irish closer to their faith by making the practice of Catholicism so difficult. Following the victory of William of Orange at the battle of the Boyne in 1690, the Irish Protestants instituted a policy of rigidly enforcing the penal code. Among the restrictions were the exile of all bishops, friars, and monks from Ireland under penalty of death, the destruction of all public crosses, and the banning of Catholic pilgrimages. These and other penalties had the effect, which is still present today, of linking the expression of Catholicism to defiance of the hated British, as can be seen from the following joke:

"Father," said the young IRA soldier, "I have sinned, for I have blown up ten English busses."

"I see," replied the priest. "For penance you'll have to blow up another ten."

Thus the priests became the spiritual leaders of the masses in more ways than one.

When the Irish arrived here in great numbers during the 1840s, they faced tremendous discrimination on account of their religious beliefs. They were assailed by nativists of all sorts, especially the Know-Nothings and the Ku Klux Klan, who accused them of owing allegiance exclusively to the pope. Samuel B. Morse, inventor of the telegraph and a strong anti-Catholic, warned that the pope intended to re-establish the Vatican in the Mississippi River Valley. In response the Irish reacted as they had in Ireland, embracing the Church even more warmly. As historian Lawrence McCaffrey has observed:

Catholicism was the glue holding the ghetto together, the one familiar institution bridging Old and New World experiences. It assuaged Irish misery, disciplined Irish conduct, and drew people from different parishes and counties in Ireland into an Irish-American community. *(The Irish Diaspora in America,* p. 173)

John Carroll, the first American bishop of the Catholic Church, had been of Irish descent, but it was not until the 1840s that the Irish became the dominant ethnic group in the Church. They had the advantage of being the first Catholic group to arrive in sizeable numbers, and they also spoke English. Finally, they seemed to have a talent for organization, one that they would use to great advantage in the political arena, and were successful in establishing, over the next fifty years, a far-flung system of schools, convents, seminaries, orphanages, and other charitable institutions. What this meant in terms of the religious involvement of the Irish was that their central institutions of Church and School were dominated by their own former countrymen. The only serious opposition to Irish control within the Church was mounted by the German Catholics, but even they were eventually forced to relinquish control of the Church hierarchy. In 1886 thirty-five of the sixty-nine bishops in the United States were Irish, followed by the Germans with fifteen.

This dominance has persisted through the years. Writing in 1972, Greeley estimated that 35 percent of the clergy and 50 percent of the hierarchy were Irish, despite the fact that the Irish represented only 17 percent of the total Catholic population. Today their control has become somewhat less significant as the influence of the growing Hispanic population in the United States begins to be felt and as those of Irish descent "give themselves" to the Church in declining numbers.

Still, the Irish remain attached, even if only sentimentally, to the Church, and for many its values continue to shape their outlook on life. Thus, William Shannon could write in the Sunday edition of the New York *Times Magazine* in a matter-of-fact way,

Being a religious group the Irish see the hand of God in human affairs. . . . Although good at worrying, they ultimately trust in Providence. The really important things in life, like good health or a happy marriage or the gift of love, cannot be planned or bargained for. So why not leave them to God's decision? (New York *Times Magazine*, March 14, 1976: 75–76)

Is Shannon correct? Are the Irish still "a religious group," as he puts it? Again Greeley provides us with an answer. In *The Education of Catholic Americans* he and co-author Peter Rossi conclude that parochial school education has a greater effect on those of Irish and German descent than on Italian and Polish Catholics. More importantly, Greeley notes in *That Most Distressful Nation* that "77 per cent of the Irish go to church every week (higher than the national average) while only 29 per cent of the Protestants and 4 per cent of the Jews attend church weekly."

Attending church and being religious are not necessarily the same thing. Indeed, for many Americans attending a religious house of worship is a purely social matter. Still, it is a measure of some degree of involvement. Moreover, on the basis of personal experience spanning over a decade in one of the newer suburban parishes, Greeley claims that current loyalties to the Church are probably stronger than in the past. Allowing for the fact that "very religious" is a relative term, one could say, based on what we know at this point, that this stereotype probably has a good deal of truth to it. Parenthetically, Catholicism still has a very strong hold on the population in Ireland.

Highly nationalistic

In America this stereotype could easily be substantiated during the nineteenth and early twentieth centuries. It has little validity today except in Ireland, where the Irish are as proud of their country as anyone else. To be sure, many Irish are proud of their heritage and identify with the mother country, but this could be said of any one of a dozen groups in the United States, including the Greeks, Jews, Italians, Croatians, and so forth. Still, the stereotype persists. In fact, it has grown in recent years.

In a 1969 study of stereotypes, about twice as many people believed that the Irish were "extremely nationalistic" than was the
case in 1933. The origins of this perception are directly linked to
historical developments in Ireland.

Most of the Irish immigrants during the nineteenth century
were very attached to the old country. In addition to the normal
yearnings and homesickness that typified the experience of most
newcomers, there was the intensity of feeling against British oppression. Combined with anti-Catholic feeling in the United
States, the net effect was to increase the sense of loyalty to Ireland. Thus the immigrants supported the Catholic Emancipation
struggle, the Young Irelanders, and the Irish Republican Broth-
erhood (the original name of the Fenians) through rallies, political pressure, and money. Sizeable numbers of Irishmen fought
on both sides during the Civil War in the United States and
many saw it as an opportunity to gain experience to be used
later in freeing Ireland. Bringing attention to the struggle in Ireland was seen as valuable not only in terms of attracting support
but also in explaining to Americans why the Irish who came
here were so poverty-stricken and uneducated. Moreover, talking about freedom must have struck a responsive chord in the
hearts of many Americans, who could relate it to the fight
against the British a century earlier.

In the early twentieth century the struggle over Home Rule
and the Easter Rebellion of 1916 again galvanized feelings of
Irish nationalism in this country. On June 11, 1921, the fighting
stopped in Ireland and shortly thereafter the Irish Free State
was created. The northern province of Ulster remained under
British control. The Irish Republican Army [IRA], outcome of a
union between the Sinn Fein and the Irish Volunteers, refused
to accept this state of affairs and has kept the flames of nationalism alive ever since through its opposition to Irish partition.

If the Irish-Americans were especially nationalistic, one would
expect their support of the IRA here to be especially strong.
This is not the case. Most Irish-Americans, while sympathizing
with the Catholics in Ulster, have not actively supported them.
Writing in the New York *Times* several years ago, William Shannon remarked,

. . . the American Irish are less emotionally engaged by the fate of
Ulster than are most American Greeks by the Turkish occupation of
Cyprus and much less than are most American Jews by the danger to
Israel. The explosive headlines . . . dominate the news from Ireland.
Funds from America help finance this strife, but . . . only a very
small and diminishing number of American Irish contribute money or
feel directly involved in the Ulster crisis. (New York *Times Magazine*,
March 14, 1976: 72–73)

It is precisely because the headlines about violence in Belfast
dominate the news that this stereotype is still current. That is
probably what lay behind the thinking of those who associated
the Irish with strong nationalistic feelings in the 1969 survey
mentioned earlier. Most experts on the Irish community agree
with Shannon. According to a 1979 *Time* magazine article, Irish-
American contributions to the IRA that year totaled about
$145,000—more than from any other country but not much con-
sidering the number of Irish-Americans in the United States.

Literary, witty, and gregarious

> We were the last romantics—chose for theme
> Traditional sanctity and loveliness;
> Whatever's written in what poet's name
> The book of the people; whatever most can bless
> The mind of man or elevate a rhyme;
> But all is changed, that high horse riderless,
> Though mounted in that saddle Homer rode
> Where the swan drifts upon a darkening flood.
>
>   (William Butler Yeats, from
>   "Coole Park and Ballylee, 1931")

The reputation of the Irish in this area was solidified in the
sixteenth century when the Irish legal profession came of age.
Thus, an English official in Dublin wrote to Henry VIII as follows: "Sir, the Irish hath most pregnant, subtle wits." In *The
Irish Mystique* Max Caulfield gives us the following description
of a judge, the Earl of Norbury, who lived in those times:

When passing sentence of death on a prisoner found guilty of stealing a watch, he remarked, "My good fellow, you made a grasp at Time, but egad! you caught Eternity." [At one point] Norbury would finally "throw open his robes . . . and pour forth an outlandish, unconnected jumble of anecdotes of his early life—jokes, quotations . . . sarcasms against the defendant's counsel; and possibly a few allusions to trial incidents. (pp. 201–2)

The Irish have certainly produced their share of distinguished and, in some cases, great writers and intellectuals. Among them have been George Bernard Shaw, James Joyce, Samuel Beckett, Oscar Wilde, Brendan Behan, J. M. Synge, Edmund Burke, Frank O'Connor, and Oliver Goldsmith. A good number were particularly known for their wit. John P. Mahaffy, a former provost of Trinity College and the author of a work called *The Art of Conversation,* was once asked by a women's rights advocate, "And just how are men and women different?" "I can't conceive," airily replied Mahaffy. Yeats once offered the following opinion of a colleague: "The worst thing about him is that when he's not drunk, he's sober." The tradition of arts and letters was continued in the United States, where the Irish contribution included the works of Eugene O'Neill, John O'Hara, F. Scott Fitzgerald, James Farrell, Elizabeth Cullinan, Flannery O'Connor, J. F. Powers and William F. Buckley.

Notwithstanding all those individuals duly cited in the above paragraph, this stereotype is of questionable validity. There are many other countries that can argue the merits of their literary history with equal, if not greater, conviction. (The entire matter is, after all, somewhat relative.) Take Ireland's neighbor, England, which has been home to such literary giants as Shakespeare, Wordsworth, Dickens, Shelley, Keats, and Byron. And let's not forget the Scot Robert Burns. Was Chaucer less witty than Shaw or Wilde? What about the French, who gave us Baudelaire, Rabelais, Molière, and Hugo? Then there is Germany, the birthplace of Goethe, Schiller, Heine, and many others. Yet it is the Irish who seem most closely associated with a literary bent, especially wit, in the common mind. Why?

Perhaps it is because words are one of the few weapons available to the conquered. Their harsh treatment at the hands of the

British made it imperative that they find some way to retain a sense of honor. Often unable to prevail physically, they chose instead to fight with words. This is common among many maligned groups. Jews and Blacks, for instance, have successfully employed humor to achieve a symbolic victory. Richard O'Connor has written in *The Irish:*

To be witty when the odds were against you was a guarantee of immortality, at least among the Irish. Thus when the short-tempered Louis XIV complained to its officers that the Irish Brigade caused him more trouble than all the rest of his army put together, one of them replied, "Please, Your Majesty, your *enemies* make just the same complaint about us." (p. 274)

The fact that Irish writers believed in the efficacy of the word also helped spread the stereotype, for they adopted and stressed this attribute in their own writings. Many books about the Irish take the uniqueness of their people's talent in this area as a given, though some authors, such as Max Caulfield, claim it is dying out in the Ireland of today.

With respect to the American scene, the entry of many Irish into politics—where a way with words, sharp riposte, and a general gift for gab mixed in with a flair for flamboyance were almost essential—drew attention to what was already a stereotype. Moreover, their command of English made their writings more likely to be read than the literature of the French, Germans, and Italians. A glance at the newspaper advertisements of the day reveals a certain fondness for the English language that is unmistakably literary. *The Irish News* of May 9, 1857, described "An Evening with Tom Moore" as follows:

The cup will sparkle and the harp of Temor speak, and the collar of gold which Malachi wore will come to light, and the swords of former days will flash out as they did at Clontarf and Yellowford, in the sweet starlight of these evenings.

The Irish propensity for drink, which we have already noted, added to the impression of sociability and gregariousness. The saloon was a place where people gathered to talk and laugh and, as everyone knows, liquor loosens the tongue. On the other hand, this writer grew up in a neighborhood where many of the

Irish he saw sitting on the stoops of their tenements or with whom he played were anything but gregarious. Their grinding poverty made them, on the whole, a rather sullen and uncommunicative lot. James Farrell was obviously a man of words, but the Studs Lonigan who he so accurately portrayed was just as clearly not. Thus, one must be careful not to generalize.

When all is said and done, it is clear that the Irish have made their mark in literature, but in so doing they join many other nations. Andrew Greeley notes, however, that this tradition is disappearing among the Irish. Oh, yes, there are still Tom McHale and other writers who keep it alive, but Irish-Americans today have, for the most part, chosen other fields, such as government, law, and medicine. In short, they have become just as American as everybody else.

The "fighting Irish"

"How does an account of an Irish party begin?"
"Among the injured were . . ."

Football fans might perhaps think that Notre Dame University coined the term "fighting Irish," but its origin probably lies in the medieval English view of the Irish as wild barbarians. This is understandable, for the Irish strongly resisted English rule, though they often came up short. There was the revolt of Silken Thomas of Kildare in 1537; that of Hugh O'Neill, Earl of Tyrone, in 1595; Owen Roe O'Neill in 1649; Wolfe Tone and the United Irishmen in 1798; and many more. In the modern period there were the Young Irelanders, the Fenians, and today's IRA. Clearly the tradition from the Middle Ages onward was not a nonviolent one, though it must be added that this was true on both sides. In addition, there was the macho culture of hard drinking and battling inspired by the bachelor societies that came into existence because Irish males were unable to support themselves.

When the Irish came to this country, both domestic events and their history and culture conspired to ensure the perpetuation of this stereotype. Impoverished, they were often compelled to take hard and unrewarding jobs that no one else wanted. Working as dockhands, railroad workers, and general day laborers, often forced to go on the road to feed their families, they lived rough-and-tumble lives often marked by violence. Having arrived here with no skills and no time in which to learn them, they were particularly threatened by other groups that followed them here, such as the Chinese and Italians, and frequently fought violent battles with them. The fights that erupted when they had a bit too much to drink are probably the source of the quick-tempered stereotype. There were also Irish gangs that fought constantly, the most famous of which was probably Chicago's Regan Colts. Arrest records show that when the Irish were apprehended, it was usually for such crimes as disturbing the peace, disorderly conduct, and assault. It must be remembered, however, that this is common to members of many discriminated against groups, and prejudice against the Irish was particularly strong in those days. A Massachusetts senator commented in 1852,

So far as they [the Irish] are mere hand-workers, they must sustain the head-workers, or those who have any element of intellectual ability. Their inferiority as a race compels them to go to the bottom; and the consequence is that we are, all of us, the higher lifted because they are here.

Edward Everett Hale, "A Plea for the Irish Immigrant." (p. 463)

There was also the exemplary military record compiled by the Irish. In addition to the thousands of first- and second-generation Irishmen who fought, more than 140,000 native-born Irish served in the Union Army, a figure considerably higher than their representation in the population. Another 40,000 or so saw combat with the Confederate Army. The most famous unit was the Union's 69th Regiment, dubbed by the media as "The Fighting Irish." As Edward Wakin tells us in *Enter the Irish-American*, they gained a reputation for courage and skill prompting even General Robert E. Lee to say, after one particularly vicious battle, "Never were men so brave. They ennobled their race by their splendid gallantry on that desperate occasion." Later, during World War I, the 69th, redesignated the 165th Infantry, fought again with distinction, inspiring Victor Herbert to compose music to Joyce Kilmer's poem, "When the 69th Comes

Back," as they marched triumphantly up New York City's Broadway on April 28, 1919.

There were other developments, too, that gave credence to the Irish reputation for fighting. They were active participants in the Draft Riots of 1863, instigated by a law allowing those who could afford to pay others to fight for them in the Army to avoid service. More than twelve hundred people were killed in what has become known as the most costly domestic riot, in terms of human life, in U.S. history. On another front there was the active support for Ireland's struggle against the British, which involved gunrunning, military training, and recruitment from the Irish-American community. Factional strife among the various groups often broke out into violence and augmented the impression of many Americans that the Irish were violence prone. Finally, there was the reputation for pugnaciousness achieved by the Irish as prizefighters. The most famous was John L. Sullivan, who captured the American public's imagination with his dare, "My name's John Sullivan and I can lick any sonofabitch alive."

There is no empirical evidence that the Irish are better fighters than anyone else. Violence has nonetheless played a major part in shaping their culture and history, though their role in it was often an unwilling one. The stereotype is therefore more or less valid when discussing the past history of the Irish. As for today, there is no basis for assuming that someone of Irish descent is more likely to physically assault you than anyone else. Nor can a propensity for physical combat be said to be a characteristic of the Irish in Ireland. The crime rate is relatively low, and though there are arrests for assault, often related to drunkenness, the problem is nowhere near as serious as, say, in Poland or Russia.

EIGHT

Poles

"What does it say on the bottom of a Coke bottle in Poland?"
"Open from other end."

Probably no stereotype in America today is as common as the one about the "dumb Polack." The thousands of jokes constantly circulating among the general population, often on a daily basis, confirms its existence. The question is: Do these jokes have a basis in fact? The answer, from a scientific perspective, is definitely not.

The first extensive use of I.Q. tests in this country occurred in the early part of the twentieth century, when large numbers of immigrants arriving here from the East and South of Europe were tested by the U. S. Army. Poles, Russians, and Italians consistently scored lowest among European immigrants. These results were widely cited at the time and eventually formed part of the basis for laws in the early 1920s that greatly limited the number of East Europeans and Europeans from the South admitted to the United States. Researchers are well aware that Jews (who constituted more than half of the Poles and Russians tested) performed better and better on I.Q. tests as time went on, but not much has been reported on non-Jewish Poles, Russians, and Italians. Dr. Thomas Sowell, however, recently analyzed data on this question for The Urban Institute. His conclusions indicate that Polish I.Q.s have "risen significantly over time, to a level at or above the national average." What happened, in Sowell's view, was that I.Q. scores increased as the immigrants' socioeconomic levels rose, and their cultural environment improved as a result.

Psychologist Richard Herrnstein, in a 1980 article that appeared in *Commentary,* cites an interesting study of I.Q. in postwar Warsaw. The tests included almost all of the children born in Warsaw in 1963 and still living there in 1974. The average I.Q. was about 109—considerably higher than the general average score of 100. The authors of the study concluded that the difference was due "to the flow of highly trained people, with their I.Q.s, toward the capital." Herrnstein points out that a study of London's population has shown that its inhabitants also have the highest I.Q. in the United Kingdom, but it is only 102, 7 points *lower* than the much maligned Poles. Thus we see that both domestic and foreign data challenge the validity of this stereotype.

Since there are no grounds for the notion that Poles are more stupid than anyone else, why is it that so many people think so? How have the people of a nation with a respected intellectual history and an old tradition of scholarship come to be perceived this way? To be sure, the Poles were depicted in most unflattering terms when they first came here in the late nineteenth and early twentieth centuries. "Wretched . . . mental cripples . . . rejects of Europe . . . vulgar" were typical terms of abuse employed to describe them. But, then again, Lithuanians, Italians, Greeks, Jews, and many other groups were also portrayed in this manner. Only the Poles seem to have retained a large number of these negative traits. Why?

One reason advanced by social scientists has been the fact that the Poles have begun moving into the middle class only in the last decade or two, having been members of the working class or on the lowest rung of the middle class until then. This has given them a newfound visibility. If this is so, then other groups should have been subject to the same stereotypes as their economic status rose. It would seem, therefore, that we need to look further.

It is difficult to say precisely when Polack jokes became popular, but it seems that the election of Senator Edmund Muskie (formerly Marciszewski) in 1959 provided the catalyst for this type of humor. Rather than blaming him, however, it would seem as though the civil rights movement, which began its active phase with the 1960 Greensboro, North Carolina, sit-ins, might have played a role in an indirect but very important way. It is well known that when people cannot take out their frustrations on that which is bothering them, they will focus on something else. This is sometimes referred to by psychologists as displaced aggression.

Whites in America were confronted by angry Blacks during the sixties. Many felt both guilty about their own prejudices and hostile at having to face up to them. Unable to openly express their racism, they returned to more acceptable forms of prejudice. The seemingly innocuous Poles (the term "white ethnics" didn't even exist in those days) seemed a perfect group on which to focus. In fact, writer Don Kovalic has suggested that Poles became the butt of such humor in part because they did not have a JDL or NAACP that could intimidate people. Thus, the Polish parachute that "opened on impact" replaced the Amos and Andy caricatures of the fifties. The fact that Poles were the largest single group of East Europeans also helped solidify them as a stereotype. (In this sense the Czechs, Hungarians, Lithuanians, Slavs, and Ukrainians were just lucky.) Reacting to this, Michael Novak wrote in *The Rise of the Unmeltable Ethnics:*

In particular, I have regretted and keenly felt the absence of that sympathy for PIGS [Poles, Italians, Greeks, and Slavs] which simple human feeling might have prodded intelligence to muster, that same sympathy which the educated find so easy to conjure up for black culture, Chicano culture, Indian culture, and other cultures of the poor . . . Why do the educated classes find it so difficult to want to understand the man who drives a beer truck, or the fellow with a helmet working on a site across the street with plumbers and electricians, while their sensitivities race easily to Mississippi or even Bedford-Stuyvesant? (p. 69)

There is a strong current of resentment against intellectuals present in this passage and in much of the book. Novak accuses intellectuals of insincerity when he uses the phrase "conjure up." He feels they should empathize with the common workingman who is white and also struggling. Intellectuals are aware of this hostility and they also know that many ethnics are angry at what they see as preferential treatment for these groups. This makes it easier for them (i.e., the intellectuals) to attack Poles in good conscience. Their prejudice becomes legitimate because it is aimed at the "bad guys," who are bigots anyway. Naturally, given the snobbery of many intellectuals, portraying the Polish people as dumb becomes the highest form of insult, one that gained legitimacy, it seems, from the fact that until recently relatively small numbers of Poles attended college.

Now that the militance (and white liberal support) of the sixties and early seventies seems to have ebbed and white ethnics have achieved cultural respectability, it would seem that Polish jokes should be on the way out. Perhaps, but they are likely to linger on for a while. In an article that appeared in *Perspectives* magazine, Novak recalled,

During the early stages of Watergate . . . the media didn't quite trust Rodino, Jaworski, and Sirica until they had "proved" themselves. (p. 24)

Lest anyone think this is no longer true, it should be noted that the *Pol-Am Journal* of Scranton, Pennsylvania, took Senator Henry Jackson of Washington to task for poking fun at Poles at a banquet held in Vancouver on October 23, 1978. The senator was reported to have suggested that the Catholic Church substitute vodka for wine to increase Church attendance now that it had a Polish pope. This is because they have become institutionalized over a period of time through repeated and almost constant reinforcement by the mass media. From Archie Bunker to books containing Polish jokes, and through constant reference to them in newspapers and magazines Poles have achieved respectability, so that even they are reluctant to make a fuss about these jokes. I know of a neighbor who makes it a point to tell his Polish neighbor the latest "Polack jokes." I am told that the neighbor laughs politely. I wonder if he would tell his Black co-workers the latest "nigger jokes."

Perhaps the most significant development in this area has been the election of Pope John Paul II and his emergence as a strong, forceful, and *intellectual* religious leader. According to persons active in the Polish community, Poles in America have begun taking more pride in their heritage. According to Archbishop John Cardinal Krol of Philadelphia, many men are now telling him for the first time that their mothers are Polish. What this will do to the stereotype of Poles as stupid no one knows, but it has certainly improved their image in this country and has given many Poles greater self-confidence, as is indicated by a story told to me by a close Polish friend.

You know, there's this group of women that I play cards with every week. And, you know, they're always making fun of the Poles, telling those jokes. Well, when they announced who the new pope was, I said to them, "You better shut up with those jokes because now we got one of our own in there!" They're mostly Irish and, you know, you could have heard a pin drop. Let's face it, I can't stand those jokes and I felt it was about time I told them off.

Dirty

"Why can't you kill a fly in Poland?"
"Because it's the national bird."

I recently told a colleague of mine that I was writing a book about racial and ethnic stereotypes. His response, half-serious, half-joking, was instructive. "Oh, I'm going to hate you if you do that." "Why?" I asked. "Because I know a lot of good Polack jokes and you're going to spoil it all if you say they're not true!"

Making Polack jokes is the racism of the middle class, especially liberals. Frequently these people are unaware of how insulting this form of humor is to Polish-Americans. Some years ago Edward J. Piszek, president of Mrs. Paul's Kitchens Inc., embarked on a half-million-dollar campaign called "Project Pole." Among other things, Piszek placed ads in various magazines and newspapers praising the Polish people's accomplishments. His efforts met with only limited success because many Americans simply did not take them seriously. In 1980 a New York State judge dismissed a bias suit brought by Poles against a store that was selling a coffee mug with the handle *inside* the cup, labeled "Polish Coffee Cup." Perhaps the Poles will have to burn down Hamtramck before anyone pays attention.

At first glance it might appear that this stereotype owes its genesis to the peasant background of most Polish immigrants who came to this country. Certainly, conditions of filth and squalor were common. The middle class was especially critical of the tendency among some of the immigrants to keep a pig or two and chickens around the house. This was often, however, a matter of necessity. Dr. Joseph Wytrwal describes some of the problems in his book *Poles in American History and Tradition.*

Placed in the anthracite region by the force of circumstances, without either the time or the means or the knowledge to look elsewhere for work, the Pole could only supply his pressing physical demands by selling his labor under conditions below the general level in the United States. Under such conditions he tolerated living in a one-room hut, built by his own hands on a hillside near the mine, of driftwood gathered in spare moments from along the highway, and roofed with tin from discarded power-cans. (pp. 223–24)

The problem with this argument is that the Poles were not unique in this respect. Jews were crowded into filthy tenements on New York City's Lower East Side, as were Italians, Irish, and other groups. Moreover, the Poles were often described by knowledgeable observers as cleaner than other immigrants. This is noted by Dr. Emily Balch, a former economics professor at Wellesley College, who spent years studying immigration to the United States in the early part of this century. Balch cites the following description of Poles by a Miss Garret, who lived in Baltimore, which appeared in a journal in 1904:

The houses [of the Poles] are cleaner than those occupied by any other group of foreigners . . . the floors are scrubbed and the rooms are kept wonderfully neat . . . Neighbors, business men, doctors, teachers all lay stress on the extreme neatness and cleanliness of the Polish people. (*Charities*, 11, December 3, 1904, p. 273, as cited in *Our Slavic Fellow Citizens* p. 374n.)

Balch also cites a resident of Wilkes-Barre who told her,

The Irish lived far worse when they first came . . . than the Slavs have ever done . . . The Irish used to make dug-outs in the hillsides, and live in them with their animals. (p. 374n.)

If the Polish immigrants did not have a monopoly on dirt, then why are there so many jokes about this subject? One possibility is that as working-class people they frequently engaged in what others might call "dirty work." One could not stay clean in a coal mine or steel mill or in any one of two dozen blue-collar occupations. In associating them with such work, it is conceivable that the stereotype of dirty work became synonymous with a dirty life.

Peter Binzen, a Philadelphia journalist who spent much time traveling to and living in various white working-class communities around the country, has written about the stress placed on neatness and cleanliness. In his book he recounts his experience in the home of one woman, the daughter of Polish immigrants, from whom he had rented a room:

Tidiness, in fact, is the hallmark of Wanda's house . . . tidiness and a kind of mausoleum decor. These are common characteristics of the better Whitetown houses . . . the basement, too, is far cleaner than my dirty cellar in suburbia . . . Wanda is still asleep. I boil an egg over her gas stove and make some instant coffee. Stacking the dishes in the sink . . . something I suspect Wanda would never do since she seems to clean up after every meal or snack . . . I leave the house and resume my wanderings. (*Whitetown, U.S.A.*, p. 132)

Stereotypes can often be explained by looking at the culture of the people who are being stereotyped, but in this case it may be more fruitful to examine the functions such images serve for the stereotyper. As noted earlier, Poles made their way into the larger society in the fifties and sixties just as anti-Black feeling was becoming unfashionable. It was therefore entirely likely that persons whose personality structure required a scapegoat would look around for someone else, and Poles, who represented a very large single group of blue-collar workers, were available. The Italians, incidentally, also came in for their share, being referred to as greasy and unclean by comedians, but they already possessed other stereotypes to satisfy the popular mind, such as Mafioso, violent, clannishness, cowards, talking with their hands, and so forth.

The idea that people transferred their stereotypes from Blacks to Poles seems to be even more plausible here than in the case of other traits because, as we saw in the discussion of Blacks, many whites associate filth with blackness. At the same time, it should be emphasized that dirt is a widely used stereotype whenever attempts are made by members of one ethnic group to put down those of another. In his classic work *The Nature of Prejudice,* Dr. Gordon Allport pointed out that in Europe, where there is no significant Black population, it is the Jew who is called dirty. In Israel it is the Arab, in Yugoslavia the Turk, and so forth. In short, calling members of a group against which one is already prejudiced dirty becomes a way of further dehumanizing them and justifying one's biases.

Summing up, there is no evidence that Poles are dirtier than anyone else. Those who hold such views would probably do well to examine their own motives for feeling this way.

Racists and bigots

The language of Spiro Agnew, the language of George Wallace, excepting its idiom, awakens childhood memories in me: of men arguing in the barbershop, of my uncle. . . . cursing the niggers in the mill below, and the Yankees in the mill above . . . millstones he felt pressing him. Other relatives were duly shocked, but everybody loved Uncle George; he said what he thought. (Michael Novak, *The Rise of the Unmeltable Ethnics,* p. 67)

Perhaps you've seen him in your neighborhood drinking beer on his porch in his sleeveless undershirt or in the local tavern after a hard day's work at the mill. You've watched him on "All in the Family" or maybe you remember him from the nationally televised hard-hat demonstrations of the early seventies. He may be a Slovak, an Irishman, or an Italian, but as far as most people are concerned he might as well, for convenience' sake, be a Polack. He hates everyone who doesn't belong to his own group, especially Jews, Blacks, and Hispanics. They're stepping on *his* family, *his* flag, and *his* country. They're turning *his* dream, for which *his* forebears struggled and suffered, into a nightmare.

Does he really exist, this stereotype, or is he wholly a creation of the mass media? The answer, as is often the case, lies somewhere in between. The Poles have, in the past, scored rather high on tests designed to measure prejudice, but there are qualifiers and disclaimers that must be made if we are to evaluate their responses properly.

In a national study of white American Catholics done in 1964, Dr. Andrew Greeley reported that Poles are more likely to have racist attitudes than any other group. These differences remain even when one measures third-generation respondents, demonstrating that even among highly Americanized Poles anti-Black attitudes continue to be expressed. Greeley's study also shows that even when parental education, income, and occupation are held constant, Poles are still more likely to score higher on measures of racism than other groups. On the other hand, a 1968 study of college graduates by the National Opinion Research Center revealed that out of ten ethnic groups asked about racist attitudes, Polish graduates ranked seventh. Moreover, a 1970 Harris Poll indicated that native Anglo-Saxon Protestants are more apt to feel hostility toward Blacks than Polish-, Italian-, or Irish-Americans.

There are many reasons for whatever animosity exists between these two groups. Many Poles (and other white ethnics) resent the gains made by Blacks in the last two decades, gains that came when Poles were entering the middle-middle and upper-middle classes. As a result, they often found themselves in competition for the same jobs. Both groups were urban, working class, and had suffered discrimination. Novak's comments point up the suspicions and hostility that are presently in the community:

Ethnic Americans agree they would not like to be black in America . . . They don't begrudge the black's gains; but they smell something very *unfair*. On television blacks are wealthier and smoother than the ones workers meet every day. "Propaganda, lies!" they think. (p. 295)

But the differences go deeper than the question of unfairness. It is also a matter of self-sufficiency, industriousness, and other values that racial quotas and affirmative hiring seem to be attacking.

Southern and eastern Europeans have strong family ideals about helping others who are in need. But they hate to ask favors; often they refuse help from government welfare programs. (p. 297)

In addition to economic competition, there is the problem of violence, which disproportionately affects those living in the inner cities. Many older Poles live in ethnic enclaves in large cities like Philadelphia, New York, and Chicago. As Blacks move into these areas, there is conflict that includes but goes beyond crime. The cultural values of these groups frequently clash. For instance, East Europeans look down on the conspicuous consumption patterns that often characterize Black ghetto culture. Their attitudes differ on clothing, saving money, child rearing, leisure-time activities, and the importance of property ownership. As a result, East Europeans are sometimes pressured into panic selling, thus increasing the resentment. A Polish-American eighth-grader in Philadelphia expressed the situation as follows:

Negro people want the same rights as the white people but they don't want the responsibility that goes with it . . . They wreck their houses and then move to other ones. They try to integrate white people's neighborhoods and they don't want to pay for their own children. They start riots because they want equal rights. They break windows into stores. They cheat . . . Negro people have new cars but they don't want to pay for the rent of their houses. Their children go around half-starved. They go around stealing because they don't have any food. They don't do anything together . . . to the Negroes, life is easy come, easy go . . . Nowadays the Negro people are asking too much. Not all the Negro people are bad, but most of them are. (Binzen, *Whitetown, U.S.A.*, pp. 261–62)

Although replete with stereotypical judgements, these comments, which appeared twelve years ago, reflect the feelings of many in the Polish-American community.

In the last ten years these attitudes have begun to shift. As the educational level of the community rises and contact with the larger society increases, many are accepting the inevitable. In a recent New York *Times* article about integration in Parma, a Cleveland suburb, various residents with East European backgrounds were cited as favoring, or at least not opposing, the entry of Blacks into the community, a sharp contrast to the violence that greeted Martin Luther King in Cicero, Illinois, more than a decade earlier.

Relations between Poles and Jews are a different story. The economic threat that Blacks pose is not there, but the mutual dislike between these two groups is hundreds of years old. Jews began arriving in Poland in great numbers during the thirteenth and fourteenth centuries to escape persecution in Germany and Bohemia. The kings and princes of Poland, realizing their value in developing the economic potential of the country, welcomed them. The Church, however, which had come to Poland relatively late (966), was afraid that Judaism would undermine Christianity. Canonical laws were passed to prevent Jews and Christians from socializing with each other. They were required to wear a special hat as well as a red cloth that was to be sewn onto their clothing. As the Polish merchant class grew, they too felt threatened by the Jews and gave their support to the Church's activities, which had come to include pogroms and blood libels.

Most of Poland's population consisted of peasants, and ultimately they, too, turned against the Jews. This was due both to the teachings of the Church and the economic position of the Jews. Forbidden to own land and long experienced in commerce, most Jews functioned as rent and tax collectors, tavern owners, petty traders, and artisans. Although the majority were not well off, their position was considerably better than that of the peasants. The Jews aroused particular bitterness because they often worked for the nobles, who oppressed and exploited the peasantry at will. In his book *Poland: Between the Hammer and the Anvil* Polish writer Konrad Syrop quotes the following statement by an eighteenth-century reformer about the condition of the peasants under the rule of the nobles:

I can see millions of people, some half naked, some dressed in skins or rough cloth, all emaciated, wasted, reduced to misery. Sullen, stunned and stupid, they feel little and think little. (p. 58)

The Jews were a convenient scapegoat for the peasants, who hated the nobles but could do little against them. As the centuries passed, their antagonism grew until it became part of the culture. Syrop writes about King Casimir the Great, who invited the Jews to settle in Poland in the fourteenth century.

Had this been Casimir's main or only claim to fame it is certain that the Poles who, on the whole, do not love the Jews, would have never called him Great. (p. 21)

Even a cultured person like Frédéric Chopin made no effort to hide his feelings about Jews.

His social vices were characteristic of the highborn Pole domiciled in Paris: he was snobbish to the point of stupidity, and often treated those he considered his inferiors with brusque discourtesy. Of a part with this was his fanatical contempt for Jews . . . unless they happened to be a Rothschild, a Mendelssohn or a Heine. He used the epithets "Jew" and "pig" interchangeably for anyone who incurred, even unwittingly, his disfavor. (*The Music Lover's Handbook*, pp. 472–73)

Dr. Greeley's research demonstrates that among white Catholics surveyed throughout the nation in 1963, only the French were slightly more anti-Semitic; the figures are 52 percent for the Poles and 54 percent for the French. Nor is such feeling likely to disappear as Poles acculturate to life in America. Among third-generation (or later) Poles, anti-Semitism is even greater, with 59 percent holding such views, compared to 43 percent among the French and a low of 25 percent among the Irish. Even writers highly sympathetic to the Polish community who are eager to defend it make no effort to deny the existence of the degree of friction between the two groups. In her textbook *Polish Americans* sociologist Helena Lopata, who probably knows more about Polish-Americans than any other American sociologist, writes,

The history of relations between Polonia [a name for the Polish-American community] and the Jewish community is one of mutual dislike and attempts at cooperation are relatively infrequent. In recent years Polonia's members have been increasingly angry over what they define as a deliberate attempt by Jews in the mass communications media to prejudice the rest of society against them, and the relations between these two communities tend not to be very cordial, especially in recent years. (p. 79)

Undocumented statements of this sort are unusual among social scientists and, if nothing else, point up the fact that this cleavage is taken for granted by insiders.

In defense of the Poles, it must be noted that Polish-Jewish relations were very good at certain times in Poland's history and that large numbers of Poles were and are pro-Jewish. Many Poles saved and hid Jews during World War II, although sometimes they were motivated more by the possibility of converting them to Catholicism than by anything else. Still, those who were caught shielding Jews were generally executed, and the risk was therefore quite great. The case for Polish kindness toward the Jews during this period is made in a book by Kazimierz Iranek-Osmecki called *He Who Saves One Life*. Against this argument must be weighed the fact that great numbers of Jews were either killed or betrayed by the Poles. The Nazis were well aware of Polish anti-Semitism when they decided to build concentration camps in Poland. Poland was the only country to have an anti-Jewish pogrom (in the city of Kielce) *after* World War II. It happened in 1947, and much of the country's latent anti-Semitism—it had subsided somewhat after most of the Jews there had died—surfaced again after the 1967 Arab-Israeli War.

If it is true that there is a considerable anti-Black and anti-Jewish bias in the Polish-American community, does this mean it is fair to say that the Poles are bigots? Not really. While sociologists have proven that those who score high on anti-Semitism and racism tests are usually prejudiced in general, no studies have been done that show Poles to be prejudiced against *all* other groups. Moreover, is it possible to say with certainty that

Poles dislike Jews more than the English hate the Irish or the Armenians the Turks? Finally, only a bigot would claim that a person who is Polish *automatically* feels hostility toward members of these groups. Nevertheless, it is not unreasonable, on the basis of the evidence at hand, to say that Poles are, as a group, more apt to dislike Jews and Blacks than members of most other groups in American society today.

Uneducated

"Did you hear about the fire in the Warsaw Library?"
"No."
"Both books were destroyed."

Such a joke is certainly not a fair statement about education in Poland, which has a tradition of scholarship dating back hundreds of years. One of the oldest universities in Europe was founded in Cracow in the fourteenth century. Moreover, today the overwhelming majority of Polish youths complete high school and thousands study at the various universities there. Finally, the Polish Academy of Sciences is only one of the numerous prestigious academic organizations in the country that are internationally respected. Americans may or may not be aware of Poland's history in this area, but it matters little in a practical sense because such jokes are usually aimed at those Poles who have immigrated here.

Most Poles who arrived here came between 1870 and 1914, about two million in all. The majority were peasants in the old country and held a generally negative attitude toward formal education and intellectuals. In her work *Our Slavic Fellow Citizens* Emily Balch writes of one Galician district that had only nine schools among thirty villages. According to a doctor who came from the area, about a fourth of the children attending these schools never even learned to read. Teachers who complained of truancy were sometimes boycotted or bribed with eggs and other small gifts. This situation was a reflection of peasant culture, where an educated person was considered something of a deviant in those days. Although there were some immigrants who were educated, especially before the 1870s, most came from this culture and viewed the intellectual tradition in Poland as one reserved for the nobility, a group that had oppressed and exploited the peasants for centuries.

Besides the values of an agricultural life-style, there was the problem of the Church. Catholicism in rural Poland did not encourage a spirit of open inquiry or love of learning in general, and these attitudes were often brought over to the United States. True, the immigrant did send his children to elementary school, but his reasons for doing so were to provide a good moral background and not to lay the foundations of an intellectual education. This was why the Polish parochial school system flourished in the United States in the early part of the century. It was seen as a place where children would learn how to behave and respect their elders. By 1911 there were three hundred schools in the Polish-American parochial school system. The quality of instruction, however, was poor, with most schools overcrowded and staffed by teachers who were overworked and poorly paid.

Although members of the Polish-American community may be reluctant to attack the Church for its failings in this area, they have done so on occasion in the publications that circulate primarily among Poles. One example is the following brief excerpt from an article that appeared in the January–March 1974 issue of *Perspectives Inc.* It was written by Gene Knox, who is described as an expert in medieval history. Knox bemoans the failure of Polonia to produce an "academic elite." This, he says,

reflects an unrealistic separation of Church and State . . . the separation of strong morals and effective science . . . America's leading Catholic layman, the late Ambassador Joseph Kennedy, resolved it in his era by sending his girls to religious schools and his boys into public education. If the religious realm continues to advocate bingo and emphasize football, prospects are dim indeed. ("Bingo Politics of Scientific Leadership," p. 133)

Another major problem was that the Poles, who tended to have large families, saw children primarily as wage earners. Considering their economic situation, this was understandable, but in terms of schooling the effect was to discourage interest in formal education, which only delayed the time when the young could begin earning a living.

Economic adversity always affects those at the bottom most severely. Since the Poles were, for the most part, unskilled workers in the 1930s, the Depression greatly slowed their progress up the social ladder. This was reflected in their level of educational attainment during the 1940s and 1950s. Beginning around 1960, however, a significant shift took place. More and more young Poles began extending their education. Despite this shift, they were constantly ridiculed in jokes such as the following:

A man asked a Polish painter: "How much will it cost to have my house painted?"

"I'll charge you $600," replied the painter.

"You've got to be crazy!" exclaimed the owner. "I wouldn't pay that kind of money to Michelangelo."

"That's your business," retorted the Pole, "but, one thing you gotta know—if that Wop is charging you less, then he doesn't belong to the union!"

Michael Novak perhaps summed it up best when, writing about Polish jokes in *Newsweek* a few years back, he stated,

Most of us who are children of Eastern European Christian immigrants know we are the children of peasants. We do not have in our family experience many models of learning, status and public grace. We have a sufficient sense of our modest origins. ("The Sting of Polish Jokes," *Newsweek,* April 12, 1976: 13)

While such humor must have been discouraging to many young Poles, figures reflecting the number of school years completed by Polish youth demonstrate that this stereotype is no longer true. According to statistics that appeared in the 1972 *Current Population Reports* of the U. S. Bureau of the Census, 24.1 percent of Poles between the ages of 24 and 35 have completed four years of college or gone on to graduate and professional schools. These figures are *higher* than those of many other ethnic groups, including the Germans, English, Italians, and even the Irish, who came here knowing English. For example, for Germans the 1972 figure was 19.2 percent, for Italians it was

16.5 and for the Irish it was 16.3. It will probably come as a shock to some people that in a 1961 National Opinion Research Center study Polish-American college graduates were more likely than any other group (including Jews) to select an academic career as an occupation.

It would appear, therefore, from the evidence available that this stereotype, while it may have been true fifty years ago, is no longer valid today and that Germans, Irish, and various other groups might be more appropriate subjects for jokes about nationalities that do not value education. Why, then, have the Poles been singled out? Largely for the same reasons that they are called stupid. There is the intellectual bias against the Poles, which we have already discussed, and there is the fact that stereotypes that have found acceptance in a culture often disappear slowly. With the increasing numbers of Poles who have achieved prominence in American society, especially in the political arena (e.g., Muskie, Brzezinski, Representative Clement Zablocki of Wisconsin, and New York's former lieutenant governor, Mary Ann Krupsak), these attitudes are bound to change.

The achievements of Poles in education ought not, however, to be exaggerated. To do so distorts reality and deludes members of the group. Knox's observations on this subject are made with a candor unusual for an insider.

The leadership of the activist elements of Polonia is not in the hands of scientists . . . but rather those who pay lip service . . . by safely praising dead Polish scientists (read Copernicus, etc.) in the hope some lustre would accrue to their person . . . Fortunately we have a small college (Alliance College in Cambridge Springs, Pennsylvania). Unfortunately it is dominated by those who enjoy an ability to sell insurance . . . (p. 133)

Knox concludes by suggesting that

one way to seek mental leadership is to advertise for the smartest Pole in America. He should be willing to challenge all others in debate . . . and be open for continual debate. In this strife we can develop a scientific Polonia. (p. 133)

Harsh as these words may seem, the letters to the editor that appeared in a subsequent issue did not challenge the author's criticism concerning the state of education in Polonia. In fact, one man, Professor Hank A. Pogorzelski of the University of Maine at Orono, asserted that at the 1973 Meeting of Scholars of Polish Descent held at Cracow's Jagiellonian University, a convention attended by an estimated 10 percent of all Polish scholars in the world, there were only three native Polish-Americans present.

The sum total of all these arguments is that Poles have not yet produced an intelligentsia in this country. On the other hand, many more attend college than the stereotype would lead one to believe. Producing an intelligentsia takes time. If Polish-Americans continue to attend school in growing numbers, an intellectual elite will emerge. With regard to Knox's allusion to the tendency among Polish-American community leaders to trot out the names of luminaries not representative of the average (all groups do this in varying degrees), perhaps the following observation can be made. Emphasizing the contributions of members of the group ought not to lull its members into complacency. On the other hand, it serves two important purposes. It boosts the egos of discriminated against groups and it demonstrates that while members of the ethnic group may not have reached a certain level of achievement for whatever reason, they are capable of doing so.

Boorish and uncultured, low class

Stella: "Stanley is Polish, you know."

Blanche: ."Oh yes. They're something like Irish, aren't they?"

Stella: "Well—

Blanche: "Only not so—highbrow? (*They both laugh in the same way.*) I brought some nice clothes to meet all your lovely friends in."

Stella: ."I'm afraid you won't think they are lovely."

Blanche: ."What are they like?"

Stella: "They're Stanley's friends."

Blanche: ."Polacks?"

(Tennessee Williams, *A Streetcar Named Desire*
Act 1, scene i)

This stereotype has been around a long time, ever since masses of peasants from Poland entered the United States around the turn of the century. Polish jokes may not have been so widespread before the civil rights era, but the support for them certainly existed within American society. Stung by the rejection that a foreign tongue, strange customs, and poverty brought upon them, Poles retreated into their own culture, establishing, as did many other groups, ethnic enclaves that highlighted their separateness and distinctiveness. Their rural background did not equip them very well for life in an urban society. High illiteracy and extreme poverty forced them into menial jobs in packing houses, factories, and the like. A certain number of immigrants were able to purchase farms in the countryside, but these were mostly German Poles who had come a half century earlier when land was still available.

Typical of the jokes about presumably uncultured Poles is the following:

Polish cocktail: a mushroom in a glass of beer.

There was and still is an intelligentsia in Poland, and the names of Chopin, Paderewski, and Leopold Stokowski are household words among music lovers. In the spheres of theater and film we have Helena Modjeska, the most prominent Shakespearean actress in America at the turn of the century; Marcella Sembrich-Kochanska, a famous soprano at the Metropolitan Opera; and Jan and Edouard de Reszke, internationally known performers at the Met. In science there was Dr. Marie Curie-Sklodowska, co-discoverer of radium; Dr. Jacob Bronowski, mathematician, historian, and author of *The Ascent of Man;* Dr. Hillary Kropowski, leading American expert on the biology of cells; mathematicians Drs. Mark Kac and Antoni Zygmunt; and many others. In literature there is Henryk Sienkiewicz, author of *Quo Vadis?* which won the Pulitzer Prize; and, of course, Joseph Conrad. Obviously, it is unfair to assume that anyone who is Polish is uninterested in classical music, art, or intellectual matters.

Many in our society equate lack of culture with occupational status. It has been noted, with some justification, that social scientists often spend a great deal of time studying the obvious. A

sociologist has been defined as someone who decides to study a
whorehouse after everyone has been there. Certainly we do not
need studies (although they have been done) to prove that jani-
tors, steelworkers, and auto workers are less likely to listen to
Beethoven than college professors, artists, and editors of the
New York *Times*. Leaving aside, for the moment, the question of
cultural relativity (who is to say that the Polish polka reflects
less culture than a Mozart symphony?), the fact is that Poles
have been attending college in increasing numbers and have
been leaving the working class in recent years. A 1969 survey
showed that 45 percent of employed Poles had white-collar jobs.

Disinterest in what American intellectuals define as high culture exists among people of all nationalities, and there is no evidence that it is more prevalent among Poles than anyone else. In
fact, in a 1961 study of college graduates, Andrew Greeley and
Joe Spaeth found that Polish Catholics ranked ahead of German
and Italian Catholics on a scale designed to measure reading
habits. The scale, incidentally, differentiated between reading
"serious fiction" and light reading and also inquired about poetry. Once a group has been stereotyped as bigoted, stupid,
uneducated, and dirty, it is not surprising that it will be further
defined as boorish. There is, however, no indication that this stereotype is true of Poles today.

NINE

WASPs

WASPs (White Anglo-Saxon Protestants) differ in several important ways from the other groups discussed in this book. Hence, some introductory comments are in order. WASPs are the standard by which groups in American society judge themselves as well as others. Although they may be loathe to admit it, minorities in American society tend to view the WASP, among other things, as the idealized image of what it's like to be on top. Studies by sociologists have shown that members of minority groups, when asked to identify those they consider socially acceptable, respond in similar ways. They consistently rank their own group as the best and then retain the rankings of the dominant American culture. Thus a Black person will rank Blacks on top and follow it with "English" or "native white American." A Jew or Italian responds in the same manner. We see, therefore, that WASPs are viewed in somewhat similar ways by other ethnics.

Two other points need to be clarified. The stereotype of the WASP is, in the minds of many, one of wealth and power. While WASPs are heavily represented in the upper crust of American society and industry, this judgement is inaccurate by definition, and it would be a crime to perpetuate it in a work that undertakes to analyze stereotypes. This is because there are various people throughout the country who are WASPs by definition but who do not fit the popular image. How rich and powerful are the poverty-stricken residents of Appalachia? How genteel are the dirt farmers of Missouri and the hog raisers of Nebraska? What about the urban poor of cities like Cincinnati, Atlanta, and Chicago, who we stigmatize as "white trash"? There are large numbers of WASPs among these subgroupings, though we scarcely think of them in the same breath as the elite white Protestants who often head our corporations and industries. While there are different subgroupings among all American ethnic groups, they are more diverse and larger in size among WASPs.

Strictly speaking, a WASP is a white Protestant whose background is Anglo-Saxon. Yet it does not seem to have worked out that way. True, the founding fathers were from the British Isles, and it was they who shaped many of the values and character traits that came to be considered "American." Yet there were other groups that, by virtue of their willingness to adapt to these values and their Protestant faith, plus their North European origins, were able to blend in and win acceptance by the Anglo-Saxons. I am speaking, of course, of the Scandinavian, Dutch, and German Protestants. Perhaps, in certain instances, they were treated as not quite equal, but in American society being a second-class WASP is better than being considered no WASP at all, and many have made their peace with their ambiguous status.

If WASPs range from upper class to lower class and come from different cultures, can we consider them as a single group? Only if we take into account this diversity. Because there are so many differences, our treatment of them must, in a sense, be more general than that of other groups. It is also more likely that WASPs, encompassing, as they do, distinctive value systems and socioeconomic backgrounds, are apt to have characteristics that appear contradictory. Some may be very liberal and others conservative, some socially conscious and others not. Nevertheless, because of their common Protestant faith and various social and historical factors, they do have a number of shared characteristics. In this last sense they can and will be viewed here as a distinct entity. Throughout the following discussion the focus will be on the upper middle and upper class WASP since it is he who is most closely associated with the WASP stereotypes in the popular mind.

Honorable

This is a rather tricky concept because virtually every society has it. A Druse leader charged with murdering a Bedouin chieftain in a fight over a seat in the Israeli Parliament explained that he did so because the chief had offended his "sense of honor." Mafia members kill because the honor of their family is violated, the Japanese may commit suicide because of honor, and so forth. Thus, when we talk about honor among WASPs it is first necessary to define it. Generally stated, honor in this community has to do with a sense of fair play, courage, honesty, forthrightness, and doing "the right thing." It is also part of the larger concept of being a gentleman or a person who is well bred.

There is a basis for this stereotype in the history of the group. It stems primarily from the values of the Quakers, whose credo, as expressed by Benjamin Franklin, was that "honesty is the best policy." Although the Quakers based this belief on religion, Franklin also noted the practical consequences of honesty: It was useful because it helped build credit. This last idea is, as we shall soon see, very important in terms of understanding what happened to this concept as time went on. If we think for a moment about the stories and anecdotes surrounding some of the great American leaders, it becomes clear that honesty and "doing the right thing" were important values. There is, for example, the story of George Washington, who confessed to having chopped down the cherry tree, thereby becoming enshrined in the childhood socialization of millions of Jacks and Jills throughout America. Then there is the one about "Honest Abe" Lincoln, who walked ten miles to return a book on time.

Further evidence of the emphasis placed upon this value can be seen from the policies of the Protestant-dominated private boarding schools that sprang up in the nineteenth century. In his book *American Boarding Schools* Dr. James McLachlan quotes the views of Henry Coit, rector of the famous St. Paul's School, on this subject.

Honour, boys . . . honour, boys, is not a Chameleon, with one phase
for gentlemen in society, and another for men pursuing their ordinary business, and another for boys at school. The honour which you
ought to show to one another is just the same which you ought to
show when you are full grown to your fellow men . . . Honour is real
manliness, which is able to look everyone full in the face; not from
the possession of vulgar brass, but from a free conscience that has
nothing to fear because there is nothing to hide. Honour is real
manliness which scorns to do or say anything in a corner, or behind
the bush . . . it has the courage to do as its better knowledge dictates, and the steadiness, when it has started on the right track, not
to fall back because of a sneering tongue, nor to turn aside to listen
and be trapped by a lying one. (p. 167)

Looking at Protestant theology, we see an emphasis on indi-
vidualism. Protestantism argues that each person must be the
judge of his or her religious convictions. In other words, they
must accept responsibility for their actions. Moreover, Protestant
theology supports the freedom of individual inquiry. A religion
that forces a person to stand on his own two feet and has a this-
worldly, action-oriented approach would appear to be fertile soil
for individuals who value honor, conviction, and moral responsibility. There is, in fact, evidence from empirical studies that
white Protestants stress such responsibility. According to Dr.
Gerhard Lenski, who studied independence training among
members of different religious groups, white Protestant mothers
expected their children to assume responsibilities at an earlier
age than Catholic mothers.

Certainly WASPs think of this concept as one belonging to
them. In *WASP, Where Is Thy Sting?* Florence King writes,

The WASP mother's fondest dream is being undercharged eleven
cents in the middle of a snowstorm, for it gives her a golden opportunity to teach a moral lesson. That very minute, she can send
Johnny back to the store with a dime and a penny clutched in his little mittened hand. (p. 183)

Or, in another vein,

Obligation haunts the WASP. Like all women, I was told by my
mother that a man's payment is "the pleasure of your company," but
I never believed it. None of my friends did either. To the money-

obsessed WASP, if a man spends a lot on you, you really ought to
go to bed with him. After all, it's the only way to keep from getting
involved with him. (p. 184)

The problem with all this is that the facts do not support the
claims. Clearly, the constant lip service given to principled behavior can backfire, with the person becoming so guilt ridden at
his inability to live up to the ideal stressed by his culture that he
must exaggerate piety to cover up its absence. Thus King observes, "We strive for the *little* honesty that shines like the morning star through a cesspool of malfeasance." According to sociological research, in reality WASPs have not proven to be any
more (or less) honorable than others. The respect given to their
assertions in this area is most probably due to the fact that they
are the dominant group in our society.

In *The Protestant Establishment* Professor E. Digby Baltzell
writes about the success of the honor system at Princeton. He is
not so sanguine about the Yale of 1900.

. . . in a survey covering three floors of a dormitory, it was found
that not a single student wrote his own themes. They bought them, of
course. After all, this sort of menial labor was only for the "drips,"
"grinds," "fruits," "meatballs," and "black men" of minority ethnic
origins and a public school education. (p. 130)

There are many other cases of WASP lack of honor. There was
Sherman Adams, who accepted bribes from Bernard Goldfine
during the Eisenhower administration, and Charles Van Doren,
who achieved notoriety during the quiz show scandals. Today
we have the involvement of WASPs (Catholics and Jews too) in
Watergate and Abscam.

It is possible that WASP probity has been defeated by the emphasis upon materialism and consumerism prevalent in America
today. As noted earlier, since WASP honesty was in part based
on the idea that it was good for business, its disappearance
might in some measure be due to the fact that in contemporary
society it is no longer as good for business. We are told that
most criminals never serve time, especially those of the white-
collar variety, and we see men in high places getting away with
all sorts of things.

Finally, it should be remembered that Protestantism is not the only religion that urges people to behave honorably. Catholicism and Judaism are also based on the Old Testament. Similarly, the Koran, and the holy works of Hinduism and Buddhism also exhort their followers to act morally. Summing up, it can be said that honor is an important component of WASP culture, but it has often been violated by its members, especially in recent times, and there is no evidence that WASPs are more likely to act honorably than other people. It should also be remembered that, as is the case with all discussions of WASP stereotypes, there are likely to be significant differences among different social classes and denominations, as well as among the various regions of the country. It is clear, nonetheless, that honor is regarded in some circles as a distinctly "American" characteristic, and that inasmuch as WASPs founded this country, they may have had some role in propagating this trait. In this regard, it is of interest to recall a recent article that appeared in the New York *Times* in which President Reagan was said to have "rejected as unworthy of the American character any 'revenge' against Iran for the hostage crisis." Of course, there are probably more than a hundred countries whose leaders might have made a similar statement about their nations' "honor."

Hardworking, industrious, and thrifty

Q: Suppose a capitalist, in employing his capital, makes large profits, would that harm the working man?

A: No. There would be more capital to pay wages.

Q: Are you sorry, then, that capitalists should have great profits?

A: Glad.

Q: Why does the foreman get more than the laborer?

A: Because the foreman's work is of more value than the laborer's.

Q: If there are two boys starting in life, one the son of a man who has accumulated capital, the other of a man who has not, shall I be right in saying that the boy without this advantage can never be a capitalist?

A: No.

Q: But what is to make him a capitalist?

A: Saving.

(Peter Binzen, *Whitetown, U.S.A.*, pp. 42–43)

This catechism appeared in a nineteenth-century edition of the widely read *American Journal of Education*. It was designed to help teachers in the public school system inculcate proper attitudes in their charges. Those who ran the public school system were primarily Protestants who viewed it as a way of both educating the masses and keeping them civil and respectful of authority. The above-quoted comments and the general values they represented were in vogue long before then. They had, in fact, been brought over from England by the first settlers in this country.

Foremost among these values was the "Protestant ethic" (the term was coined by Max Weber), which equated prosperity with eternal salvation and poverty with damnation. Protestants believed that worldly success was a sign that God favored them. Unlike the otherworldly monks of an earlier age, one did not have to withdraw from the world to merit salvation. In this atmosphere a person's work, or his "calling," became extremely important because it was seen as a way in which he fulfilled his divine mission on earth. Whereas in earlier centuries accumulation of wealth had often been associated with greed, it now became acceptable and was even encouraged.

Another important value was that of thrift. Accumulation of savings meant that greater amounts of capital could be invested, thus creating more opportunities for proving that one was in God's good grace (or graces). Of course, the pursuit of financial gain purely for its own sake and conspicuous consumption were still condemned. Needless to say, temptation got the better of many people in this area.

These attitudes made their appearance in the New World when the Puritans settled in New England, the Dutch Reformed in Manhattan, and the French Calvinists in Charleston, South Carolina, and in New Rochelle, New York. As Professor Baltzell notes in his excellent book *Puritan Boston and Quaker Philadelphia*, "Even the first settlers of Virginia were essentially in sympathy with the Puritan wing of the Anglican church." The founding fathers who defined and shaped the moral values of this country were mainly from this background, men such as Washington, Franklin, Jefferson, Adams, and Madison. From their writings, most notably *Poor Richard's Almanac*, it is clear that "virtuous industry," as Franklin put it, was a basic value.

As Daniel Boorstin observes in *America and the Image of Europe*, we "skipped the aristocratic phase" that was such an essential part of European history. The shedding of feudalism had been rendered possible by the Founding Fathers' assertion that all men were created equal, one that conveniently ignored Blacks. Those who were here during the formative years of the nation did, in fact, have opportunities that were virtually unlimited, and this probably had a great deal to do with the emphasis they placed on hard work. For those who came a century or two later, the situation was quite different. The work ethic had far less meaning for those who came at a time when America was in the midst of an industrial revolution and the frontiers were receding. What did the virtue of labor mean to an Irish railroad worker, a Lithuanian laborer in a Chicago slaughterhouse, or a Polish coal miner? In *The Work Ethic in Industrial America, 1850–1920* Dr. Daniel Rodgers shows how values shifted over time. As the content of work became less rewarding, those who worked with the immigrants began to play down the Protestant emphasis on the moral benefits of work, stressing instead how hard work could create leisure time and money with which to buy things. Of course, the work ethic did not really disappear, but it found itself sharing the stage with other, often contradictory, goals.

It seems clear from all this that the stereotype of WASPs as hardworking, industrious, and thrifty was certainly true in the past. Both the religion and the opportunities present in colonial America supported it. Have these attitudes survived into the present? In a tongue-in-cheek description of her WASP family, Florence King writes,

The best time to see Protestantism in full flower is not in church but on report-card day in a Wasp home. When Gail Parent's hero David Meyer brought home all A's, he was praised as "a regular Einstein." When the Wasp child brings home all A's, he is paid off in cold cash, so much for each A. The Jewish parent cares about what his child has actually *learned*. The Wasp parent is concerned with how hard his child worked. Therefore, report-card day is really payday.

Comparing our loot was standard practice for my classmates and me on day-after-report-card day. I got a dollar for every B and three dollars for every A, and considered myself gainfully employed; school was my "job." (*WASP, Where Is Thy Sting?*, p. 117)

Without meaning to disillusion Ms. King, I know plenty of Catholic and Jewish schoolchildren who were similarly rewarded. Then again, perhaps they got the idea from the Protestants.

Of greater significance is the existence of various empirical studies of the question of whether or not this value continues to be important among white Protestants. The evidence, while interesting, does not lend strong support to the stereotype. In 1961 the National Opinion Research Center conducted a study of the aspirations of college graduates based on a sample of 40,000 graduating seniors from 135 institutions of higher learning. In one part of the study conducted by Dr. Andrew Greeley, about 2,000 Protestant respondents answered questions about their personality traits. Protestants scored higher on the drive or ambition scale than did either Catholics or Jews. When asked why they attended college, Protestants were also more likely to respond "career training" than were Jews or Catholics. These differences remained even when the study accounted for social and economic status. According to Florence King,

Wasp parents nag about other things. Committed to practical (i.e., $) knowledge and harboring a fundamental distrust of pure scholarship, they are constantly on the lookout for "horse sense." (p. 117)

Perhaps, but Greeley's evidence raises some questions about these claims. In his study Catholics were more apt to say they were entering business and a larger proportion of them considered "making a lot of money" important in one's choice of career.

Other studies indicate that the work ethic is shared by more Protestants than Catholics. For example, in a 1955 survey of a national sample, respondents were asked whether they enjoyed their hours on the job more than those off the job. While 32 percent of the Catholics answered yes, 48 percent of the Protestants replied in the affirmative. An analysis of the results, however, revealed that these differences disappeared when urban Catholics and Protestants were compared. Apparently this value is held primarily by rural Protestants. Most of the research indicates that leisure and work values are changing in the direction of less emphasis on hard work as an end in itself. This is probably due as much to the general improvement in our material well-being as to the fact that social barriers among different cultures continue to break down. For those WASPs who are well off, the work ethic seems rather irrelevant. Not only do they not have to work hard but their money, often in the family for generations, is, in a sense, living proof that adherence to this value has been a family trait for a long time. If they still feel guilty about not *earning* money, they can always sublimate by doing "good works," a subject that we shall subsequently treat at greater length.

What about the poor WASPs? Have their values changed? The majority of these people come from or live in the Appalachian or Ozark Mountains. They are descended from the surplus poor of England's seventeenth- and eighteenth-century cities. After paying off the price of their passage through hard labor on the plantation, thousands headed west and settled in the hinterlands of the Carolinas and Virginia, in West Virginia, Kentucky, Tennessee, and beyond. Writing about them in *Night Comes to the Cumberlands,* Harry Caudill, an ex-legislator from Kentucky, remarked,

It is apparent that such human refuse, dumped on a strange shore in the keeping of a few hundred merciless planters, was incapable of developing the kind of stable society under construction in the Puritan North. Instead of the hymn-singing Pilgrim to whom idleness was the badge of shame, we must start with the cynical, the penniless, the resentful and the angry. (p. 6)

Still, life on the frontier was hard and demanded a great amount of work as well as independence of spirit. Despite the hardships, the mountaineers cherished their freedom. This was the land that gave birth to authentic American folk heroes such as Daniel Boone and Kit Carson.

Ultimately, however, these proud people lost that independence. They were cheated out of their land by greedy WASP timber and coal speculators from the North and the East. They sold their land for a fraction of its value and in so doing began a slow but sure descent into second-class status. Loss of their land was followed by the Depression, which affected them severely, as it did all of America's underprivileged. During this period welfare made deep inroads into the area, with 75 percent of Appalachia's inhabitants receiving some form of public assistance. To the surprise of many outsiders, the mountaineers did not reject the dole. In his book *Everything in Its Path* sociologist Kai Erikson somberly reflected:

Now it may well be that many of the mountaineers visualized welfare as a part of nature's bounty rather than as a form of human charity, for they had long lived in an area where the necessities of life were taken casually from the land; but the long-range effects of the arrangement certainly took their toll on patrician dignity. (p. 110)

It appears that those who encountered the mountain folk in the cities generally developed an unfavorable image of them with regard to work. In his book *White Southerners* sociologist Lewis Killian reports that officials in industrial plants were generally willing to hire them only as a last resort, charging, among other things, that they were unreliable workers and lazy. Whether or not this is true is open to question, since prejudice against "hillbillies" undoubtedly played a role in such perceptions.

Given the problems that faced these WASPs, it is not surprising that they failed to develop the work ethic of their northern co-religionists. The hardships they endured—loss of their land, work in the mines—bred in them a resignation and fatalism that gave the lie to the idea that success was possible through struggle. It seemed to them that their whole existence was permeated by struggle. Yet there were few, if any, tangible rewards. It would therefore be unfair to judge the accuracy of the stereotype by their experiences.

It would seem that industry and thrift were certainly dominant features of Protestant theology in the early days of this country, having been brought here from England by the Puritans and their sympathizers. Because they were here first, their values took hold and became an integral part of the value system. Today, however, there is no clear-cut evidence that Protestants are more likely to consider these ideas of central importance to their lives than Catholics or Jews. In fact, the evidence points to a sharing and intermingling of values among the various groups that make up American society. The stereotype is therefore of questionable validity.

Cold and insensitive

We are simply not "people people." Close emotional contact with our own species presents too many threats. Charming and exquisitely polite we may be, and fair-minded to an extreme, but we are not warm. (Florence King, *WASP, Where Is Thy Sting?* p. 158)

Ms. King has written an entire book about WASPs. She speaks from experience, having been one all her life, and one presumes that she knows what she is talking about. Moreover, academic researchers seem to be in general agreement with her sentiments. For example, Dr. Paul L. Adams, professor of psychiatry at the University of Louisville, in a chapter called "The WASP Child" that appeared in the *Basic Handbook of Child Psychiatry*, has written, "Privatism, a pattern that holds one uninvolved until oneself or one's immediate world are touched, or encroached on, also lurks wherever the spirit of Protestantism reigns." The question is: How much concrete evidence is there to support what appears to be a widespread view of WASPs?

In a study of college graduates done by Dr. Greeley in 1961, respondents were asked to circle various traits that, in their view, best described their personalities. In his book *Religion and Career* Greeley summarizes his findings, including one that claimed that Protestants score lower on emotionalism than either Catholics (who place second) or Jews (who rank highest). Community studies done by sociologists also lend support of an indirect nature to the idea that WASPs are cold—at least to outsiders. In a study of a Connecticut community in the 1940s, Dr. C. Wendell King found that WASPs maintained a great deal of social distance between themselves and other groups, with the exception of a small number of Scandinavians. Another study conducted by Dr. Elin Anderson compared social exclusiveness among different ethnic groups in Burlington, Vermont. He concluded that WASPs were less likely to intermingle with outsiders than members of other groups, with 87 percent reporting that all of their close friends were also WASPs or, as he put it, "Old Americans." More support for the reluctance of WASPs to mix with others comes from the famous "Yankee City" studies carried out by Professors W. Lloyd Warner and Paul S. Lunt, which drew conclusions similar to those of King and Anderson.

Closely associated with the stereotypes of cold and insensitive are those of stoicism and reserve. While they are not precisely the same, all four imply a reluctance to show emotion. If it can be demonstrated that WASPs are less apt to show emotion in certain circumstances, this may provide further support for the general validity of the stereotype. In a fascinating book entitled *People in Pain*, Dr. Mark Zborowski conducted 242 in-depth interviews in an effort to determine how persons from different cultures reacted to pain. The four ethnic groups he focused on were Irish, Jews, Italians, and "Old Americans." This last group was defined by Zborowski as persons of "Anglo-Saxon origin, usually of Protestant creed, whose ancestors have dwelt in the United States more than three generations." The results demonstrated that Old Americans and Irish subjects bore their pain with far less emotionality and were much more uncomplaining than either Jews or Italians. Moreover, in a finding that bears on the stereotype in question, Old Americans were most likely to withdraw from other people when in pain. Some of the remarks typically made by Old Americans were:

I wouldn't holler. Not unless I didn't know what I was doing . . . I'd clench my teeth.

Well, see, I'm not the complaining type, you know. I don't complain unless it's very serious or something like that. Then I tell the doctor.

I never scream. I can take pain like a man. (pp. 51–54)

This last statement evokes memories of dozens of war and cowboy movies, from *Patton* to *Hondo*, in which the hero is always removing an arrow or bullet from his body while claiming he didn't feel a thing. Whether or not the origins of the stereotype are WASP would be difficult to prove, but it is definitely a part of American culture. These traits are also present in British culture, where they are referred to as "manliness" and "keeping a stiff upper lip." A more recent example of the stereotype is the unemotional and bitchy WASP, as played by Mary Tyler Moore in the film *Ordinary People*.

In looking at the evidence, one wonders whether regionalism is not a stronger factor than religion in explaining this stereotype. Most of the studies done on this question were based on samples drawn from New England communities. What about "Southern hospitality," a phrase presumably encompassing many WASPs of that region? While this, too, may be something of a myth, it certainly does not conform to the image of the white Protestant as cold and insensitive. Perhaps the answer lies in Puritanism, which was, of course, strongest in New England. It seems reasonable to assume that asceticism, an emphasis on obedience to authority, and the general repression that characterized Puritanism might have encouraged the development of a personality lacking in warmth. Such assumptions can, however, only be made tentatively, inasmuch as no evidence exists that such values are directly related to Protestantism itself.

One other factor of importance here is the dominant position of WASPs in American society. Because of this, WASPs tend to have more of what members of other groups want. As a result, they are often in a position to reject. WASPs are far less likely to be turned down by Catholic- and Jewish-dominated golf clubs than the other way around. They are far more apt to blackball members of other groups from certain jobs, organizations, schools, and so forth. As a result, the chances are greater that they will be judged insensitive—perhaps rightly so. Moreover, it should be added, in all candor, that WASPs are probably aware that in many situations they need not accommodate themselves to those of lower status, and that this may lead them to act in a callous manner that leads to accusations of coldness, lack of concern for others, and so forth. This, of course, has nothing to do with how warm or cold they may be among themselves.

Well-mannered, polite, genteel

One's clothes should be of the very best fabrics and make, but
should never be highly styled, of bright colors, or new-looking . . .
Good jewels should be worn sparingly . . . For the children it was a
world of discipline and ritual . . . of little boys in dark blue suits
and fresh white gloves, little girls in dresses of fuchsia satin, learning
to bow from the waist and curtsy . . .

These words might have been uttered by a proper white
Anglo-Saxon Protestant woman of the early twentieth century—
only they were not. They are the views of Mrs. Philip J.
Goodhart, as described by Stephen Birmingham in his book *Our
Crowd* (p. 15). Mrs. Goodhart, the sister of Herbert Lehman,
was, of course, Jewish and her observations underscore the
doubtful accuracy of this stereotype. As a rule, manners are a
function of class, not religion or ethnic background. Moreover,
they are a relatively recent development in Western society.

Were it possible to travel back in time to the Europe of the
Middle Ages, the picture of the aristocracy would be a rather
unpleasant one insofar as manners are concerned. One would
find members of "high society" blowing their noses into their
hands, eating meat with their hands from a common pot, and
spitting, farting, and defecating in public. In his work *The
Civilizing Process: The History of Manners* Professor Norbert
Elias explains how things changed. As time went on, impulses
and habits came under stricter control, mostly as a result of restrictions set up by the ruling classes to control the behavior of
those under them. Gradually these limitations became self-en-
forcing and people accepted them as part of the progress of civilization. Elias based his conclusions, in large part, on an examination of etiquette books that had appeared in various European
countries through the centuries.

There is no indication from Elias' work that the British possessed a monopoly on genteel behavior, but there are all sorts of
claims that they did on the part of writers and travelers to that
country. For example, Ralph Waldo Emerson, who was considered an expert on manners, wrote that the English were

inexorable on points of form . . . A Frenchman may possibly be clean; an Englishman is conscientiously clean. A certain order and complete propriety is found in his dress and in his belongings . . . Cold, repressive manners prevail. No enthusiasm is permitted except at the opera . . . They require a tone of voice that excites no attention in the room. (*English Traits*, pp. 101–2, 107)

It is difficult to determine the truth of such assertions empirically. Yet novels about life in England often included characters of the working class who were well-mannered and polite to a fault. In Somerset Maugham's classic *Of Human Bondage* the main character speaks deprecatingly of Mildred Rogers, a waitress, describing her as common and vulgar. But he also notes her efforts at courteousness: ". . . and he remembered the little finger carefully extended when she held her glass to her mouth; her manners, like her conversation, were odiously genteel."

Whatever the reasons for such behavior in England, they were not successfully implanted in this country. The belief that the upper classes in America were well-mannered is an exaggeration, though it would be fair to say that they tried. English visitors to the States were said to have been shocked at the lack of manners that prevailed in New York high society, and Birmingham tells us that such views were "largely justified." Nor was such a lack of propriety limited to Gotham. In *The Proper Bostonians* Cleveland Amory wrote that "Boston's 'men of high degree,' it would seem, have established a wide reputation for their want of social graces."

Amory was referring to the nineteenth century, a period during which Boston ranked first in the publication of books on etiquette. The proliferation of such works indicates that American high society was indeed concerned about the proper social graces and regarded them as the mark of the well-bred person. Amory writes about one three-year-old girl who "would *never* help herself at table from a dish unless it was one passed from the left side." Since high society consisted primarily of WASPs, it was only natural that people equated them with proper behavior. Thus, in *I Can Get It for You Wholesale* novelist Jerome Weidman has his Jewish protagonist observe, "I had to laugh at these *goyim* and their politeness."

Despite the failings of many adult members of the establishment, gentility was assiduously cultivated in the boarding schools attended by their sons, such as St. Paul's, Groton, Lawrenceville, Hotchkiss, Choate, Phillips Exeter, and Phillips Andover. Here the concept of the gentleman meant more than politeness and table manners. A properly trained graduate was expected to have acquired a respect for age, a sense of fair play and honor, as well as a certain degree of scholarship and a healthy interest in sports. Such values were supported by the country's leaders. Financier J. P. Morgan was reported to have said, on one occasion, "You can do business with anyone, but only sail with a gentleman."

Morgan's comment is of more than passing interest because it tells us something about an important function served by the emphasis on a code of personal conduct: It enabled members of the establishment to preserve their power and influence. Proper breeding became associated with certain schools, resorts, summer camps, parties, and so forth, run by WASP society. The manners learned in these places could be employed at will by those who had attended them to identify themselves as members of a certain class. The importance of this ability was underscored by Woodrow Wilson, who explained his criteria for choosing preceptors at Princeton as follows: "If their qualities as gentlemen and scholars conflict, the former will win them the place." Child psychologist Robert Coles describes this process very well in volume five of *Children of Crisis,* where he analyzes the children of the privileged.

These children are brought up not only to "have" manners, but to use them as a means of distinguishing themselves in several senses of the word . . .

Politeness, however, becomes *politesse*—a code of behavior that excludes as well as includes. It is not "polite" to speak with people one does not "know," one has not formally "met." It is not "polite" to ask questions of so-and-so, or talk with someone else in any but a prescribed, almost ritualized fashion. Even within the home, it is not "polite" to get "too friendly" with a maid or a cook or a gardener or a handyman . . . When good manners are found lacking in others, they become a "them." (pp. 529–30)

According to Coles, such children strongly believe in the efficacy of good behavior. They are certain—until, as adults, they learn otherwise—that if you show people that you know how to conduct yourself, things will turn out all right.

Manners, gentility, and so forth, are perhaps no longer even class-based, or at least limited to the upper class. It seems quite possible that the middle class, millions of whose members avidly follow the dictates of Amy Vanderbilt and her colleagues and are probably more self-conscious about such things, may behave more properly than the "aristocracy." On the other hand, if one is to believe authorities such as Cleveland Amory, manners are probably passé by now. In any event, there does not seem to be any evidence that today's WASPs have cornered the market in this area of human conduct.

Snobbish

It may be useful to first distinguish between snobbishness and prejudice. Generally speaking, snobbishness exists when people are looked down upon because of their social or economic class, while prejudice is directed against members of certain ethnic, religious, or racial groups. The terms often overlap because people who are in a lower economic or social class are often there because of racial, religious, or ethnic backgrounds. Thus snobbishness and prejudice are often interrelated. For example, Frederick P. Keppel, dean of Columbia College in 1914, wrote in his book *Columbia* that detractors of the college were often fond of saying, "Isn't Columbia overrun with European Jews who are most unpleasant persons socially?" Another case demonstrating the fuzziness between class and ethnicity occurred several years ago in an affluent New York City suburb. Conflict, sometimes violent, erupted between students in a Roslyn, Long Island, high school. Some of the students came from Albertson, a nearby working-class area, while others came from Roslyn itself, a wealthy community. Although the conflict was often explained in economic terms, it was also defined as religious. This was so because most of Albertson's residents are Christian and most of Roslyn's are Jewish.

On the other hand, conflict can often be related to class alone.

I know of an elementary school located in an upper-class suburb that also has students who come from the inner city located near that suburb. Occasionally there will be a conflict, and if it involves children from the city (who are, as a rule, less well off), they will sometimes accuse the school of insensitivity because "we're not rich and all you care about is the almighty dollar." People often express their feelings in class terms, though these may conceal ethnic prejudice. An acquaintance of mine who lives in a wealthy, lily-white community once remarked to me, "I don't care if Blacks move in here; if they can afford it, then they're of a class that I can accept."

Having established that snobbishness emphasizes class but is also related to religion, race, or ethnicity, can we say that WASPs are more likely to be snobs? The answer is yes and no. Since WASPs are the highest status group in our society, they are most likely to be sought after. Therefore, they have the most chances to rebuff others. As for other groups, it's hard to be snobbish if no one cares. If Poles, Puerto Ricans, Italians, or other low-status groups display snobbishness, people are not likely to pay much attention because they do not think that highly of them. Thus Jews will be referred to as "clannish" and Blacks as "uppity" rather than as "snobs."

"There can be no in-group without an out-group" goes the popular saying. Snobbishness is an almost universal phenomenon and can be found among high-, middle-, and low-status groups. In his autobiography *Name and Address* T. S. Matthews, former managing editor of *Time* and a bona fide WASP, wrote,

The Matthewses did in fact consider themselves a cut above the Procters, partly because they thought themselves better bred—their Welsh-English descent being, in their eyes, superior to the Irish-English line of the Procters—but principally for two other snobbish reasons: they had been Americans for nine generations to the Procters' three; and no Matthews, so they said, had ever been "in trade." The Procters, on the other hand, had grown rich by the somehow shameful process of making soap, and also tallow candles, to begin with. (p. 106)

And so we see that there exists intramural snobbishness among WASPs. Yet WASPs are only one of hundreds of groups about whom this can be said. Northern Italians are sometimes contemptuous of their southern brethren and German Jews have often expressed similar feelings about East European Jews. Urban Poles may look down upon rural dwellers as less sophisticated, a tendency present in many countries. Among Blacks one sometimes sees snobbery based on how white one's features are (even after the Black pride movement of the last twenty years) or how much "Indian blood" a person has.

To understand why snobbery is so common, we need to examine its functions. For one thing, it makes people feel good. When you are uncertain about your status, a way of ensuring it is by finding someone who is regarded by others as inferior. Thus you reduce your insecurity while at the same time showing how insecure you really are. Snobbishness also serves the practical function of maintaining the privileges of certain groups, and it is here that we begin to understand why WASPs are labeled by many as snobs. As long as WASPs were overwhelmingly dominant, there was no need for them to "put on airs." Once their position was threatened, snobbishness became an important weapon in the struggle for power. In *The Protestant Establishment* Professor Baltzell observed,

Thus a leader of the D.A.R. [Daughters of the American Revolution] saw a real danger in "our being absorbed by the different nationalities among us," and a president-general of the Sons of the American Revolution reported that: "Not until the state of civilization reached the point where we had a great many foreigners in our land . . . were our patriotic societies successful. (p. 115)

That this was true can be seen, as Baltzell notes, from the relatively late dates many of these societies were founded: Sons of the American Revolution (1883) DAR (1890), the Colonial Dames (1890), the Society of Mayflower Descendants (1894), and so forth. The need for establishing such organizations was not only due to mass immigration to this country from other parts of the world but also to the increasing emphasis on material goods. In a society where money was so important, the disdain of those who belonged to a lower social class (e.g., nouveau riche) became the last line of defense. The problem was and is that such disdain is increasingly ignored.

WASP snobbery still exists today. When I taught at Yale several years ago, one professor, a well-known and respected scholar, informed me, at one of those interminable sherry parties so characteristic of the institution, "You know, I've been here a long time. We celebrate Christmas and all, but among some people things never change. The fact that I'm one quarter Jewish is still held against me." Yale, however, is not America, and those who practice genteel bigotry of this sort are increasingly coming to be viewed as relics of the past.

Summing up, there is nothing intrinsic about WASPs that makes them more snobbish than others, and no social scientific studies that I know of have ever documented it. On the other hand, since wealthy WASPs occupy a privileged position in America's social hierarchy, their snobbishness is likely to be both noticed and expressed more often.

Wealthy and powerful

. . . the model of the upper *social* classes is still "pure" by race, by ethnic group, by national extraction. In each city, they tend to be Protestant; moreover Protestants of class-church denominations, Episcopalian mainly, or Unitarian, or Presbyterian. (C. Wright Mills, *The Power Elite*, p. 60)

These words were written in 1956, and although things have changed considerably since then, there is a good deal of truth to them. The major proportion of wealth and power in the United States still resides among WASPs. On the other hand, it is not correct to say that most WASPs have wealth and power. The majority are middle class or lower class, with many poor white Protestants as impoverished as poor Blacks, Hispanics, and American Indians. Regarding Mills's statement about the various denominations, it appears that Lutherans, Baptists, and various fundamentalist sects are underrepresented among the nation's elite, but this is somewhat deceiving since there is a tendency among Protestants to join higher-status denominations as they move up the socioeconomic ladder.

Books such as *The Power Elite*, G. William Domhoff's *Who Rules America?* and Baltzell's *The Protestant Establishment* are among the many works that assert the predominance of WASP influence in the higher circles of the U.S. establishment. Domhoff and Mills, who have been called "conspiracy theorists" by many, are especially keen on showing us how power is vested in the hands of military, industrial, and political elites, who form a sort of club bent on preserving power for its members. Much of their evidence comes from an examination of the different schools attended by these people, their social background, and the fact that they sit on the boards of many powerful corporations. For example, Professor Domhoff notes in *The Higher Circles* that people who in 1963 sat on the board as outsiders at IBM also belonged to the boards of twenty-three industrials, thirteen banks, five utilities, one oil company, three insurance firms, and one railroad.

There is a good deal of evidence that Protestants have had a disproportionate share of power throughout the history of this country. This is important to establish because wealth and power are often passed on from one generation to the next, and those with a head start are therefore at a decided advantage. In a 1925 study of American millionaires sociologist Pitirim Sorokin found that a majority of them were of British origin. Several sociological studies of American communities in the 1930s and 1940s substantiated the idea that WASPs dominated the higher-status positions within these communities. In one study of New Haven, Connecticut, WASPs represented 12 percent of the total population. Yet they occupied two thirds of all professional and managerial positions in the city.

How did all this start? Were WASPs smarter than everyone else? Did they have better business acumen? Not really. They simply possessed several advantages over other immigrants. As the first group to arrive in substantial numbers, they were able to seize the opportunities presented by an underpopulated land with tremendous resources. Having a highly developed work ethic derived from Calvinism didn't hurt either, as we have already seen. Besides the early colonists, approximately two million British immigrants arrived here in the nineteenth century. These immigrants were well equipped for the rigors of life in a new country because they possessed certain skills that were particularly well suited to the industrial expansion that marked the nineteenth century. They had acquired experience working in the coal mines and mills of England and, as a result, moved ahead very rapidly in similar jobs in the United States. That they were overwhelmingly literate, had smaller families than most other immigrating groups, and were WASPs also helped them immeasurably. As pioneers in virtually every industrial field in America, WASPs gained control of the top positions in a host of fields, including steel, copper, coal, iron, railroads, and related businesses.

Partly to preserve cultural values but also to consolidate their power in America, WASPs (both colonists and later arrivals) created a network of schools, clubs, churches, and resorts that catered to their needs and interests. This can perhaps be called "sustained clannishness." As Peter Schrag tells us in his scathing book *The Decline of the WASP,*

If money alone made men equal, as the historians suggested, then how could you keep Jews out of the eating clubs and spades out of the fraternity? And how could you keep a lot of upstarts from competing? Clean up, sanitize, talk manners, talk background, talk new money as against old money . . .

So they cheated in the name of "character"; they imposed quotas in their colleges, gutted the requirements, created special prep schools or converted old ones, glorified the gentleman's C . . .

Making it, in short, did not merely grow out of the Puritan tradition; it required, in some form, the maintenance of that tradition for use as a means of curbing sheeny shysters, Irish pols and Italian hoods who applied the ethic according to their own standards and according to whatever conditions WASP exclusiveness imposed. (pp. 30–34)

In 1964 Dr. Baltzell wrote in *The Protestant Establishment* that unless the WASP establishment opened up its ranks to other groups it would continue to decline in power. From what we know it has apparently been declining, albeit very slowly, for a long time. In *Beyond the Ruling Class* Dr. Suzanne Keller of Princeton University reported that the proportion of top WASP executives in America's biggest companies had decreased from 87 percent in 1870 to 77 percent in 1900 to 65 percent in 1950. On the other hand, 85 percent of those in the highest positions in 1950 were of the Protestant faith, thus indicating that WASP membership had been extended to such non-WASPs as Germans and Scandinavians. A 1968 article in *Look* magazine shed further light on this question. According to the author, Fletcher Knebel, the overwhelming majority of directors in the fifty largest American corporations were WASPs. Protestants in general were also significantly overrepresented in banking, insurance, and other major industries. Knebel also noted that almost all of the presidents of the nation's colleges and universities at that time were white Protestants, as were the vast majority of trustees among the country's ten largest universities.

The last ten years have seen many changes. Far more university presidents and trustees are Catholic or Jewish. A lower-status Protestant, a Baptist, has been elected president and has, in turn, been followed by a president whose ancestry is part Irish Catholic. Innumerable clubs have opened their doors to non-WASPs and major law firms that once accepted only token members from minority groups now actively recruit them, using academic excellence as the prime criterion. The same is true of the prep schools. Still, it would be foolish to underestimate the power of the WASP in the corporations, government (most members of Congress are WASPs even today), and the military. Power built up over two hundred years does not vanish overnight. Nor does prejudice.

Guilt-ridden do-gooders

Whatever is moral, *that* WASPS thirst to be. Seeing that others are less morally concerned, they cannot hold back too long an irrepressible condescension . . . Of no other group, perhaps, is such self-criticism and plasticity to be expected; there seems to be no limit to their willingness to "update" their moral sensibilities. (Michael Novak, preface to *The Rise of the Unmeltable Ethnics,* p. xxvii)

The origins of this stereotype, often a code word for liberalism, may be traced back to the Social Gospel Movement of the 1890s, which attempted to shift the focus of religion from the salvation of the individual to concern over social issues. Led by theologians such as Washington Gladden and Horace Bushnell, its proponents, mostly Protestants, believed that Christianity remained unfulfilled unless it became actively involved with the larger problems facing society. The movement, however, was opposed by the salvation-oriented fundamentalists, such as Billy Sunday and Dwight L. Moody, who argued that religion's prime focus should be on the individual.

During the 1920s prosperity resulted in a loss of influence on the part of the social reformers, and the end of Prohibition in the 1930s signaled a decline in the fortunes of the fundamentalists, but both groups have survived till today. The liberal wing of the Church established orphanages, schools for the handicapped, and hospitals in the early part of the century, but it really came into its own during the 1950s and 1960s, taking up the fight against poverty, racial discrimination, capital punishment, the Vietnam War, and pollution. The heavy commitment of the churches to these causes helped popularize the notion that WASPs were "do-gooders."

Despite a history of involvement in social causes, the validity of this stereotype can be seriously questioned on several grounds. It is well known that slavery was far less compassionate in parts of the New World where Protestants prevailed than in those governed by Catholics. Moreover, although men such as John Wesley were concerned with doing good works as early as the eighteenth century, their emphasis was on eliminating individual rather than social vices. Thus the tradition of social concern is a relatively recent one. Most importantly, however, the emphasis on human rights has never been supported by the majority of lay Protestants. The National Council of Churches, for example, is a powerful organization in the area of human rights, but does it speak for the average Protestant in the street? According to most studies it does not. In *The Gathering Storm in the Churches* Dr. Jeffrey Hadden reports that only about a third of a sample of Americans interviewed were sympathetic to Northern ministers and students who had gone South to work for civil rights. Almost half felt that members of the "clergy should stick to religion and not concern themselves with social, economic, and political questions." A National Opinion Research Center survey conducted by Dr. Andrew Greeley found that

WASPs held less favorable attitudes toward Blacks than did those of Irish, Polish, Jewish, or Italian extraction.

Recently there has been a tremendous resurgence in fundamentalism. Organizations like The Moral Majority have gained prominence, and with their rise has come a renewed emphasis on personal salvation and a de-emphasis of concern for societal ills. The evangelists, revivalists, and their followers are, by and large, conservative in their social and political outlook. They are more interested in a government that supports school prayer in the public schools and right-to-life amendments than one that talks about helping the poor and promoting affirmative action. The millions of Protestants who support these leaders cast serious doubt on the validity of this stereotype.

It is also important to note that tens of thousands of Catholics and Jews have played prominent roles in "do-gooder" movements over the years. They have been involved in civil rights, prison reform, environmental movements, and similar issues at both the individual and organizational levels. In fact, most studies confirm that Jews are most involved in such causes among the three denominations.

Those who have carefully examined the role of Protestants in civic causes have observed that it is far more likely to be related to status than anything else. Higher-status Protestants are more liberal and more involved in social issues. This is probably due not only to their philosophical orientation but to the simple fact that the better off you are, the more time you have for the problems of others. A dirt farmer in Arkansas cannot think about solving the world's problems when his immediate dilemma is how to put food on the table for his family.

Many writers have dwelt on the seeming capacity of liberal Protestants to feel guilty about those less fortunate than themselves. To the extent that Protestants have always had the benefit of being considered the most socially desirable group in American society, one can see a basis for this view. But the issue is somewhat more complex than this. There is a certain ambivalence within Protestant theology that promotes feelings of guilt. On the one hand, there is the notion of "the Christian thing to do," as exemplified by the concern of Jesus for his fellow man. Albert Schweitzer pointed out in his autobiography that as a child he had learned that the good Protestant showed compassion and concern for others. On the other side is the Calvinist notion that the poor are responsible for their own problems, that their misfortune is their destiny. Resolving the dilemmas inherent in these two approaches can easily make one feel guilty. Sometimes an individual solves the problem through involvement in the difficulties facing others. Blacks are an especially inviting target because slavery thrived during a period when America was overwhelmingly Protestant.

There *is* a tradition of caring about others within Protestantism, a sort of noblesse oblige. It appears, however, to be led by religious leaders whose congregants often do not share their views. Numerically, those denominations that rank low on social issues would seem to outnumber those that rank high. One must be careful, however, not to generalize. There are probably a few Southern Baptists who are more active in social issues than certain Episcopalians. Most significantly, perhaps, various studies have shown that Protestants are not more likely to show concern about do-gooder issues than either Catholics or Jews. Finally, the trend today among Protestant groups seems to be away from social activism. For these reasons this stereotype would seem to be just that, an exaggeration of an existing category.

TEN

Hispanics

Like WASPs, Hispanics are a large group with many distinctive subcultures. Because Mexican-Americans (also called Chicanos) and Puerto Ricans are the most numerous and widely known of these groups, and because they are the recipients of the most negative stereotypes, this chapter will focus on them. Since all Hispanics share certain common cultural features, such as Catholicism (Protestantism is a relatively recent development), a common language, and a Latin heritage, immigrants to the United States from countries such as Ecuador, the Dominican Republic, Cuba, and Colombia are often lumped together by Americans. There are many important distinctions between members of these groups, but in terms of most of the stereotypes discussed here the differences are not that great, especially between Puerto Ricans and Chicanos.

In addition to religion, language, and Latin heritage, there are other common characteristics. Chicanos and Puerto Ricans in this country suffer from low income and educational achievement, as well as serious discrimination and prejudice. Most live in urban areas and tend to have large families. The United States has a special relationship to both countries that is related to historical events and the fact that both Mexico and Puerto

Rico are near the United States. This nearness also means that immigrants from these lands often retain a special relationship with the homeland and those who still live there. This is not the case, by and large, with inhabitants of the other countries of Latin America. On the other hand, together with all Hispanics they share a consciousness of that which is similar in their cultures. Although socioeconomic problems and geographical distances have contributed to the difficulties of forging a strong national movement in this country, coalitions such as the Forum of National Hispanic Organizations do exist.

At the same time, it should be remembered that there are differences between Mexican-Americans and Puerto Ricans. While both are descended from a combination of Indian, African, and Spanish stock, Indian ancestors are likely to be more numerous among Chicanos because the Indians were not killed in such great numbers in Mexico. In Puerto Rico, where the native Taino Indians were virtually eliminated and replaced by African slaves, the proportion of Indian blood is considerably less.

The implications of this fact have never been fully investigated. Chicanos, who have been here longer, have made greater gains than Puerto Ricans. They are also more numerous. According to rough estimates, there are about eight million Chicanos (not counting the vast numbers of illegal aliens) and two million Puerto Ricans living in the United States today. Culturally there are differences in food preferences, music and art, family patterns, and so forth, but, again, there are enough similarities in terms of stereotypes to justify treating them in a general sense under the same heading. This should become clearer in the pages that follow.

Big on machismo

Juan was riding on a burro while his wife was walking behind him. "Why isn't your wife riding?" asked his Anglo friend.
"Because she doesn't have a donkey," responded Juan.

Machismo is a rather complicated concept. Therefore we need to properly define it before we can talk about whether or not it is prevalent among Hispanics. One of the best articles on the subject has been written by Dr. Evelyn P. Stevens, a political scientist. Called "Machismo and Marianismo," the article explains that machismo has several meanings, one of the most important of which is pride and dignity. Sometimes this is manifested by a desire on the part of the individual to have his own way. As Stevens notes, males, or *machos,* in the community often avoid frank discussion of issues for fear that they will feel compelled to literally fight to preserve their honor if a disagreement develops. With the exception of sporting events, men will go to considerable lengths to avoid disagreeing with each other. Also related to the concern with dignity or, as it is referrred to by insiders, *dignidad,* is the tendency toward stubbornness that often forces men into positions from which there is no retreat.

The other area is relations with women. Stevens observes that the purported sexual aggressiveness of Latin American males is "the behavioral trait that has given *machismo* its bad press at home and abroad." Basically, it is the identification of potency and fertility with manliness. Worried that others may not believe his claims, the male often seeks proof of his virility in extramarital conquests. It is also expected that he will show "callousness" toward other women. Machismo of this sort is not confined to any particular class, though it may be more overt among the poor, such as the families described by Oscar Lewis in *La Vida.* When this trait appears among the middle or upper classes, the individual may be stereotyped as "a romantic Latin."

How true are these statements? Since machismo is, more than anything else, a state of mind, it is a difficult concept to measure. How quickly a person is ready to fight, his motives for marital infidelity, and similar questions are hard to assess quantitatively. We are therefore forced to rely on the judgements of insiders, or at least those who have observed the culture closely. Judging from this literature, it appears that machismo is widely accepted as a characteristic of Hispanic culture. The following quotes are selected from scores of observations on this subject:

A boy always has to prove himself. Like when a boy throws his first rock and breaks some boy's head, he'll get spanked for it, but his father will say, "Oh, did you see him break that boy's head." So a boy has to do it again and again. He grows up to be a man and he is still a boy, trying to prove himself, to show his *macho*. So he never grows up.

(Beatrice Colon in *The Islands,* by Stan Steiner, p. 459)

Mexican American males were reluctant to seek public help because of pride and their attitudes of *machismo*.

(Matt S. Meier and Feliciano Rivera, *The Chicanos,* p. 158)

In such instances [moving from Mexico to the United States] the father's *machismo,* or maleness, suffered, and his role as the dominant figure in the family would suffer as well.

(Tony Castro, *Chicano Power,* p. 98)

The idea that machismo is an integral part of Hispanic culture is not only widely accepted by insiders but by outsiders too. In this country it is so widely used that it has practically become an English word. If extramarital sexual activity is cited as a criterion of machismo, one can point to the idea of having "a woman on the side," which is widely accepted in countries such as Puerto Rico. On the other hand, this is also accepted in Japan. Moreover, having heart, showing courage, and manliness are present in a host of cultures. Why, then, has the word machismo gained such wide popularity?

In the American context, the presence of machismo can perhaps be partly explained as a response to the insecurities brought about by the move to a new country. This can be seen from the following comment appearing in Steiner's *The Islands:*

. . . our men are "de-balled." Since they can't prove their manhood economically, they try to do it sexually, at the expense of their women. (Connie Morales, former minister of education of the Bronx Young Lords, p. 454)

An unidentified woman elaborates further on this subject. Although she is Puerto Rican, the oppression of which she speaks has been the fate of millions of Chicanos, Dominicans, Colombians, and Hispanics from other countries who have immigrated to the United States:

Try to rationally figure why a virgin is so necessary to a *macho*. To start with our men have been castrated by colonizers as far back as our history goes. They have been deprived of their freedom economically, socially and politically. The result is a nation of very insecure men. Insecure in his masculinity and the right to be master of his own nation. The only thing left to call his own becomes his woman. With her he can take out all his frustrations. She becomes the only property left to him, so he holds on as tight as possible. He starts making demands on her he can't make on his oppressor. (p. 455)

While it is true that in Puerto Rico women occupy important posts in academic and political life, this is not the case in most Latin nations. Moreover, we are speaking more of an attitude, a way of relating, that goes beyond the granting of formal rights or jobs. One professional who works closely with male Hispanics told me that generally they will not accept counseling from a woman. He noted that even those who speak little English are more likely to confide in an English-speaking male counselor than a Spanish-speaking female counselor.

To understand the origins of machismo it is necessary to look a bit more closely at the history of Spain. There is, of course, the bravery of the bullfighter, the leadership of the *conquistadores*, and the image of Don Juan, but parallels for bravery and sexual prowess exist in most cultures of the world. Here, however, the tradition seemed to have been especially powerful and deep-rooted. In ancient times Spain was governed by the Romans, who believed strongly in male supremacy. Under Roman law the unity of the family reigned supreme and the authority of the father was nearly absolute. He held virtually all property rights, including his wife's dowry. If his wife was charged with a crime, she was remanded into his custody and could be put to death if he so decreed. He was also permitted to sell his wife, a practice that occurred with such alarming frequency that the Romans were eventually forced to pass a law forbidding it. When Spain, or Iberia, as the Romans called it then, was conquered by Italy, these values were introduced into the area.

Under the influence of the Arabs, notions of male superiority were reinforced, reaching their greatest heights in the sixteenth century during the reign of King Philip II. As Will and Ariel Durant have described it,

Female purity was guarded not only by religion and law, but by the *punto*, or point of honor, which required every male to defend or

avenge by the sword the threatened or violated chastity of any
woman in his family . . . Decent women were usually kept at home
in a semi-Arabic seclusion; they dined apart from the men, seldom
accompanied them in public, and used closed coaches when they
stirred outside their homes. (*The Story of Civilization*, vol. VII, p.
276)

The sixteenth century was also the period of the Spanish conquests in the New World. Those who came here found Indian
societies where women had far greater influence and power than
in Spain, but it was the Spaniards who defeated the Indians, and
thus their version of civilization emerged triumphant.

What of the other component of machismo, namely, pride?
Here, too, it is clear that pride, or honor, was especially valued
throughout Spanish history. The Partidas, a thirteenth-century
legal code, made a point of defining honor, describing it as "the
reputation a man has acquired by virtue of his rank, his high
deeds, or his bravery." According to the Partidas, public insults
cast shame on the individual, and within Spanish society it was
expected that public dishonor be avenged in order to save one's
reputation. In his book *The Spanish Character* historian Bartolomé Bennassar remarks that foreign nations often commented
on the passion for honor as a "national trait" of the Spaniards.
Indeed, Bennassar carefully analyzes the concept and shows
how it was integral to Spanish life, appearing as a dominant
theme in plays and novels, especially during the Golden Age of
Spain. Concern with honor was not limited to the upper classes
in Spain. As Professor Julio Caro Baroja points out in an essay
called "Honour and Shame," novels dealing with this subject
were the "favorite reading of drovers, farm-hands and other
working people."

If one looks at the Black community or the early experiences
of Italians, Jews, Irish, and so forth, in this country, it becomes
clear that Hispanics are only one of many groups who suffered
from discrimination. Therefore this fact alone should not lead to
excessive machismo. The difference is that not all groups have
the same combination of historical origins and oppression that
were and still are present among Hispanic peoples. We may note
that one other group in which males have enjoyed considerable

authority are the Italians, who obviously share common historical elements in terms of the Roman and Arabic influence.

Recent studies of the Hispanic community have concluded
that the authority of the male has decreased as contact with
American culture grows and as the feminist movement begins to
make its influence felt among Latinos. A study by Professors Leo
Grebler, Joan Moore, and Ralph Guzman of sex roles in the family demonstrates that Mexican-American men are gradually accepting responsibilities that have traditionally been regarded as
"feminine." Similarly, a 1976 doctoral dissertation by V. T.
Cromwell shows that many of the stereotypes about male dominance in the Hispanic community are no longer true.

Machismo is obviously a characteristic of Hispanic culture.
Nevertheless, the available evidence does not support the view
that male authority *today* is far greater among Hispanics than
among any other group. To the extent that this has been true in
the past, it is a function of the Spanish heritage and the oppression suffered by Hispanic peoples, many of whom are poor and
discriminated against.

Lazy

. . . the Anglo books, movies, television, advertising, and the press
all work to reduce the Mexicano to a certain stereotype image: stupid, lazy, dirty, ignorant, sneaky, violent, unreliable, sinister . . .
Most of the time, the Mexicano is asleep under a big sombrero. He
wakes up just long enough to say a few words in broken *Engleesh*
before going back to his endless siesta. So much for the children of
Cuauhtemoc, Hidalgo, Morelos, Juárez, and Zapata. They have been
washed away. (Elizabeth Sutherland Martínez and Enriqueta Longeaux y Vásquez, *Viva La Raza*, p. 141)

Perhaps the authors were thinking of the old L & M cigarette
commercial featuring "Paco," who never "feenishes" anything,
"not even the revolution." Possibly they remembered the popular song that contained the lines: "Mañana, mañana, mañana is
good enough for me; my poppa's always working, he is working
very hard; but every time he looks for me I'm sleeping in the
yard." Or they may have had in mind the countless movies and

TV serials in which the Mexican village is portrayed as the home of sleepy, indolent idiots.

Social scientists, while often well-intentioned, have also contributed to this perception by neglecting to stress that the slower life-styles of rural Mexico or Puerto Rico are not necessarily followed by those who have gravitated to the cities. Irrespective of who may be most responsible for this image, it is a common one among many Americans. This is confirmed in a study of Mexican-Americans by Dr. Norman Humphrey, an anthropologist, which appeared in the *American Journal of Economics and Sociology*.

In an attempt to discover the accuracy of this laziness stereotype, Professors Leo Grebler, Joan Moore, and Ralph Guzman interviewed several thousand Chicanos living in San Antonio and Los Angeles. In one part of the study they questioned people about the Protestant ethic. The results indicated that Mexican-Americans tended to agree with the work ethic attributed to Americans in general. Respondents were also asked whether shorter working hours and "lots of free time" were important considerations when choosing a job. These "attractions" received a very low rating, thus challenging the notion that Chicanos are only interested in taking it easy. Other studies, such as one done by Dr. Celia Heller, a sociologist, confirm this pattern. In her book *Mexican American Youth* Heller found that Chicano youngsters "did not differ significantly in mobility goals and values." She also observed that the quality of the school experience may be the most important factor in determining ambition among Mexican-American youths.

The laziness stereotype is somewhat less common among Puerto Ricans, but it exists. For example, in the film *The Pawnbroker* Jesus Ortiz, who works for the pawnbroker, is portrayed as forever coming to work late. In one scene he tells his employer, "I'm gonna be here practically early on Monday." Another case in point is the late Freddie Prinze's portrayal of a Puerto Rican janitor in the now defunct TV program "Chico and the Man," whose favorite rejoinder was, "Ees not my job." In a study of aspirations among Puerto Rican migrants to New York in the late 1940s, Professors C. Wright Mills, Clarence Senior, and Rose Goldsen found that most persons interviewed wanted to change their socioeconomic status but were not really doing anything about it. Rather than assuming that Puerto Ricans are congenitally lazy, these findings may be interpreted in light of the lack of opportunity awaiting the migrants who came here then. The Chicano sample mentioned earlier was interviewed in the 1960s, a time when government programs and general opportunity were greater and discrimination less pronounced.

Interestingly, a study of attitudes among native-born Mexican-Americans by Dr. Anthony Dworkin revealed that 78 percent of them believed that Chicanos were "lazy, indifferent, and unambitious." According to Dworkin, the respondents had successfully internalized the stereotypes held by the Anglo majority in the United States. Further evidence of this came from the fact that only 28 percent of the foreign-born Mexican-Americans agreed with this stereotype. In Dworkin's view they had simply not been here long enough to adopt this negative image.

People who are quick to characterize Hispanics (or other disadvantaged groups) as lazy often neglect to consider how they would react if they faced similar problems. Prejudice, language difficulties, poverty, and lack of education and skills can easily destroy existing motivation. It's hard to get excited about being a dishwasher or fruit picker earning the minimum wage. The problem is exacerbated when those who choose not to work seem to be making more money in other ways. In a 1978 *Time* magazine article on Hispanics, a Puerto Rican youngster was quoted as saying,

A lot of kids want an education to get out of here. But in order to survive, they're dealing [drugs]. Kids ten and eleven make more money than their old man in the factory. ("It's Your Turn in the Sun," *Time*, October 16, 1978: 58)

The problem here is one of a vicious cycle. Poor job opportunities and inferior schools lead to loss of ambition, and this, in turn, means even fewer chances at improving one's life. Until the cycle is broken the problem will exist. There is, however, no evidence that laziness is intrinsic to Hispanic culture. Where it exists it is due to conditions in the larger society, conditions that have caused similar traits to appear among Blacks, poor whites from Appalachia, and other groups. The dilemma was perhaps most eloquently stated by a Chicano youth, who wrote,

Who am I? I am a product of myself . . . We came to California long before the Pilgrims landed at Plymouth Rock . . . You know we owned California—that is, until gold was found here. Who am I? I'm a human being. I have the same hopes that you do, the same fears, the same drives, same desires, same concerns, same abilities; and I want the same chance that you have to be an individual. Who am I? In reality I am who you want me to be. (Wayne Moquin [ed.], A *Documentary History of the Mexican Americans*, p. 386)

In the last eight years I have taught hundreds of Hispanic students at City College (CUNY), and my impression is that they are anything but lazy. In fact, in many instances they seem to exert more effort than the stereotypically hardworking Jewish students. The results, in terms of grades, may contradict this assertion, but it should be remembered that many Hispanics have difficulty mastering not only English but also the jargon peculiar to each discipline. A student who must rely on a foreign language dictionary as a study aid is not likely to find explanations for words in "sociologese," such as ethnocentrism, acculturation, mortification, total institution, and so forth, as they are used by specialists in the field.

Of even greater importance is the fact that most of the students at City College work and many are also trying to support families. This leaves them little time for study. I think of the doorman on East End Avenue from the Dominican Republic who puts in forty hours a week and has five children but takes fifteen credits a semester. I recall the young woman who traveled by subway every day from Far Rockaway, holding her infant in her arms. I think of the countless students in my evening courses who, at the end of a long day—be it in the mailroom of a publishing house, in a secretarial pool at the Federal Building, or selling tokens in the subway—drag themselves to the college to earn six credits a semester. At that rate most will take up to eight years to graduate, all this while they read about how a bachelor's degree doesn't do you any good. These individuals, both Hispanic and Black, are duplicating the immigrant Jewish experience of fifty years ago, but hardly anyone seems to notice —or care.

One of my fondest memories is that of the Puerto Rican student who received a grade of 60 on his midterm in a "Racial and Cultural Minorities" course. "How am I going to get into law school with a D in this course?" he wailed disconsolately. "Why didn't you think of that before you took the exam?" I asked. "I just didn't realize it would be so hard," he replied. "Well, now that you know, why don't you study really hard so you'll do better on the final," I said. "But I would probably have to get a 90 or 100 to really improve my grade." "That's correct," I replied. Mr. Gonzalez studied and, to my surprise, received the only 100 in the class on the final exam. He also got an A in the course, was admitted to law school, and is today a successful attorney. While not every student does as well as Mr. Gonzalez, very few have struck me as unwilling to work. All they need, like everybody else, is encouragement and a real chance to make it.

Refuse to learn English

The language of a people expresses the soul of that people, their whole culture. Imposing the Anglo's language—English—is a way of destroying our soul. This is what we call cultural genocide.

(Elizabeth Sutherland Martínez and
Enriqueta Longeaux y Vásquez, *Viva La Raza*, p. 142)

It would not be fair to assert that Hispanics refuse to learn English since millions of them speak it rather well and have never rejected it. At the same time, studies of language loyalty in the United States indicate that Spanish is more prevalent than any other foreign tongue spoken by immigrants. The majority of Hispanics are bilingual—in itself a reflection of their strong cultural ties to their countries of origin. People often say, "Why can't they be like everybody else? Italians, Poles, Jews—they all had to learn English." The case of the Hispanic community is special, however, and for many reasons.

Spanish has a long tradition in this country dating back to the time of the Spanish conquests in the New World. As former Congressman Herman Badillo put it recently in an article that appeared in *U.S. News & World Report,* "We do not consider ourselves immigrants. We feel we were here first, and so we have a different psychology." Although it is true that the French and the Dutch could make similar claims, neither can say that their languages were legally supported by the U. S. Government at any time. Spanish, on the other hand, occupied a special status. Throughout much of the nineteenth century, Mexican-Americans were a majority in Arizona, New Mexico, and California. As early as 1849 California passed a law requiring that all regulations and state laws be translated into Spanish. Although it was later rescinded when Anglos wrested power from the Mexican-Americans, the existence of such a requirement was unique. In New Mexico Hispanics fared better. Bilingualism became an official state policy early in the twentieth century, with Spanish and English considered equal languages by the government. Puerto Rico, which was acquired by the United States in 1898 following the Spanish-American War, was also viewed as a special case. Its citizens, while discriminated against on the mainland, were not viewed as foreigners in quite the same way.

One of the most important reasons for the survival of Spanish was and is geography. Both Puerto Rico and Mexico are within easy traveling distance of the United States. The Italian, Greek, Chinese, or Jewish immigrant had a much more difficult time getting back to the old country. He certainly was not able to visit it very often. Chicanos and Puerto Ricans take advantage of the easy access to their homelands by visiting them often, and this quite naturally reinforces both the native language and other aspects of the culture. There is also the need to communicate with relatives, and this provides yet another reason for remaining well versed in the language. Those who stay in the United States for long periods of time and lose their facility in Spanish are often looked down upon and are sometimes ridiculed by those in the homeland.

The mass media have also played an important role in maintaining the language. Hispanics have tended to concentrate in the Southwest, in Miami and New York, and to a somewhat lesser degree in Chicago. Wherever they are found in large numbers, there are radio and TV stations broadcasting either partly or totally in Spanish. The Puerto Rican child is exposed to Spanish-language programs *before* he reaches school age, as is his Chicano counterpart. He and his parents can listen to sports events, soap operas, and music—all in his native tongue. Among other things, this has the effect of legitimizing retention of the language.

Hispanics suffer disproportionately from discrimination in the United States, and their path to the better life is often blocked. Frustrated in their efforts at improving their social and economic situation, many find comfort in retaining the cultural values that characterized their lives before coming here. Not surprisingly, studies of the Hispanic population in the United States have found that those Hispanics with the lowest income and educational levels are most likely to communicate primarily in Spanish. If it is true that they refuse to learn English, perhaps it is because they see little gain in doing so. It must be remembered that those who come here are generally already severely disadvantaged economically. Moreover, the millions of illegal aliens who are Spanish-speaking are in a particularly difficult position. Relegated to the worst jobs and always on the lookout for those seeking to deport them, they cannot mix freely outside their communities. On the other hand, by their mere presence among legal Hispanic residents they contribute heavily to the tendency to use Spanish as the language of communication.

Hispanics are one of the largest ethnic groups in the United States, second only to Blacks, and according to most estimates they will soon be *the* largest group. It is an axiom of social science research that the larger the group the *slower* the rate of assimilation. Not only are Hispanics encouraged to retain their culture by force of numbers, but the size of the community forces Anglos who have contact with them to learn their language. This includes social workers, teachers, businessmen, government officials, foremen in factories where they are employed, and anyone else with whom they have dealings.

There are also the positive aspects of language retention. As Dr. Ellwyn Stoddard notes in his book *Mexican Americans,*

The differences in language structure and word meanings from one part of society to another restrict the manner in which society

members perceive the real world. . . . The language of one's people and of one's culture has deep personal meaning. (pp. 115–16)

For the immigrant the native language is crucial not simply
because it is a way of communicating but because it reflects his
cultural values. To force a person to give up his native language
is to deprive him of an outlet for cultural expression. Most important, perhaps, is the fact that Spanish is one of the main components of Hispanic identity and is therefore a difficult one for
many members of the community to give up. The roots of this
issue are historical. For many years public schools in Hispanic
areas viewed the use of Spanish as the reason why members of
the community failed to progress rapidly. In many instances its
use in the schools was specifically prohibited, and those who
insisted on speaking it were punished. One disciplinary method
involving keeping the child in school after hours was referred to
by those in the community as "Spanish detention." Thus, speaking Spanish became for many a way in which Hispanics could
rebel against Anglo oppression. Moreover, the fact that Puerto
Rico and Mexico were both defeated at one time or another by
the United States caused many to view the right to speak
Spanish as a way of maintaining at least some vestige of dignity
and self-respect.

Beginning with the 1960s, the Hispanic community grew far
more militant. Groups such as Alianza, the Brown Berets, MAPA
(Mexican American Political Association), and the Young Lords
were formed. These groups had many goals, ranging from political power to land rights, but they often included pride in speaking Spanish. As a result, what was already an established pattern
in the community received strong support from yet another
quarter. Those who refused to go along with the demands of the
militants were often branded "Tío Tomás" (Uncle Toms).
Under such circumstances many in the community who were not
really militant felt pressured to keep up the language simply as
an expression of ethnic solidarity.

Today, of course, Spanish has gained greater acceptance than
ever. Voting booths have instructions in Spanish, as do banks in
cities with sizeable Hispanic populations, thus further legitimizing the language. There are those who argue that bilingualism

hurts the community in the long run because many jobs require proficiency in English. In a recent column in *Newsweek* magazine the former U.S. ambassador to El Salvador, Henry E. Catto, Jr., stated, "If education in Spanish is a right, the melting-pot principle is in serious danger." Catto argues that the trend in bilingualism has gone too far and has become very costly. Under the present system, he notes, students have the right to be taught in sixty-odd languages, including Yiddish, Aleut, Navajo, Apache, and Japanese. Those who favor bilingualism point out that the emphasis on Spanish helps Hispanics adjust to life in this country. They also feel that expression of one's culture should be a basic right and not a debatable issue. To those who say that other immigrant groups did not have the same opportunity they respond, "Why perpetuate a wrong that is a hundred years old? The earlier immigrants should also have had the right to a bilingual education." Both sides have produced studies supporting their position. Regardless of which side is correct, and notwithstanding the negative attitude toward bilingualism of the Reagan administration, bilingualism is apparently here to stay. Its prevalence in the Hispanic parts of the country is indicative of the importance placed on Spanish by members of the community.

There are clearly many reasons why Hispanics are likely to retain their native language. At the same time, many, if not most, recognize the necessity of knowing English. Gaining fluency in both languages is not easy, and the difficulty of doing so probably has a good deal to do with the existence of this stereotype.

Don't care if they're on welfare

Now, you look at the Puerto Ricans. I can't believe these people. They come here from P.R. and the first thing you know they're on welfare. They don't give a damn because they have no pride.

These remarks were made by a Black woman in a class of mine at City College held in February of 1981. From the reaction that ensued, it became clear that they reflected the sentiments of many others in the class. This is a classic case of blaming the victim. Most people, regardless of background, have a

certain degree of pride. Besides, the payments given welfare recipients are not enough to make someone rich. As one Puerto
Rican woman put it in a May 12, 1980, New York *Times* article
by reporter David Vidal, "They give you a hard time, but the
money helps for now."

We have already seen the important role of machismo in the
Hispanic community. It is particularly evident when Hispanics
explain their feelings about welfare. A young Chicano farm
worker has said,

It eats up a man's soul to beg from the government. We are asked
to sell our souls for the welfare. We must or our bodies will starve.
Yes, but I say, what if our souls starve? (Stan Steiner, *La Raza: The
Mexican Americans*, p. 254)

In *Growing Up Puerto Rican*, consisting of a collection of essays, a young woman named Fernanda writes about her father,
who suffered a serious heart attack at the age of thirty-seven.

He was a very independent self-assertive man and suddenly he could
no longer work. Even worse, he had always looked down on people
who got welfare checks, and suddenly he was also. His pride as a
father, a man and a provider were totally shattered. (p. 5)

Dr. Ellwyn Stoddard, an expert on the Mexican-American community, asserts that Chicanos have a greater sense of pride than
other groups.

The stereotype of the Mexican American seeking a "welfare dole" is
ridiculous and misleading but generally believed. The author's experience in disaster relief studies has been that Mexican American
families, more than other ethnic groups, would subject their families
to starvation rather than accept relief from persons they do not know
or cannot trust. (*Mexican Americans*, p. 164)

Even if it were true that Hispanics do not care if they are on
welfare, such evidence would be hard to document. Textbooks
on ethnic groups, which, on the whole, try hard to portray them
sympathetically, are not apt to quote people who feel this way.
A better approach is to ask people who work in the community,
especially those in charge of welfare. Interviews with a number
of welfare workers in New York City revealed that Hispanics

were no more or less likely to be ashamed of accepting public assistance. Murray Gewirtz is presently a supervisor for New York City's Department of Social Services. He has been with the department for over fifteen years and has dealt with hundreds of recipients of public assistance on a day-to-day basis in a variety of settings. In his opinion,

You can't generalize. I have met many people who are embarrassed at being on welfare who are Hispanic. I've also dealt with many who are not bothered by it. The same is true of Blacks, poor whites, and any other group. Some care, some don't.

My own experiences as a caseworker in the heavily Hispanic Melrose section of the Bronx more than a decade ago were similar. Some of the people approached the department for aid with great reluctance, while others seemed to regard it as their right. Concerning this last point, people often forget that welfare *is* a right for those who are eligible. Its abuse has caused it to be viewed so negatively. On the other hand, those who dispense aid are often overzealous in their efforts to track down malfeasance. I recall being instructed by my supervisor to check under the beds of families who claimed abandonment by the father for men's shoes, a sure assault on the dignity of the many who just happened to be telling the truth. In *La Raza* Stan Steiner writes of one Chicano woman's reaction to such efforts.

Mrs. Elisa Valencia says, "I heard a knock on the door at 1:30 A.M." It was a state investigator trying to discover whether her husband was sleeping with her. "Somebody had report [sic] that my husband was at my house, staying with me while I was getting ADC. I went to my case worker and told her everything and told her to discontinue my checks because my girls and myself were very embarrassed and felt terrible. So I decided to do the best without ADC. I didn't think that $107 a month was worth the nightmare we went through." (p. 255)

I also remember the case of a woman who received aid under five different names. On one occasion I visited her about a request for new furniture and arrived a half hour early, just in time to discover her moving a pretty living room set into her neighbor's apartment. Flustered, she admitted her duplicity and begged me not to report it. Clearly, one cannot generalize.

While there is no real evidence to support the idea that Hispanics don't care about being on the dole, it is a fact that they are probably more likely to receive public assistance than any other group, including Blacks. They are also worse off than any other group. According to statistics published in *Time* magazine in 1978, almost 27 percent of Hispanic families in the United States earn under seven thousand dollars a year, compared to 16.6 percent for the country as a whole. Only 40 percent have completed high school, as contrasted with 46 percent for Blacks and 67 percent for whites. The problem is especially acute among Puerto Ricans. A 1979 study by the National Puerto Rican Forum reported that Puerto Ricans earn, on the average, less than half as much as Americans in general and over two thousand dollars less per year than Afro-Americans.

There are other reasons why Puerto Ricans are over-represented on the welfare rolls. The difference in the amount of money received by a family if the father is absent is very great, thus encouraging abandonment. Even if the father visits the family surreptitiously, the situation can hardly contribute to family stability. The weakening of the family structure prevents it from helping migrants adjust to life in this country, thereby increasing their dependence on public assistance. The significance of this is underscored when one thinks of the important role played by the family in the lives of the millions of Europeans who immigrated here in the last century. In addition, certain features of the culture are also responsible. Dr. Joseph P. Fitzpatrick, a sociologist and noted expert on the Puerto Rican community, writes in his book *Puerto Rican Americans,*

Traditional features of Puerto Rican culture (machismo, the practice of the mistress, consensual unions, the culture of poverty) have created a problem of abandonment in the past. In the process of migration, the cultural patterns whereby people sought to cope with the consequences of abandonment are easily lost. (p. 159)

Thus we see that both culture and the way in which the larger society responds to disadvantaged and discriminated against groups are factors contributing to the stereotype. Researchers have also observed that Puerto Ricans in New York City have higher death rates resulting from drug addiction, diabetes, cirrhosis of the liver, and accidents than any other group. Their children under fifteen years of age are more likely to die from pneumonia, bronchitis, and influenza. All this contributes heavily to the cycle of poverty, dependence, and even greater poverty.

One other point needs to be made. Unlike the situation of other groups who immigrated here, the United States bears considerable responsibility for the problems facing Chicanos and Puerto Ricans today. As a result of the United States victory over Mexico, many Mexican-Americans suffered the loss of their land in ways that were unfair or illegal. By compelling landowners to initiate expensive legal proceedings and by using physical intimidation, government agencies and private individuals forced many Mexican-Americans off their land. Lacking education and disliked by Anglos, many became downwardly mobile, forced into taking menial jobs as laborers, domestics, and farm hands. This was how the poverty-stricken barrios came into existence. One common practice in the late nineteenth century was to increase taxes on the land. Then, when Hispanics, desperate to pay their bills, sold their property to landholding companies, the taxes were lowered. It is estimated that up to 80 percent of Hispanic landholders in New Mexico met with this fate.

American culpability for the widespread poverty in Puerto Rico is equally great, though no one has argued that it would have been a wealthy country in the absence of American involvement. The United States acquired Puerto Rico in 1898 as a result of the Spanish-American War. From that time on it completely dominated the island politically until 1917, when it granted Puerto Ricans American citizenship. It appointed the governor and the executive council, which were responsible for running the country. No justification was given for taking over the country beyond the idea that Puerto Rico should be part of the United States simply because the United States needed it. Most importantly, the United States exploited Puerto Rico economically. Among other things, it was an absentee landlord for one hundred thousand acres of sugar plantations, thus earning

Puerto Rico the title of "Uncle Sam's Sweatshop." The island was allowed to sell its products only to the United States and was forced to purchase virtually all its finished products from our country.

Because of the historical relationships between the United States, on the one hand, and Mexico and Puerto Rico, on the other, one could argue that there is an issue of moral responsibility. Regarding the stereotype, Hispanics are no more likely to "care" about being on welfare than anybody else. They are, however, among the most likely groups in this country to require it.

Don't value education

The Mexicans, as a group, lack ambition. The peon of Mexico has spent so many generations in a condition of servitude that a lazy acceptance of his lot has become a general characteristic. (Lillian Graeber, "A Study of Attendance at Thomas Jefferson High School, Los Angeles, California," Master's thesis, University of Southern California, 1938)

This quote, which is cited by Dr. Joan Moore in her textbook *Mexican Americans,* typifies the stereotypes held by many Americans about Hispanics, especially of Chicanos and Puerto Ricans. Yet according to research on the subject, the stereotype, while perhaps true of the peasant classes forty years ago, is false today. In the 1950s Professors Melvin Tumin and Arnold Feldman did an exhaustive study of Puerto Rican society. Interviews with one thousand persons revealed the following: Almost all respondents agreed with the statement, "The more one studies, the better off one is." People were generally aware that a good education meant better jobs and more influence within the community. The favorable attitude toward education existed in varying degrees among all classes, but it was considerably higher among urban residents. Another study by Dr. James Coleman and others found that, compared to other racial and ethnic groups, Mexican-Americans "ranked high in their determination to stay in school, be good students and attend class regularly." Nevertheless, they were rated lower than Anglo-Americans in the degree to which they valued education.

If these groups value education, it is not apparent from their performance levels, which are quite poor. Chicano and Puerto Rican students are left back in classes far more often than other ethnic groups, drop out more frequently and at an earlier age than their Anglo counterparts, and do quite badly on achievement tests. In 1978 only 32 percent of Puerto Ricans in the United States were high school graduates. The national rate for Hispanics was 40 percent, which was lower than that of Blacks and far lower than that of Anglos.

How do we account for the lack of educational attainment on the part of a group whose members seem to consider learning very important? One possible answer is that aspirations are not the most important variable. Of greater significance, perhaps, is self-confidence. A study done by Professors William Kuvlesky, David Wright, and Rumaldo Juarez of Chicano youths in Texas concluded that they had higher aspirations than Black or Anglo youths but were far less sure of their ability to achieve their goals. In other words, just because a person *values* education does not mean that he believes in his ability to do well in school, which is ultimately the most important criterion for educational success.

If lack of self-confidence is the problem, how is it inculcated? In an article that appeared in *The New Leader*, Richard Margolis explains the role of the schools in this process:

A teacher stands at the classroom door each morning and sprays entering Chicano children with perfume—"because they smell," she explains to a visitor.

A girl in the first grade is made to stand in a corner for saying something in Spanish to a teacher. What she said was, "I don't understand."

Little Federico is told that from now on in school he will be called "Fred," because "It's more American."

The assignment in class is to draw a picture, but Jacinta tells her teacher she has no crayons. "If your father got off Welfare and went to work," says the teacher, "you'd have crayons."

(*The New Leader*, February 12, 1979: 13)

Children exposed in this fashion to formal education are not likely to perform very well. There are other problems too. Although Hispanics value education in a general sense, economic pressures often dampen their enthusiasm. There are clothes and shoes as well as supplies that must be bought for school. Low-income families, especially migrant laborers, are inclined to view teenagers who continue in school as potential wage earners whose immediate value is not being realized. For the younger children migrant labor means that their chances of staying in the same school for any length of time are slim. After all, the harvesting season and the academic year do not run concurrently. Conditions of slum life, such as overcrowding, diet deficiencies, lack of privacy, and broken homes, also affect school performance. The schools that serve Hispanics in the United States have consistently been shown, in study after study, to be inferior in quality, with larger than average classes, lack of facilities, and teachers who view their assignment to such schools as dead-end jobs. Faced with such obstacles, Hispanic parents, often uneducated themselves, find it difficult to provide the moral support for getting an education that is the norm for middle-class families. Moreover, the absence of role models for good study habits also hurts.

Summing up, there does not appear to be any basis for saying that Hispanics do not value education. It is true that many do not do well in school, but the reasons are more related to circumstances than to culture. As time goes on, however, this situation will change. There are today hundreds of respected Chicano and Puerto Rican scholars throughout the United States—far more than twenty or even ten years ago.

Warm, expressive, and emotional

Puerto Ricans are loud and emotional. I'm very sentimental. If you're one of my best friends and you say something I don't like, I start crying. I cry a lot.

(Sixteen-year-old girl in *Growing Up Puerto Rican*, p. 53)

Puerto Ricans use the telephone and the mails, but to "really get things done," there is no substitute for a face to face meeting . . .

Puerto Ricans are in unanimous agreement that the *americano* has a
"colder" personality, because of his penchant for mechanical communication and for "going by the book."

(Kal Wagenheim, *Puerto Rico: A Profile*, p. 213)

Although it is difficult to prove, there seems to be almost universal agreement among both professionals and lay people as to
the validity of this stereotype. Within the community of Latins it
is called *personalismo*, or personalism. What it means is a belief
in the inner worth and uniqueness of the individual in all areas.
For example, Latin American politics is known for its focus on
personal relationships and guarantees and is based on mutual
trust rather than written agreements. It plays a role in business
relationships as well, as described by anthropologist John Gillin:

. . . the impersonal confidence which, say, a buyer has toward a
salesman of a large established corporation in the United States is
not yet part of the pattern in Latin America. There you have to know
him as an individual and to understand his "soul" really to have
confidence in him. (*Contemporary Cultures and Societies of Latin
America*, p. 510)

Traits such as the above find their clearest expression in the
Hispanic family. In the introduction to his classic work *Five
Families*, Oscar Lewis notes that all the families he studied were
characterized by warm emotional ties, especially between the
mother and child. In a May 12, 1980, New York *Times* article, a
Dominican man summed it up as follows: "A Hispanic will greet
you by inquiring into your family in detail out of sincerity. An
American will find this an intrusion."

The sensitivity mentioned earlier has also been noted by many
observers. An excellent description of it appears in Dr. Joseph
Fitzpatrick's book *Puerto Rican Americans*.

Puerto Ricans are much more sensitive than Americans to anything
that appears to be personal insult or disdain; they do not take to
practical jokes which are likely to embarrass, or to party games in
which people "make fools of themselves." They do not "horse
around," as Americans would say, in an offhand, informal manner;
they are unusually responsive to manifestations of personal respect
. . . (p. 90)

There are several possible explanations that might account for the warmth of Latin Americans where it exists. In any society the family is one of the most important shapers of the individual. It is there that the child first learns how to act when among others. In an article that appeared in the *Basic Handbook of Child Psychiatry*, two medical doctors, Alberto Serrano and Fortunato Castillo, point out that Chicano mothers provide "more cuddling and kissing of the infant than would be true with Anglo parents." They are intensely involved with their children in general throughout their lives. In the same passage the authors observe:

The imprint of the oral stage on the child's personality lasts the lifetime through. Among other factors, it can be discerned in such adult attitudes as the following: The Mexican-American is affectionate and uses terms of endearment very readily as an adult; he talks not only with his voice but readily embraces people he likes and is spontaneous in the exchange of physical affection.

The Mexican-American thinks that the Anglo-Saxon is stuffy and unfriendly. The Anglo-Saxon perceives the Mexican-American as mushy and overfriendly.

The Anglo-Saxon cannot understand why, if the Mexican-American is poor, he "wastes" his money on great amounts of food for friends and relatives. The Mexican-American, on the other hand, cannot understand why, if the Anglo-Saxon has money, he only gives his guests what is perceived as too little to eat. (p. 258)

From this lengthy quote it becomes clear how such traits function in a variety of circumstances. In addition, the extended family structure common among Hispanics and the fact that "family" often includes people who live in the same place but are not necessarily related are also considerations. As a result of this pattern of living, the child learns to regard a greater number of people with warmth and affection, as opposed to the typical American nuclear family. As Serrano and Castillo observe, infants receive attention not only from the mother but from other relatives and friends as well.

In attempting to explain the origins of personalism, Dr. Fitzpatrick argues that because the average Puerto Rican was, in past generations, "born into his social and economic position" he tended to place greater importance on personal qualities to distinguish among those with whom he lived. This is certainly a factor, but it can be said about many cultures throughout the world where mobility is limited, including India, China, Haiti, and Saudi Arabia, to mention only a few. Some researchers have argued that climate may play a role, noting that Mediterranean people in general seem more expressive, emotional, and open. They feel that the warm climate brings people into greater contact with one another. Such assertions are, however, purely speculative. One could also argue the reverse, namely, that colder climates, because they force families to stay together indoors, result in more closely knit families. Yet no one has taken that position, much less proven it. Besides, there are plenty of examples of totally different cultures developing side by side in the same climate.

A more logical possibility is the presence of machismo as a cultural value. Machismo emphasizes the importance of the person, both negatively and positively. One of its main components is honor, and just as an insult can lead to serious retribution, conferring honor upon an individual can prompt expressions of great warmth and friendship. Any society that places importance on personal qualities of this sort is likely to encourage a mode of expression that is highly personal.

Based on the observations of researchers familiar with the community, it would seem that there is a good deal of truth to this stereotype, though there is room for a wealth of research on the subject. Its origins can be traced to the family structure and the cultural values of the community.

Violent and hot-tempered

This is a difficult stereotype to evaluate. Where no crime is recorded it is obviously difficult to know whether violent behavior has occurred. Also, national statistics on violent crimes are not, as a rule, divided according to ethnic groups, and information on this question is therefore hard to obtain. Nevertheless, there is considerable evidence to support the notion that Hispanics are more likely than many other ethnic groups to engage in crimes involving violent acts. Whether this is also true of everyday situations, such as losing one's temper and pushing some-one or shouting at the top of one's lungs, can only be guessed at.

Research on stereotypes suggests that this view of Hispanics is a popular one. In an article entitled "Ethnic Images and Stereo-types of Mexicans and Americans" Dr. Norman Humphrey re-ports that the Mexican is likely to be perceived by middle-class Americans as "given to ready expression of emotion (a knife wielder, jealous, capable of extreme cruelty, hot tempered)." Such views often appear rather innocently in the context of arti-cles in the mass media about other subjects. For example, a re-cent piece in the New York *Times* dealt with the reluctance of British residents of the Falkland Islands, one of Britain's last colonies, to be placed under the control of Argentina, which claims the islands as its own. Most of the article was devoted to an assessment of political and economic matters, but the last paragraph claimed, in almost routine fashion, that cultural differences were also involved.

"I like Latin people," said Harold Rowlands, the financial secretary and main cog in the government here, "but we're different. We have a British temperament, more reserved, not fiery and excitable. To go and change that we can't do." (Edward Schumacher, "Stubborn Brit-ons Cling to Embattled Atlantic Islands," New York *Times*, February 5, 1981)

Although they would undoubtedly reject the idea that His-panics are apt to be gun-toting hoodlums, studies by Dr. Anthony Dworkin and others have shown that Hispanics themselves agree with the general view that they are an emotional people.

Research on Hispanics points to a definite tendency toward vi-olent crime. Homicide was the most frequent cause of death among Puerto Ricans between the ages of 15 and 44 according to a study conducted in the early 1970s by Fordham University's Hispanic Research Center. Of those arrested, Chicanos are far more likely than Anglos to be charged with assault and battery. Evidence of this comes from police reports in cities such as Los Angeles, San Antonio, and El Paso, all of which have high pro-portions of Mexican-Americans. While most Americans are fa-miliar with the Italian-dominated Cosa Nostra, not as many have heard of the Nuestra Familia or the Mexican Mafia, both of which are reputed to be quite violent. Of greater interest, perhaps, are figures that compare violence in Latin America with that in other parts of the world. In 1973 six Latin American nations were among the ten countries with the highest rates of violent death. This trend has been going on for some time. Colombia, with a population of about 10 million people, had about 300,000 homicides between 1948 and 1965. In Mexico the figures have also been very high, prompting a popular saying there that the chances of dying a violent death in Mexico City are greater than was the case during the London Blitz of World War II.

It goes without saying that most violent crimes by Hispanics in the United States are committed by those at or near the bottom of the socioeconomic ladder, and there are many reasons for this. Poverty, discrimination, and the prevalence of gangs, drugs, weapons, and so forth, all combine to create an environment supportive of violent behavior. Children brought up in such communities look to the gang as a place where they can feel accepted. As one gang member named Carlos put it,

I don't need no cops because I got plenty of protection from my gang. If you're with a gang and you get hit, you're not alone. You've got friends who will help you and that's important. (Paulette Cooper [ed.], *Growing Up Puerto Rican*, p. 104)

Sometimes the violence is not directed at people but at property. In a recent article in the New York *Times Magazine* about graffiti in New York City's subways, writers Caryl Stern and Robert Stock observed that "there has been a rising incidence of graffiti-related vandalism—India ink spread over seats, windows cracked . . . attacks by graffitists against car cleaners." In the authors' view these incidents are most often caused by youths, many of them Hispanic and Black, who have a confused self-image, a strong sense of territoriality, and a need to attack authority. In another article on the subject, urban expert Carl Horowitz argues that the crowning achievement of individuals who act in this manner "may yet be their contribution to the decay of public facilities and urban neighborhoods."

The problems described until now could be applied to Blacks and other segments of America's poor as well as Hispanics. There are other factors, however, that contribute to the violence stereotype directed against Hispanics. The first settlers who came here from England already harbored negative images of Spain. Much of the literature in that country described Spain as "treacherous, fanatical, violent," and so forth. According to writer Philip Wayne Powell, "we [Americans] transferred some of our ingrained antipathy toward Catholic Spain to her American heirs." This can be seen from the following statement that appeared in William Robertson's 1822 work *The History of America:* "In almost every district of the Mexican Empire, the progress of the Spanish arms is marked with blood, and with deeds so atrocious, as disgrace the enterprising valour that conducted them to success." This perception was reinforced during the mid nineteenth century when Mexico and the United States were at war. Our own atrocities were not emphasized as much because Mexico was the enemy and the U. S. Government was not about to indict itself for cruelties against its antagonist any more than it was willing to accept the blame for its crimes against the Indians.

In the late nineteenth and early twentieth centuries such stereotypes helped justify economic exploitation and social discrimination. Then came the zoot suit riots of 1943. As a result of a controversial court decision involving a murdered Mexican-American youth, conflict broke out in Los Angeles between U.S. servicemen and Chicanos. The police often sided openly with the servicemen, arresting Chicanos even when they were clearly victims of unprovoked attacks. The riots spread to other American cities and lent new support to the violence stereotype. Later investigations by a government commission placed the blame for the riots upon prejudice and unfair press coverage, but the damage, with respect to the image of Chicanos, had already been done. Finally, the continuing influx from Mexico and Puerto Rico, as well as from other Latin American countries, of predominantly poor people who settle in high-crime areas has strengthened the association held by many of violence with Hispanics.

Violence is also related to machismo. Anthropologist Julian Pitt-Rivers has observed, "The ultimate vindication of honour lies in physical violence." Moreover, "When challenged to fight it is not honourable to demand police protection." The well-known

Mexican writer and diplomat Octavio Paz has depicted the essence of machismo in his book *The Labyrinth of Solitude:* ". . . the essential attribute of the *macho*—power—almost always reveals itself as a capacity for wounding, humiliating, annihilating."

Nowhere is this tendency more prevalent than among the impoverished classes, where culture and economic desperation provide mutual reinforcement. Take, for example, the following excerpt from Oscar Lewis' *The Children of Sanchez.* The speaker is Manuel, the oldest of the Sanchez children.

Mexicans, and I think everyone in the world, admire the person "with balls," as we say. The character who throws punches and kicks, without stopping to think, is the one who comes out on top. The one who has guts enough to stand up against an older, stronger guy, is more respected. If someone shouts, you've got to shout louder. If any so-and-so comes to me and says, "Fuck your mother," I answer, "Fuck your mother a thousand times." And if he gives one step forward and I take one step back, I lose prestige. (p. 38)

There is no question that the use of physical force is an essential element of Hispanic culture. There are, in addition to many accounts and literary descriptions, scientific studies pointing to its existence. Of course, it would be silly to assume that *all*, or even most, Hispanic persons are likely to respond in a violent fashion to any affront. Moreover, the socioeconomic position of middle- and upper-class Hispanics is likely to strongly influence such temptations. Finally, these perceptions have been heightened by both prejudice and historical events in America. Nevertheless, there is, under certain conditions, more than a grain of truth to this stereotype.

ELEVEN

Are stereotypes valid?

"Stereotype" has been something of a dirty word for a long time among social scientists, many of whom have taken the position that when it comes to racial and ethnic groups, they are an indication of one's prejudices. As a result, many researchers have turned their attention to why people stereotype without so much as a second glance at the stereotypes themselves. Perhaps it is time to change our thinking on this matter.

At the beginning of this book we asked a basic question: Why are some groups described as having certain traits more often than others? Are WASPs really more honorable and hardworking? Are Jews really shrewd businessmen? Do Italians really talk with their hands more often than people from other cultural backgrounds? Are Black people more musically inclined than others? After examining more than seventy-five widely held stereotypes, it is clear that this connection is not accidental. Every single stereotype discussed turns out to have a reason, or reasons. Moreover, as stated in the introduction, the latter have to do either with the group's culture and history or with those outside the culture who had contact with it.

Are the stereotypes accurate? A good many are, but the majority are not. In only a few cases can it be categorically stated

that a stereotype is definitely true or false. For most one can
only say "usually false" or "usually true." After all, we are talking about large numbers of people. I have always told my sociology students that when social scientists try to deal with complicated questions—ethnic identity, the basis of human love,
prejudice, the origins of social movements, and similar issues—
they cannot achieve the accuracy of the natural scientist. Nor
should they feel bad about this. Human beings are not like
chemical solutions, which, when mixed under the proper conditions, invariably produce the same compound. They are unpre-
dictable and much more complex.

Having accepted the existence of limits to our understanding,
it should be evident that definite answers about stereotypes are
almost impossible. On the other hand, a great deal of research
has been done about different cultures, and we can make some
tentative judgements. It turns out that approximately one third
of the stereotypes can be said to have a good deal of truth to
them. Furthermore, of those that are false at least twenty had
more than a kernel of truth to them in the past. It is only as the
various groups became more Americanized that those elements
in the culture that made them true started to disappear. Thus, if
we include both past and present conditions, it can be said that
almost *half* the stereotypes have a strong factual basis. This does
not, of course, mean that virtually every member of the group
conforms to the trait described. There are impolite Chinese,
physically weak Blacks, and unemotional Hispanics. Still, there
are such things as tendencies and traits that are rooted in a
group's history and culture. Ignoring or minimizing them can be
as bad as exaggerating them.

Bigots will not, however, find much support for their prejudices from the relatively high number of valid stereotypes. This
is so because most of the stereotypes for which support can be
found are positive and flattering to the group involved, whereas
those that seem highly inaccurate tend, by and large, to be negative. It is here that we see the linkage between stereotypes and
prejudice most clearly. Stereotypes are used by prejudiced people to rationalize their biases, and it is important to refute them.

Whether or not sensitive topics should be discussed is open to
debate. I have obviously indicated my position by writing about

them. I'm in favor of the idea, provided it is carefully handled. Part of the joy, or at least the excitement, of living in this world is learning how and why people think and act the way they do. Creating myths and distortions about a people's history and their culture prevents us from doing so. Moreover, the uniqueness and variety represented by the different nationalities that comprise the American people ought not to be something we are ashamed to speak about. It should be a source of pride. Those aspects of a culture that are negatively perceived by others cannot, however, be ignored since most people are aware of them anyway, at least on a subjective level. Perhaps by examining their origins we can make people more tolerant and understanding of each other. Hopefully this book represents a step in that direction.

Antin, Mary. *The Promised Land*. Boston: Houghton Mifflin, 1912.

Cohn, Norman. *Warrant for Genocide*. New York: Harper & Row, 1966.

Compaine, Benjamin M. (ed.). *Who Owns the Media? Concentration of Ownership in the Mass Communications Industry*. New York: Harmony, 1980.

Coon, Carleton. "Have the Jews a Racial Identity?" *In* Isacque Graeber and Stuart Henderson Britt (eds.), *Jews in a Gentile World*. New York: Macmillan, 1942: 30–37.

Durant, Will. *The Story of Civilization. Part III: Caesar and Christ*. New York: Simon & Schuster, 1944.

Encyclopaedia Judaica. Jerusalem: Keter, 1972.

Fishberg, Maurice. *The Jews: A Study of Race and Environment*. New York: Scribner, 1911.

Glock, Charles Y. and Stark, Rodney. *Christian Beliefs and Anti-Semitism*. New York: Harper & Row, 1966.

Gold, Michael. *Jews Without Money*. New York: Liveright, 1930.

Goldin, Milton. *Why They Give: American Jews and their Philanthropies*. New York: Macmillan, 1976.

Goldstein, Sidney. "American Jewry, 1970: A Demographic Profile." *In* Marshall Sklare (ed.), *The Jew in American Society*. New York: Behrman House, 1974: 94–160.

Herskovitz, Melville J. "Who Are the Jews?" *In* Louis Finkelstein (ed.), *The Jews: Their History, Culture, and Religion*. New York: Harper & Brothers, 1949.

Higham, John. "Social Discrimination Against Jews in America, 1830–1930." *American Jewish Historical Quarterly*, September 1957: 9–10.

Isaacs, Stephen. *Jews and American Politics*. New York: Doubleday, 1974.

Lesser, Gerald S.; Fifer, Gordon; and Clark, Donald. "Mental Abilities of Children from Different Social-class and Cultural Groups." *Monographs of the Society for Research in Child Development*, vol. 30, no. 4, 1965: 82–84.

Patai, Raphael. *The Jewish Mind*. New York: Scribner, 1977.

——, and Wing, Jennifer Patai. *The Myth of the Jewish Race.* New York: Scribner, 1975.

Ringer, Benjamin. *The Edge of Friendliness.* New York: Basic Books, 1967.

Rottenberg, Dan. "Supergelt." *Jewish Living,* September–October 1979: 41–47.

——. "How to Succeed in Business Without Being Gentile." *Jewish Living,* December 1979: 39–42.

Sartre, Jean-Paul. *Anti-Semite and Jew.* New York: Schocken Books, 1948.

Sklare, Marshall. *America's Jews.* New York: Random House, 1971.

Tonner, Leslie. *Nothing but the Best: The Luck of the Jewish Princess.* New York: Coward, McCann & Geoghegan, 1975.

Van Den Haag, Ernest. *The Jewish Mystique.* New York: Delta Books edn., 1971.

Van Impe, Jack. *Israel's Final Holocaust.* Nashville: Thomas Nelson, 1979.

Wolfe, Ann G. "The Invisible Jewish Poor." *Journal of Jewish Communal Service,* Spring 1972: 1–7.

Yaffe, James. *The American Jews.* New York: Random House, 1968.

Barzini, Luigi. *The Italians*. New York: Atheneum, 1964.

Campisi, Paul J. "Ethnic Family Patterns: The Italian Family in the United States." *American Journal of Sociology*, 53, May 1948: 443–49.

Cordasco, Francesco, and Bucchioni, Eugene (eds.). *The Italians: Social Backgrounds of an American Group*. Clifton, N.J.: Augustus M. Kelly, 1974.

Covello, Leonard. *The Social Background of the Italo-American School Child*. Leiden: E. J. Brill, 1967.

De Conde, Alexander. *Half Bitter, Half Sweet: An American Excursion into Italian American History*. New York: Scribner, 1971.

Della Femina, Jerry, and Sopkin, Charles. *An Italian Grows in Brooklyn*. Boston: Little, Brown, 1978.

Dixon, Norman. *On the Psychology of Military Incompetence*. New York: Basic Books, 1976.

Efron, David. *Gesture and Environment*. New York: King's Crown Press, 1941.

Gambino, Richard. *Blood of My Blood*. New York: Doubleday, 1974.

Gans, Herbert. *The Urban Villagers: Group and Class in the Life of Italian-Americans*. New York: Free Press, 1964.

Handlin, Oscar. *Race and Nationality in American Life*. Boston: Little, Brown, 1957.

Higham, John. *Strangers in the Land*. New York: Atheneum, 1968.

Ianni, Francis A. J. "The Mafia and the Web of Kinship." *The Public Interest*, Winter 1971: 78–100.

LaGumina, Salvatore J. (ed.). *The Immigrants Speak: The Italian Americans Tell Their Story*. New York: Center for Migration Studies, 1979.

Lopreato, Joseph. *Italian Americans*. New York: Random House, 1970.

Mangione, Jerre. *Mount Allegro*. Boston: Houghton Mifflin, 1943.

Nelli, Humbert S. *Italians in Chicago, 1880–1930*. New York: Oxford University Press, 1970.

Panella, Vincent. *The Other Side: Growing Up Italian in America*. New York: Doubleday, 1979.

Smith, Sandy. "The Mob." *Life*, 63, September 1 and 8, 1967: 15–22, 42B–45, 91–94.

Talese, Gay. *Honor Thy Father*. New York: World, 1971.

Whyte, William Foote. *Streetcorner Society*. Chicago: University of Chicago Press, 1943.

Williams, Phyllis H. *South Italian Folkways in Europe and America*. New Haven: Yale University Press, 1938.

Wundt, Wilhelm. *The Language of Gestures*. The Hague: Mouton, 1973.

Allport, Gordon W. *The Nature of Prejudice.* New York: Anchor Books edn., 1958.

Bennett, Lerone. *Before the Mayflower,* rev. edn. Baltimore: Penguin Books edn., 1966.

"The Black Consumer." *Black Enterprise,* November 1973: 17–26, 62.

Carmichael, Stokely, and Hamilton, Charles V. *Black Power: The Politics of Liberation in America.* New York: Random House, 1967.

Cash, W. J. *The Mind of the South.* New York: Vintage Books, 1960.

Clark, Kenneth B. *Dark Ghetto: Dilemmas of Social Power.* New York: Harper Torchbooks, 1967.

Cleaver, Eldridge. *Soul on Ice.* New York: McGraw-Hill, 1968.

Cobb, William M. "Physical Anthropology of the American Negro." *American Journal of Physical Anthropology,* 29, 1942: 158–59.

Coon, Carleton S. *The Living Races of Man.* New York: Knopf, 1965.

Daniels, Lee A. "Blacks Pursue More Active Role in Dealing with Crime by Blacks." *New York Times,* November 9, 1980.

Davis, George. "Bitters in the Brew of Success." *Black Enterprise,* November 1977: 32–39.

Dollard, John. *Caste and Class in a Southern Town.* New Haven: Yale University Press, 1937.

Dreyfuss, Joel. "Black Americans Speak Out: A Self-Portrait." *Black Enterprise,* August 1980: 47–49.

DuBois, W.E.B. *The Souls of Black Folk.* New York: Washington Square Press, 1970.

Eysenck, Hans J. *The I.Q. Argument: Race, Intelligence and Education.* New York: Library Press, 1971.

Fisher, Seymour. "Dirt-Anality and Attitudes Toward Negroes." *Journal of Nervous and Mental Diseases,* April 1978: 280–90.

Gibson, D. Parke. *The $30 Billion Negro.* New York: Macmillan, 1969.

———. *$70 Billion in the Black.* New York: Macmillan, 1978.

Goldaper, Sam. "Campy Who? Now Is Campy Russell." *New York Times,* November 13, 1980.

Goodman, Mary Ellen. *Race Awareness in Young Children.* New York: Collier, 1964.

Graham, H. D., and Gurr, T. (eds.). *Violence in America: Historical and Comparative Perspectives.* National Commission on the Causes and Prevention of Violence. Washington, D.C.: Government Printing Office, 1969.

Greeley, Andrew M., and Sheatsley, Paul M. "Attitudes Toward Racial Integration." *Scientific American.* December 1971: 13–19.

Grier, William H., and Cobbs, Price M. *Black Rage.* New York: Bantam Books, 1969.

Herrnstein, Richard. "I.Q." *Atlantic Monthly,* 228, 1971: 44–64.

Herzstein, J. N. "A Comparison of the Jumping Ability of American Negro Male College Students with American White Male College Students as Measured by the Sargent Vertical Jump Test." Master's thesis, University of Maryland, 1961.

"How Whites Feel About Negroes: A Painful American Dilemma." *Newsweek,* October 21, 1963: 44–54.

Jencks, Christopher. "Heredity, Environment, and Public Policy." *American Sociological Review,* 45, October 1980: 723–36.

Jensen, Arthur. "How Much Can We Boost I.Q. and Scholastic Achievement?" *Harvard Educational Review,* 39, Winter 1969: 1–123.

Jones, LeRoi. *Blues People.* New York: William Morrow, 1963.

Jordan, Winthrop D. *White Over Black.* Baltimore: Penguin Books edn., 1969.

Kardiner, Abram, and Ovesey, Lionel. *Mark of Oppression: A Psychosocial Study of the American Negro.* New York: Norton, 1951.

Klineberg, Otto. *Race Differences.* New York: Harper & Brothers, 1935.

Kovel, Joel. *White Racism: A Psychohistory.* New York: Pantheon Books, 1970.

Kronus, Sidney. *The Black Middle Class.* Columbus, Ohio: Charles E. Merrill, 1971.

Laeding, L. "Assessment of the Difference in Power, Agility, Strength, and Reaction Time of Negro and White Male Subjects at the Tenth-Grade Level." Master's thesis, Michigan State University, 1964.

Malcolm X. *The Autobiography of Malcolm X.* New York: Grove Press, 1966.

Malina, Robert M. "Growth, Maturation, and Performance of Philadelphia Negro and White Elementary School Children." Ph.D. dissertation, University of Pennsylvania, 1968.

———. "Growth and Physical Performance of American Negro and White Children." *Clinical Pediatrics,* 8, August 1969: 476–83.

Montagna, William, and Parakkal, Paul F. *The Structure and Function of the Skin*. New York: Academic Press, 1974.

Myrdal, Gunnar. *An American Dilemma*. New York: Harper & Row, 1944.

The Negro Handbook. Chicago: Johnson Publishing Company, 1966.

Pinckney, Alphonso. *Black Americans*. Englewood Cliffs, N.J.: Prentice-Hall, 1975.

The President's Commission on Law Enforcement and Administration of Justice. Washington, D.C.: Government Printing Office, 1967.

Rosenberg, Bernard, and Howton, F. William. "Ethnic Liberalism and Employment Discrimination in the North." *American Journal of Economics and Sociology*, 26, October 1967: 387–98.

Shafer, Ronald G. "Negroes' Rising Income Prompts Auto Makers to Woo New Market." *Wall Street Journal*, December 2, 1966: 1, 20.

Silberman, Charles E. *Criminal Violence, Criminal Justice*. New York: Random House, 1978.

Smith, Lillian. *Killers of the Dream*. New York: Anchor Books edn., 1963.

Sowell, Thomas. *Race and Economics*. New York: McKay, 1975.

Steinberg, Stephen. *The Ethnic Myth: Race, Class and Ethnicity in American Life*. New York: Atheneum, 1981.

Taylor, Howard. *The I.Q. Game: A Methodological Inquiry into the Heredity-Environment Controversy*. New Brunswick, N.J.: Rutgers University Press, 1980.

Williams, Robert L. "The BITCH Test." St. Louis: Black Studies Program, Washington University, 1972.

Wilson, William J. *The Declining Significance of Race*. Chicago: University of Chicago Press, 1978.

Arkoff, Abe. "Need Patterns in Two Generations of Japanese Americans in Hawaii." *Journal of Social Psychology*, 50, 1959: 75–79.

Bell, Reginald. *Public School Education of Second-Generation Japanese in California*. Palo Alto: Stanford University Press, Education-Psychology Series, nos. 1 & 3, 1935.

Bellah, Robert. *Tokugawa Religion*. New York: Free Press, 1957.

Benedict, Ruth. *The Chrysanthemum and the Sword*. Boston: Houghton Mifflin, 1946.

Boesen, Victor. "The Nisei Come Home." *The New Republic*, April 26, 1948: 16–19.

Bosworth, Allan R. *America's Concentration Camps*. New York: Norton, 1967.

Caudill, William, and DeVos, George. "Achievement, Culture and Personality: The Case of the Japanese Americans." *American Anthropologist*, 58, 1956: 1102–26.

Connor, John W. *Tradition and Change in Three Generations of Japanese Americans*. Chicago: Nelson-Hall, 1977.

Daniels, Roger. *The Politics of Prejudice*. Berkeley: University of California Press, 1962.

Gibney, Frank B. "Doing Business With the Japanese Teaches a Lesson in Cultural Differences." *Publishers Weekly*, October 16, 1978: 80–85.

Gulick, Sidney L. *The American Japanese Problem*. New York: Scribner, 1914.

Hane, Mikiso. *Japan: A Historical Survey*. New York: Scribner, 1972.

Hayner, Norman S. "Delinquency Areas in the Puget Sound Region." *American Journal of Sociology*, 39, 1934: 314–28.

Hearst, William Randolph. "Editorial." Los Angeles *Examiner*, February 21, 1940.

Hosokawa, Fumiko. *The Sansei: Social Interaction and Ethnic Identification Among the Third Generation Japanese*. San Francisco: R & E Research Associates, 1978.

Hosokawa, William K. *Nisei: The Quiet Americans*. New York: Morrow, 1969.

Irwin, Wallace. *Seed of the Sun*. New York: George H. Doran, 1921.

Jacobson, Alan, and Rainwater, Lee. "A Study of Management Representative Evaluations of Nisei Workers." *Social Forces*, 32, 1953: 35–41.

Kitano, Harry H. L. "Changing Achievement Patterns of the Japanese in the United States." *Journal of Social Psychology*, 58, 1962: 257–64.

———. *Japanese Americans: The Evolution of a Subculture*. Englewood Cliffs: Prentice-Hall, 1969.

Lifton, Robert Jay. *History and Human Survival*. New York: Random House, 1970.

Lippmann, Walter. "Editorial Column." New York *Herald Tribune*, February 20, 1942.

Maykovich, Minako K. *Japanese Americans: Identity Dilemma*. Tokyo: Waseda University Press, 1972.

McClatchy, V. S. "Japanese in the Melting Pot: Can They Assimilate and Make Good Citizens?" *Annals of the American Academy of Political and Social Science*, January 1921: 29–34.

McDowell, Bart. "Those Successful Japanese." *National Geographic*, March 1974: 323–59.

McWilliams, Carey. *Prejudice: Japanese Americans: Symbol of Racial Intolerance*. Boston: Little, Brown, 1944.

Meredith, Gerald M., and Meredith, Connie G. W. "Acculturation and Personality Among Japanese-American College Students in Hawaii." *Journal of Social Psychology*, 68, 1966: 175–82.

Modell, John. *The Economics and Politics of Racial Accommodation: The Japanese of Los Angeles, 1900–1942*. Urbana, Illinois: University of Illinois Press, 1977.

Ogawa, Dennis. *From Japs to Japanese: An Evolution of Japanese-American Stereotypes*. Berkeley: McCutchan Publishing Corporation, 1971.

Petersen, William. "Success Story: Japanese American Style." The New York *Times Magazine*, January 9, 1966.

———. *Japanese Americans*. New York: Random House, 1971.

Robertson, Nan. "The Life of a Japanese Journalist in New York." New York *Times*, February 20, 1981.

Schrieke, Bertram. *Alien Americans: A Study of Race Relations*. New York: Viking, 1936.

Seward, Jack. *The Japanese*. New York: Morrow, 1972.

Strong, Edward K. *The Second Generation Japanese Problem*. Palo Alto: Stanford University Press, 1934.

Suzuki, Daisetsu T. *Zen and Japanese Culture*. New York: Pantheon, 1959.

Yutang, Lin (ed.). *The Wisdom of Confucius*. New York: Random House, 1938.

Axthelm, Pete. "An Inscrutable Passion for Gambling." *New York Magazine*, September 27, 1971: 55–57.

Barth, Gunther. *Bitter Strength: A History of the Chinese in the United States, 1850–1870*. Cambridge, Mass.: Harvard University Press, 1964.

Cantril, Hadley, and Strunk, Mildred (eds.). *Public Opinion, 1935–1946*. Princeton: Princeton University Press, 1951.

Chrysler, K. M. "Chinese Americans: Stereotypes Won't Do." *U.S. News & World Report*, July 7, 1980: 37.

Clark, Helen F. "The Chinese of New York Contrasted With Their Foreign Neighbors." *The Century Magazine*, November 1897: 104–13.

Durant, Will. *The Story of Civilization. Part I: Our Oriental Heritage*. New York: Simon & Schuster, 1935.

Fong, Stanley L. M. "Identity Conflicts of Chinese Adolescents in San Francisco." *In* Eugene B. Brody (ed.), *Minority Group Adolescents in the United States*. Baltimore: Williams & Wilkins, 1968: 111–32.

"How Children's Books Distort the Asian American Image." *Interracial Books for Children Bulletin*, vol. 7, nos. 2 and 3, 1976: 3–5.

Isaacs, Harold R. *Scratches on Our Minds: American Images of China and India*. New York: John Day, 1958.

Jones, Dorothy. *The Portrayal of China and India on the American Screen, 1896–1955*. Cambridge, Mass.: Center for International Studies, 1955.

Karlins, Marvin; Coffman, Thomas L.; and Walters, Gary. "On the Fading of Social Stereotypes in Three Generations of College Students." *Journal of Personality and Social Psychology*, 13, 1969: 1–16.

Katz, Daniel, and Braly, Kenneth W. "Racial Stereotypes of 100 College Students." *Journal of Abnormal and Social Psychology*, 28, 1933: 280–90.

Kingston, Maxine Hong. *China Men*. New York: Random House, 1980.

Klineberg, Otto. *Social Psychology*. New York: Holt, Rinehart and Winston, 1940.

Kung, S. W. *Chinese in American Life*. Seattle: University of Washington Press, 1962.

Latourette, Kenneth S. *The Chinese: Their History and Culture*, 4th edn. New York: Macmillan, 1962.

Lee, Rose Hum. *The Chinese in the United States of America*. Hong Kong: Hong Kong University Press, 1960.

Lyman, Stanford M. *Chinese Americans*. New York: Random House, 1974.

Maloney, Don. *Japan: It's Not All Raw Fish*. Tokyo: The Japan Times, 1975.

Miller, Stuart C. *The Unwelcome Immigrant*. Berkeley and Los Angeles: University of California Press, 1969.

Rohmer, Sax. *The Insidious Dr. Fu Manchu*. New York: McKinlay, Stone & Mackenzie, 1916.

Schrieke, Bertram. *Alien Americans: A Study of Race Relations*. New York: Viking, 1936.

Siu, Paul. "The Chinese Laundryman: A Study in Social Isolation," Ph.D. dissertation, University of Chicago, 1954.

Sung, Betty Lee. *Mountain of Gold*. New York: Macmillan, 1967.

———. *Chinese American Manpower and Employment*. Washington, D.C.: Manpower Administration, U. S. Department of Labor, 1975.

———. *Gangs in New York's Chinatown*. Washington, D.C.: Office of Child Development, Department of Health, Education, and Welfare, 1977.

Wong, Jade Snow. *Fifth Chinese Daughter*. New York: Harper & Brothers, 1945.

Wu, Cheng-tsu (ed.). *Chink! A Documentary History of Anti-Chinese Prejudice in America*. New York: World Publishing/Times Mirror, 1972.

Yutang, Lin (ed.). *The Wisdom of Confucius*. New York: Random House, 1938.

Bales, Robert F. "Cultural Differences in Rates of Alcoholism." *Quarterly Journal of Studies on Alcohol*, 6, March 1946: 480–500.

Bestic, Alan. *The Importance of Being Irish*. New York: Morrow, 1969.

Caulfield, Max. *The Irish Mystique*. Englewood Cliffs: Prentice-Hall, 1973.

Connery, Donald S. *The Irish*. New York: Simon & Schuster, 1968.

Everett, Edward. "A Plea for the Irish Immigrant." *In* Edith Abbott (ed.), *Historical Aspects of the Immigration Problem, Selected Documents*. Chicago: University of Chicago Press, 1926: 460–66.

Farrell, James T. *Studs Lonigan; A Trilogy: Young Lonigan, The Young Manhood of Studs Lonigan, Judgment Day*. New York: Modern Library edn., 1938.

Glad, Donald D. "Attitudes and Experiences of American-Jewish and American-Irish Male Youth as Related to Differences in Adult Rates of Inebriety." *Quarterly Journal of Studies on Alcohol*, 8, December 1947: 406–72.

Glazer, Nathan, and Moynihan, Daniel P. *Beyond the Melting Pot*, 2nd edn. Cambridge, Mass.: The M.I.T. Press, 1970.

Greeley, Andrew M. *That Most Distressful Nation*. Chicago: Quadrangle, 1972.

——. *The Denominational Society*. Glenview, Ill.: Scott, Foresman, 1972.

——. *The American Catholic: A Social Portrait*. New York: Basic Books, 1977.

——, and Rossi, Peter H. *The Education of Catholic Americans*. Chicago: Aldine, 1966.

Handlin, Oscar. *Boston's Immigrants*, rev. edn. Cambridge, Mass.: Harvard University Press, 1959.

Jackson, Kenneth H. *The Oldest Irish Tradition: A Window on the Iron Age*. Cambridge, Eng.: Cambridge University Press, 1964.

Levine, Edward M. *The Irish and Irish Politicians*. Notre Dame, Ind.: University of Notre Dame Press, 1966.

Mahaffy, John P. *The Art of Conversation*. Philadelphia: Pennsylvania Publishing Co., 1902.

McCaffrey, Lawrence J. *The Irish Diaspora in America*. Bloomington: Indiana University Press, 1976.

McCord, William and Joan. *Origins of Alcoholism*. Palo Alto: Stanford University Press, 1960.

Messenger, John C. "Sex and Repression in an Irish Folk Community." *In* Donald S. Marshall and Robert C. Suggs (eds.), *Human Sexual Behavior*. New York: Basic Books, 1970.

O'Connor, Edwin. *The Last Hurrah*. Boston: Little, Brown, 1956.

O'Connor, Richard. *The Irish: Portrait of a People*. New York: Putnam, 1971.

"Passing the Hat for the Provos." *Time*, November 26, 1979: 92.

Royko, Mike. *Boss: Richard J. Daley of Chicago*. New York: New American Library (Signet), 1971.

Shannon, William V. *The American Irish*, rev. edn. New York: Macmillan, 1966.

———. "The Lasting Hurrah." New York *Times Magazine*, March 14, 1976.

Stivers, Richard. *The Hair of a Dog*. University Park, Pa.: Pennsylvania State University Press, 1977.

Strauss, Robert, and McCarthy, Raymond G. "Nonaddictive Pathological Drinking Patterns of Homeless Men." *Quarterly Journal of Studies on Alcohol*, 12, December 1951: 601–11.

Wakin, Edward. *Enter the Irish-American*. New York: Crowell, 1976.

Williams, Roger J. *Alcoholism: The Nutritional Approach*. Austin: University of Texas Press, 1959.

Wittke, Carl. *The Irish in America*. Baton Rouge: Louisiana State University Press, 1956.

Allport, Gordon. *The Nature of Prejudice.* New York: Anchor Books edn., 1958.

Balch, Emily G. *Our Slavic Fellow Citizens.* New York: Arno Press, 1969.

Binzen, Peter. *Whitetown, U.S.A.* New York: Random House (Vintage Books), 1970.

Brockway, Wallace, and Weinstock, Herbert. "Frédéric Chopin." *In* Elie Siegmeister (ed.), *The Music Lover's Handbook.* New York: Morrow, 1943.

Duncan, Beverly, and Duncan, Otis D. "Minorities and the Process of Stratification." *American Sociological Review,* vol. 33, no. 3, June 1968: 356–64.

Durham, Michael. "Crusade Against the Polish Joke." *Life* magazine, January 14, 1972: 70–71.

Greeley, Andrew M. *Why Can't They Be Like Us?* New York: Dutton, 1971.

Heller, Celia S. *On the Edge of Destruction.* New York: Columbia University Press, 1977.

Herrnstein, Richard J. "In Defense of Intelligence Tests." *Commentary,* February 1980: 40–51.

Huntley, Steve. "Polish Americans: Pride vs. Prejudice." *U.S. News & World Report,* July 7, 1980: 35–36.

Iranek-Osmecki, Kazimierz. *He Who Saves One Life.* New York: Crown, 1971.

Knox, Gene. "Bingo Politics of Scientific Leadership." *Perspectives Inc.* January–March 1974: 133.

Kovalic, Don F. "The Polish Joke Syndrome." Chicago: privately printed, 1978 (pamphlet).

Lopata, Helena. *Polish Americans.* Englewood Cliffs: Prentice-Hall, 1976.

Novak, Michael. *The Rise of the Unmeltable Ethnics.* New York: Macmillan Paperbacks edn., 1973.

——. "The Sting of Polish Jokes." *Newsweek,* April 12, 1976:13.

——. "Ethnicity Is Not a Dirty Word." *Perspectives: The Civil Rights Quarterly,* Summer 1980: 24.

"Perspectives Inc. Notebook: Anti-Polish Bias Grows!" *Perspectives Inc.*, March–April 1979: 479.

Pogorzelski, Hank A. "Reader Reactions." *Perspectives Inc.*, April–June 1974: 138.

Sowell, Thomas (ed.). *Essays and Data on American Ethnic Groups.* Washington, D.C.: The Urban Institute, 1978.

Spaeth, Joe L., and Greeley, Andrew M. *Recent Alumni and Higher Education.* New York: McGraw-Hill, 1970.

Syrop, Konrad. *Poland: Between the Hammer and the Anvil.* London: Hale, 1968.

Thomas, William I., and Znaniecki, Florian. *The Polish Peasant in Europe and America,* 5 vols. Boston: Richard G. Badger, 1918–20.

Szczepanski, Jan. *Polish Society.* New York: Random House, 1970.

United States Bureau of the Census. *Current Population Reports,* series P-20, nos. 221 and 249, 1971.

Vinocur, John. "East Germans Are Hardly Fraternal Toward the Poles." New York *Times,* December 14, 1980.

Williams, Tennessee. *A Streetcar Named Desire.* New York: New Directions, 1947.

Wytrwal, Joseph A. *Poles in American History and Tradition.* Detroit: Endurance Press, 1969.

Adams, Paul L. "The WASP Child." *In* Joseph D. Noshpitz (ed.), *Basic Handbook of Child Psychiatry. Volume I: Development.* New York: Basic Books, 1979: 283–90.

Amory, Cleveland. *The Proper Bostonians.* New York: Dutton, 1947.

———. *The Last Resorts.* New York: Harper & Brothers, 1948.

Anderson, Charles H. *White Protestant Americans.* Englewood Cliffs: Prentice-Hall, 1970.

Anderson, Elin. *We Americans.* Cambridge, Mass.: Harvard University Press, 1938.

Baltzell, E. Digby. *The Philadelphia Gentleman.* Glencoe, Ill.: The Free Press, 1958.

———. *The Protestant Establishment.* New York: Random House (Vintage Books), 1964.

———. *Puritan Boston and Quaker Philadelphia.* New York: The Free Press, 1979.

Binzen, Peter. *Whitetown, U.S.A.* New York: Random House (Vintage Books), 1970.

Birmingham, Stephen. *The Right People.* Boston: Little, Brown, 1958.

———. *Our Crowd.* New York: Dell, 1968.

Boorstin, Daniel J. *America and the Image of Europe.* New York: Meridian Books, 1960.

Broom, Leonard, and Glenn, Norval D. "Religious Differences in Reported Attitudes and Behavior." *Sociological Analysis,* 27, Winter 1966: 187–209.

Caudill, Harry M. *Night Comes to the Cumberlands.* Boston: Little, Brown, 1962.

Coles, Robert. *Children of Crisis. Volume V: Privileged Ones.* Boston: Little, Brown, 1977.

Collins, Randall. "Weber's Last Theory of Systematization." *American Sociological Review,* 45, December 1980: 925–42.

Domhoff, G. William. *Who Rules America?* Englewood Cliffs: Prentice-Hall, 1967.

———. *The Higher Circles.* New York: Random House (Vintage Books), 1971.

Elias, Norbert. *The Civilizing Process: The History of Manners*, trans. Edmund Jethcott. New York: Urizen Books, 1978.

Emerson, Ralph Waldo. *The Works of Ralph Waldo Emerson. Volume V: English Traits*. Philadelphia: The Nottingham Society, n.d.

Erikson, Kai T. *Everything in Its Path*. New York: Simon & Schuster, 1976.

Greeley, Andrew M. *Religion and Career*. New York: Sheed & Ward, 1963.

———. *Why Can't They Be Like Us?* New York: Dutton, 1971.

Gwertzman, Bernard. "President Sharply Assails Kremlin; Haig Warning on Poland Disclosed." *New York Times*, January 30, 1981.

Hadden, Jeffrey K. *The Gathering Storm in the Churches*. Garden City, N.Y.: Doubleday, 1969.

Keller, Suzanne. *Beyond the Ruling Class*. New York: Random House, 1963.

Keppel, Frederick P. *Columbia*. New York: Oxford University Press, 1914.

Killian, Lewis M. *White Southerners*. New York: Random House, 1970.

King, C. Wendell. "Branford Center: A Community Study in Social Change." Ph.D. dissertation, Yale University, 1943.

King, Florence. *WASP, Where Is Thy Sting?* Briarcliff Manor, N.Y.: Stein & Day, 1977.

Knebel, Fletcher. "The WASPS: 1968." *Look*, July 23, 1968: 69–72.

Lenski, Gerhard. *The Religious Factor*. Garden City, N.Y.: Doubleday, 1961.

Link, Arthur S. *Wilson: The Road to the White House*. Princeton: Princeton University Press, 1947.

Matthews, T. S. *Name and Address*. New York: Simon & Schuster, 1960.

Maugham, W. Somerset. *Of Human Bondage*. New York: Pocket Books, 1950.

McConnell, John W. "The Influence of Occupation upon Social Stratification." Ph.D. dissertation, Yale University, 1937.

McLachlan, James. *American Boarding Schools*. New York: Scribner, 1970.

Mills, C. Wright. *The Power Elite*. New York: Oxford University Press, 1956.

Morris, Richard B. (ed.). *Encyclopedia of American History*, rev. edn. New York: Harper & Row, 1965: 661–808.

Novak, Michael. *The Rise of the Unmeltable Ethnics*. New York: Macmillan Paperbacks edn., 1973.

Rodgers, Daniel T. *The Work Ethic in Industrial America, 1850–1920.* Chicago: University of Chicago Press, 1978.

Schrag, Peter. *The Decline of the WASP.* New York: Simon & Schuster, 1970.

Schweitzer, Albert. *Memoirs of Childhood and Youth.* New York: Macmillan, 1955.

Sorokin, Pitirim. "American Millionaires and Multi-Millionaires." *Social Forces,* 3, May 1925: 627–40.

Warner, W. Lloyd, and Lunt, Paul S. *The Social Life of a Modern Community.* New Haven: Yale University Press, 1941.

Weber, Max. *The Protestant Ethic and the Spirit of Capitalism,* trans. Talcott Parsons. New York: Scribner, 1958.

Weidman, Jerome. *I Can Get It for You Wholesale.* New York: Random House (Modern Library), 1937.

Zborowski, Mark. *People in Pain.* San Francisco: Jossey-Bass, 1969.

REFERENCES FOR CHAPTER TEN

Baroja, Julio Caro. "Honour and Shame: A Historical Account of Several Conflicts." In J. G. Peristiany (ed.), Honour and Shame. Chicago: University of Chicago Press, 1966: 79–137.

Bennassar, Bartolomé. The Spanish Character, trans. Benjamin Keen. Berkeley: University of California Press, 1979.

Castro, Tony. Chicano Power. New York: Saturday Review Press/E. P. Dutton, 1974.

Catto, Henry E., Jr. "Our Language Barriers." Newsweek, December 1, 1980: 25.

Coleman, James et al. Equality of Educational Opportunity. U. S. Department of Health, Education, and Welfare, 1966.

Cooper, Paulette (ed.). Growing Up Puerto Rican. New York: New American Library (Mentor), 1973.

Cordasco, Francesco, and Bucchioni, Eugene, The Puerto Rican Experience. Totowa, N.J.: Littlefield, Adams, 1975.

Cromwell, V. T. "A Study of Ethnic Minority Couples." Ph.D. dissertation, University of Missouri, Kansas City, 1976.

Demographic Yearbook (United Nations). New York: United Nations Publishing Service, 1973.

Durant, Will and Ariel. The Story of Civilization. vol. VII: The Age of Reason Begins. New York: Simon & Schuster, 1961.

Dworkin, Anthony G. "Stereotypes and Self-Images Held by Native-born and Foreign-born Mexican-Americans." Sociology and Social Research, January 1965: 214–24.

Fitzpatrick, Joseph P. Puerto Rican Americans. Englewood Cliffs: Prentice-Hall, 1971.

Gillin, John. "Ethos Components in Modern Latin American Culture." In Dwight B. Heath and Richard N. Adams (eds.), Contemporary Cultures and Societies of Latin America. New York: Random House, 1965: 503–17.

Grebler, Leo; Moore, Joan W.; and Guzman, Ralph C. The Mexican-American People: The Nation's Second Largest Minority. New York: The Free Press, 1970.

Hechinger, Fred M. "U.S. Ruling Fuels Controversy Over Bilingual Teaching." New York Times, January 20, 1981.

Heller, Celia S. *Mexican American Youth: Forgotten Youth at the Crossroads.* New York: Random House, 1966.

Horowitz, Carl F. "Portrait of the Artist as a Young Vandal: The Aesthetics of Paint Graffiti." *Journal of American Culture,* Fall 1979:376–91.

Humphrey, Norman D. "Ethnic Images and Stereotypes of Mexicans and Americans." *American Journal of Economics and Sociology,* April 1955: 305–13.

"It's Your Turn in the Sun." *Time,* October 16, 1978: 48–61.

Kihss, Peter. "Study Finds Puerto Ricans in an 'Awesome Crisis.'" New York *Times,* November 2, 1980.

Kuvlesky, William; Wright, David; and Juarez, Rumaldo. "Status Projections and Ethnicity: A Comparison of Mexican American, Negro, and Anglo Youth." *Journal of Vocational Behavior,* 1, 1971: 137–51.

Lewis, Oscar. *Five Families.* New York: New American Library (Mentor), 1959.

——. *The Children of Sanchez.* New York: Random House (Vintage Books), 1961.

——. *La Vida.* New York: Random House (Vintage Books), 1965.

Lynch, Pat. "Hispanics: It's in My Soul." *U.S. News & World Report,* July 7, 1980: 34–35.

Margolis, Richard J. "States of the Union: Tales Out of Schools in Colorado." *The New Leader,* February 12, 1979:12–13.

Martínez, Elizabeth Sutherland, and Longeaux y Vásquez, Enriqueta. *Viva La Raza.* New York: Doubleday, 1974.

Meier, Matt S., and Rivera, Feliciano. *The Chicanos: A History of Mexican Americans.* New York: Hill & Wang, 1972.

Mills, C. Wright; Senior, Clarence; and Goldsen, Rose Kohn. *The Puerto Rican Journey.* New York: Harper & Row, 1950.

Mirandé, Alfredo. "The Chicano Family: A Reanalysis of Conflicting Views." *Journal of Marriage and the Family,* November 1977: 747–56.

Moore, Joan W., and Cuéllar, A. B. *Mexican Americans.* Englewood Cliffs: Prentice-Hall, 1970.

Moquin, Wayne, and Van Doren, Charles (eds.). *A Documentary History of the Mexican Americans.* New York: Praeger, 1971.

Paz, Octavio. *The Labyrinth of Solitude.* New York: Grove Press, 1961.

Pitt-Rivers, Julian. "Honour and Social Status." *In* J. G. Peristiany (ed.), *Honour and Shame.* Chicago: University of Chicago Press, 1966: 19–78.

Powell, Philip W. *Tree of Hate.* New York: Basic Books, 1971.

Robertson, William. *The History of America.* 2 vols. London: Strahan, 1822.

Schumacher, Edward. "Stubborn Britons Cling to Embattled Atlantic Islands." New York *Times,* February 5, 1981.

Serrano, Alberto C., and Castillo, Fortunato G. "The Chicano Child and His Family." *In* Joseph D. Noshpitz (ed.), *Basic Handbook of Child Psychiatry. Volume I: Development.* New York: Basic Books, 1979: 257–63.

Steiner, Stan. *La Raza: The Mexican Americans.* New York: Harper & Row, 1969.

———. *The Islands: The Worlds of the Puerto Ricans.* New York: Harper & Row, 1974.

Stern, Caryl S., and Stock, Robert W. "Graffiti: The Plague Years." The New York *Times Magazine,* October 19, 1980.

Stevens, Evelyn P. "Machismo and Marianismo." *In* Irving Louis Horowitz and Charles Nanry (eds.), *Sociological Realities II.* New York: Harper & Row and Transaction Books, 1971.

Stoddard, Ellwyn R. *Mexican Americans.* New York: Random House, 1973.

Tumin, Melvin M., and Feldman, Arnold S. *Social Class and Social Change in Puerto Rico.* Princeton: Princeton University Press, 1961.

Vidal, David. "City's Growing Hispanic Minority Tries to Keep Separate Identity." New York *Times,* May 11, 1980.

———. "Hispanic Residents Report Hardships, but They Find Some Gains." New York *Times,* May 12, 1980.

Wagenheim, Kal. *Puerto Rico: A Profile.* New York: Praeger, 1970.

Weber, David J. (ed.). *Foreigners in Their Native Land.* Albuquerque: University of New Mexico Press, 1973.

INDEX